# Language Hub

## ADVANCED Student's Book

JEREMY DAY
GRAHAM SKERRITT

C1

# Contents

| | LESSON · OBJECTIVES | GRAMMAR | VOCABULARY | PRONUNCIATION |
|---|---|---|---|---|
| **U1** | **TRENDS** | | | |
| 1.1 | **Dress for success** (p2)<br>Talk about style and fashion<br>Give fashion advice | nominal clauses | clothes and fashion<br>metaphors | linking and intrusive /r/ |
| 1.2 | **Trendsetting** (p6)<br>Compare different trends<br>Make a podcast or vlog | comparatives and superlatives | experimenting with prefixes and suffixes | emphatic stress |
| 1.3 | **Café Hub** Diet and lifestyle (p10)<br>Pitch your own business idea | | *give it a go* | |
| | **UNIT REVIEW** (p12) | **WRITING** (p156) Write a blog post  |  **KEY SKILL** Making your blog post successful | | |
| **U2** | **CREATIVITY** | | | |
| 2.1 | **The story behind it** (p14)<br>Give a presentation about art<br>Talk about creative projects | narrative tenses | describing art | contrastive stress |
| 2.2 | **Creative people** (p18)<br>Talk about finding inspiration<br>Describe a life-changing moment | future in the past | ideas and inspiration<br>compound adjectives | questions for comment or criticism |
| 2.3 | **Café Hub** Art and design (p22)<br>Discuss a work of art | | *nowhere* phrases | |
| | **UNIT REVIEW** (p24) | **WRITING** (p157) Write a review  |  **KEY SKILL** Writing concisely | | |
| **U3** | **PROGRESS** | | | |
| 3.1 | **Progressive design** (p26)<br>Make predictions about the future<br>Use persuasive language to sell something | future structures | sustainability<br>forming verbs from adjectives | sounding persuasive |
| 3.2 | **Better … or worse?** (p30)<br>Discuss progress and society<br>Evaluate costs and benefits | negative inversion | verb–noun collocations | stress-shift words |
| 3.3 | **Café Hub** Sustainability (p34)<br>Discuss renewable energy | | the 'rule of three' | |
| | **UNIT REVIEW** (p36) | **WRITING** (p158) Write a persuasive email  |  **KEY SKILL** Persuasive techniques | | |
| **U4** | **INTELLIGENCE** | | | |
| 4.1 | **Brain training** (p38)<br>Discuss improving the brain<br>Talk about future technology | conditionals without *if* | conceptual metaphors | adding information |
| 4.2 | **Thinking and thought** (p42)<br>Talk about regrets<br>Discuss intelligence | wishes and regrets | science and research<br>thinking | adding information or changing the topic |
| 4.3 | **Café Hub** Life-changing tech (p46)<br>Recount events | | *straight out of* | |
| | **UNIT REVIEW** (p48) | **WRITING** (p159) Write a report  |  **KEY SKILL** Hedging | | |
| **U5** | **GAMES** | | | |
| 5.1 | **21st century games** (p50)<br>Discuss problem-solving tasks<br>Discuss gaming and game design | the passive | competition and cooperation | expressing disbelief |
| 5.2 | **Serious gaming** (p54)<br>Identify generalisations<br>Discuss ideas for solving a challenge | passive reporting structures | reporting verbs<br>motivation and manipulation | *-ate* words |
| 5.3 | **Café Hub** Win or lose (p58)<br>Plan a fundraising event | | ellipsis | |
| | **UNIT REVIEW** (p60) | **WRITING** (p160) Write a formal report  |  **KEY SKILL** Using depersonalisation | | |

# Contents

| READING · LISTENING | SPEAKING · WRITING |
|---|---|
| read an article about how clothes affect the way you think<br>listen to a conversation about how to look good for less<br>**KEY SKILL** Listening for recommendations | discuss trends in clothes and fashion<br>**SPEAKING HUB**<br>roleplay a conversation about fashion |
| read a blog post about the lifecycle of a trend<br>**KEY SKILL** Using contrasts to work out meaning<br>listen to a podcast about how to be a trendsetter | compare trends from different time periods<br>**SPEAKING HUB**<br>plan and make a podcast or vlog |
| ▶ watch a video about veganism<br>▶ watch someone pitching a business idea | **KEY SKILL** Using circumlocution<br>**SPEAKING HUB**<br>plan and give a short pitch |
| listen to a radio programme about a famous painting<br>**KEY SKILL** Anticipating content before listening<br>read a newspaper article about how the Eden Project was made | give a short presentation about a work of art<br>**SPEAKING HUB**<br>tell a story about a project |
| listen to a conversation about how creative people get inspiration<br>read an article about famous people who were discovered by accident<br>**KEY SKILL** Inferring meaning | discuss suggestions for finding inspiration<br>**SPEAKING HUB**<br>tell a story about a life-changing moment |
| ▶ watch a video about the London Design Festival<br>▶ watch people giving their interpretation of a work of art | **KEY SKILL** Managing a discussion<br>**SPEAKING HUB**<br>discuss a painting |
| read a newspaper article about an architect's plans for a city in the future<br>listen to a conversation about smart materials<br>**KEY SKILL** Listening to identify persuasive techniques | discuss future developments and changes<br>**SPEAKING HUB**<br>persuade someone to buy a product |
| listen to a radio show about declinism<br>read a magazine article about voluntourism<br>**KEY SKILL** Reading to determine costs and benefits | discuss whether life is getting better or worse<br>**SPEAKING HUB**<br>discuss the costs and benefits of a project |
| ▶ watch a video about seaweed farming in Bali<br>▶ watch people discussing alternative fuels | **KEY SKILL** Maintaining a conversation<br>**SPEAKING HUB**<br>talk about the pros and cons of renewable energies |
| listen to a radio discussion about brain training<br>**KEY SKILL** Identifying logical fallacies<br>read an article about brain augmentation | compare products to boost intelligence<br>**SPEAKING HUB**<br>discuss responses to hypothetical situations |
| read two articles about embarrassment<br>**KEY SKILL** Identifying different writing styles<br>listen to part of a debate about the disadvantages of being highly intelligent | talk about a time when you did something you regret<br>**SPEAKING HUB**<br>have a debate about intelligence and education |
| ▶ watch a video about Neil Harbisson<br>▶ watch someone tell an anecdote about a technology fair | **KEY SKILL** Recounting events<br>**SPEAKING HUB**<br>tell an interesting and complex anecdote |
| listen to a conversation about escape rooms<br>read a blog post about urban games<br>**KEY SKILL** Understanding colloquial asides | suggest creative solutions to a problem<br>**SPEAKING HUB**<br>design an urban game |
| listen to a presentation about Game Theory<br>**KEY SKILL** Distinguishing generalisations from preferred solutions<br>read an article about the gamification of life | talk about generalisations, expectations and assumptions<br>**SPEAKING HUB**<br>use gamification and game theory to solve a problem |
| ▶ watch a video about risk-taking in games<br>▶ watch people come up with strategies while playing a game | **KEY SKILL** Building relationships<br>**SPEAKING HUB**<br>discuss and plan a fundraising event for a charity |

| | LESSON · OBJECTIVES | GRAMMAR | VOCABULARY | PRONUNCIATION |
|---|---|---|---|---|
| **U6** | **DISCOVERIES** | | | |
| 6.1 | **Challenging journeys** (p62)<br>Speculate and make deductions about the past<br>Plan an amazing journey | past modals of speculation and deduction | journeys and adventures<br>three-part phrasal verbs | showing your attitude |
| 6.2 | **Inquisitive minds** (p66)<br>Discuss rewarding jobs<br>Give a presentation about someone you admire | *-ing* and infinitive forms | binomial expressions | pauses and pitch in presentations |
| 6.3 | **Café Hub** Word of knowledge (p70)<br>Plan and perform an interview | | engaging listeners | |
| | **UNIT REVIEW** (p72) | **WRITING** (p161) Write an expository essay  \|  **KEY SKILL** Structuring an expository essay | | |
| **U7** | **EXTREMES** | | | |
| 7.1 | **Beyond the limits** (p74)<br>Describe reactions to extreme experiences<br>Describe extreme situations and achievements | *it* clefting | feelings | intonation in question tags |
| 7.2 | **Extreme jobs** (p78)<br>Discuss extreme jobs<br>Deal with difficult interview questions | *what* clefting and *all* clefting | polysemy<br>intensifiers | *any* and *quite* |
| 7.3 | **Café Hub** Push your limits (p82)<br>Tell a story about an exciting journey | | fronting | |
| | **UNIT REVIEW** (p84) | **WRITING** (p162) Write a cover letter  \|  **KEY SKILL** Using power verbs | | |
| **U8** | **WELL-BEING** | | | |
| 8.1 | **Health and wellness** (p86)<br>Discuss wellness treatments<br>Talk about health and technology | relative clauses with complex relative pronouns | health problems | building suspense |
| 8.2 | **Sport and wellness** (p90)<br>Talk about sports psychology<br>Discuss nutrition and fitness | pronouns and determiners | idioms<br>describing taste | pronunciation of idioms |
| 8.3 | **Café Hub** Health hacks (p94)<br>Explain and give instructions about a process | | reformulating | |
| | **UNIT REVIEW** (p96) | **WRITING** (p163) Write a summary  \|  **KEY SKILL** Paraphrasing | | |
| **U9** | **BEHAVIOUR** | | | |
| 9.1 | **Language and behaviour** (p98)<br>Talk about group behaviour<br>Discuss factors that affect behaviour | noun phrases | slang | pronouncing vague expressions |
| 9.2 | **Animal behaviour** (p102)<br>Discuss animal behaviour<br>Talk about behavioural experiments | participle clauses and verbless clauses | verb + object + infinitive<br>gestures and body language | intrusive stops |
| 9.3 | **Café Hub** Model behaviour (p106)<br>Give and justify your opinion on social engagement | | *end up* | |
| | **UNIT REVIEW** (p108) | **WRITING** (p164) Write a conclusion to an academic report  \|  **KEY SKILL** Linking in academic writing | | |
| **U10** | **SOCIETY** | | | |
| 10.1 | **Urban problems** (p110)<br>Discuss issues related to tourism<br>Present solutions to urban problems | discourse markers | culture and heritage<br>nouns with *to* | introducing new information |
| 10.2 | **How to change the world** (p114)<br>Talk about political activism<br>Discuss how to make a difference | ellipsis and substitution | word building | managing conversations |
| 10.3 | **Café Hub** Changing cities (p118)<br>Debate for and against a motion | | describing a scene in real-time | |
| | **UNIT REVIEW** (p120) | **WRITING** (p165) Write a persuasive essay  \|  **KEY SKILL** Using counter-arguments and rebuttals | | |

**Irregular verbs** (p121)  **Grammar Hub** (p122)  **Vocabulary Hub** (p142)  **Communication Hub** (p149)  **Writing lessons** (p156)  **Audioscripts** (p166)

# Contents

| READING · LISTENING | SPEAKING · WRITING |
|---|---|
| read an article about a famous explorer<br>**KEY SKILL** Prediction strategies for reading<br>listen to a discussion about travel challenges | make speculations about historical mysteries<br>**SPEAKING HUB**<br>design and present an original travel challenge |
| read an article about investigative journalism<br>listen to a presentation about an inventor<br>**KEY SKILL** Taking notes while listening | compare different types of job<br>**SPEAKING HUB**<br>give a presentation about an inspirational person |
| ▶ watch a video about nature and the universe<br>▶ watch an interview with a scientist | **KEY SKILL** Conducting an interview<br>**SPEAKING HUB**<br>roleplay an interview between Veronica Matos and a journalist |
| read an extract from a story<br>listen to a TV show about hysterical strength<br>**KEY SKILL** Identifying causation | describe your experiences of mental states<br>**SPEAKING HUB**<br>conduct a media interview about extreme abilities/achievements |
| read an article about working in extreme places<br>listen to a talk about extreme job interviews<br>**KEY SKILL** Understanding reference within texts | give advice to a job applicant<br>**SPEAKING HUB**<br>interview candidates for a job |
| ▶ watch a video about extreme driving<br>▶ watch a phone call between two people | **KEY SKILL** Changing and recycling topics<br>**SPEAKING HUB**<br>perform a conversation about an exciting journey |
| read a newspaper article about new wellness treatments<br>**KEY SKILL** Identifying writers' opinions<br>listen to a conversation about technology and health | talk about the value of wellness treatments<br>**SPEAKING HUB**<br>design and pitch a health/wellness product |
| listen to a podcast about sports psychology<br>**KEY SKILL** Understanding speech with background noise<br>read an article about a gluten-free diet | discuss the benefits of sports psychology techniques<br>**SPEAKING HUB**<br>design a fitness plan for an athlete |
| ▶ watch a video about food packaging<br>▶ watch two people discuss a recipe | **KEY SKILL** Repairing misunderstandings<br>**SPEAKING HUB**<br>explain a process you know well to your partner |
| listen to a conversation about a psychology experiment<br>**KEY SKILL** Understanding rapid colloquial speech<br>read a newspaper article about how language affects behaviour | discuss the problems of group behaviour<br>**SPEAKING HUB**<br>analyse and present evidence for or against an idea |
| read an article about understanding animal behaviour<br>**KEY SKILL** Identifying outcomes of scientific research<br>listen to a radio show about behavioural psychology | discuss experiences and opinions of animal intelligence<br>**SPEAKING HUB**<br>plan and carry out a behavioural experiment |
| ▶ watch a video about group behaviour<br>▶ watch people discuss sociological experiments | **KEY SKILL** Backtracking and reformulating<br>**SPEAKING HUB**<br>present your opinion on social engagement |
| read three short articles about the problems caused by tourism<br>**KEY SKILL** Integrating information from different texts<br>listen to a radio report about building design | talk about the importance and problems of tourism<br>**SPEAKING HUB**<br>discuss how to solve problems in your city |
| read a newspaper article about political activism<br>listen to a conversation about finding a job after university<br>**KEY SKILL** Recognising shifts in register | discuss world problems and activism<br>**SPEAKING HUB**<br>persuade people to support a charity |
| ▶ watch a video about cable cars in Mexico City<br>▶ watch people argue about the benefits of urban development | **KEY SKILL** Using vague language<br>**SPEAKING HUB**<br>debate whether vehicles should be banned from city centres |

# Welcome

## GRAMMAR
### Verb tenses and structures

**A** Choose the correct option to complete the conversation.

A: Hello. Could you tell me ¹*where is the conversation class / where the conversation class is*?

B: Yes, just follow me! ²*I'm going / I'll go* there now. I actually study here myself.

A: Cool. ³*Did you / Have you* been studying English for long?

B: Let me think. Actually ⁴*I'll have been / I'll be* at this school for two years at the end of this month. Don't worry. You ⁵*don't have to / mustn't* bring anything. Just yourself. And there is only one rule: you ⁶*needn't / mustn't* speak in your own language in class.

A: Great, that's really important. In my last school we ⁷*used to / get used to* do a lot of grammar. But I wasn't ⁸*taught / didn't teach* any speaking or pronunciation. So I really need to ⁹*used to / get used to* speaking more.

B: Yes, me too. I ¹⁰*was learning / am learning* on my own for a bit, but stopped because I didn't feel I'd made much progress.

### Articles, determiners and quantifiers

**B** Find and correct the mistakes in the sentences.

1 It's ~~the~~ good to watch videos in English to practise your listening.
2 A lot problems when learning a language come from lack of confidence not lack of ability.
3 It's best to get personal recommendations when finding the English courses.
4 When you first learn a language you should spend a great deal time on grammar.
5 A childhood is a good time to start learning a language.
6 There's never time enough when you're working and learning at the same time.
7 Most the people feel demotivated at some point when learning a new language.
8 Every languages has it own unique pronunciation and grammar and you can't easily compare them.
9 Languages are neither fixed and completely stable but are constantly changing.

**C SPEAK** Work in pairs and discuss the questions.

1 Do you agree with the speakers in Exercise A? Why/Why not?
2 Do you agree with the statements in Exercise B? Why/Why not?

## VOCABULARY
### Collocations

**A** Choose the correct words to complete the collocations.

1 It's *highly / deeply / absolutely* likely that even jobs in education will be automated in the future.
2 Concerning future problems, I'm *bitterly / deeply / ridiculously* concerned about extreme weather conditions.
3 There is the possibility *for / of / about* colonising another planet to relieve human overpopulation.
4 Young people should have *knowledge / ideas / opinions* of news sources and searching online to deal with the problem of fake news.
5 Understanding your *focus / target / regular* audience is important for being an entrepreneur.
6 Not all regeneration projects get a *positive / high / key* reaction from local communities.

### Compound adjectives and nouns

**B** Complete the sentences with the compound adjectives and nouns in the box.

> community spirit    last-minute    old-fashioned
> six-bedroom    street parties    up-to-date

1 Visit our website for the most _____ travel times and _____ deals.
2 Mark and Susan have just bought a huge _____ house in the countryside. It's a bit _____, but they're planning on renovating it.
3 There is great _____ in my village. The local council often organise _____ for national holidays.

**C SPEAK** Work in pairs. Do you agree with the statements in Exercise A?

## PRONUNCIATION

**A** Circle the arrows to predict which intonation will be used. Then listen and check.
0.1

1 Is this meeting finishing soon? [↗] / [↘]
2 How often do you come to these classes? [↗] / [↘]
3 Unless there is a good reason [↗] / [↘], you shouldn't work late. [↗] / [↘]
4 Take some chocolate bars [↗] / [↘], in case you need a quick snack. [↗] / [↘]

**B** Listen to the sentences. Draw (‿) between any words
0.2 that link together.

1 He's improved a lot despite having a few problems.
2 We went out at night a lot to see the city.
3 Plenty of people find it difficult at first.
4 Hundreds of people came out to see her talk.

**C** Practise saying the sentences in Exercise B.

# 1 TRENDS

> The majority have no other reason for their opinions than that they are the fashion.
>
> Samuel Johnson

A flamingo amongst geese, egrets, swans and herons.

## OBJECTIVES

- talk about style and fashion
- give fashion advice
- compare different trends
- make a podcast or vlog
- pitch your own business idea
- write a blog post

Work with a partner. Discuss the questions.

1. Look at the picture. How does it relate to trends?
2. Read the quote. What do you think it means? Do you agree?
3. How important are trends in the following areas to you?
   - fashion
   - design
   - music
   - lifestyle

TRENDS 1

# 1.1 Dress for success

- Talk about style and fashion
- Give fashion advice

**V** — clothes and fashion; metaphors  **G** — nominal clauses  **P** — linking and intrusive /r/  **S** — listening for recommendations

## VOCABULARY
### Clothes and fashion

**A** Work in pairs. Do the quiz.

**B** Go to the Vocabulary Hub on page 142.

## READING

**A** PREDICT  Work in pairs. Read the title of the article. Look at pictures 1–3. How might what the people are wearing affect their behaviour?

**B** SCAN  Read *Style speaks* and check your predictions from Exercise A.

1. Do you carefully plan your **outfits** or just wear the first thing to hand?
2. Have you ever had to attend an event with **a dress code**?
3. If you had to go to a fancy dress party, what **costume** would you wear?
4. Are people more productive when they wear **uniform** or **casual** clothing?
5. Would you describe yourself as a **trendsetter** or a **trend follower**?
6. Is it better to **fit in with** or **stand out** from **the crowd**?
7. Do you ever wear **baggy** or **scruffy** clothes to relax at home?

# STYLE speaks

We've all heard the old adages …
*Dress for the job you want, not the job you have. Look good, feel good.* These clichés are rather worn out. How can the way we dress affect our lives? But it seems there may be some truth in them after all. People do form first impressions based on what we're wearing. Not only that but maybe even part of our own self-worth is tied up in the clothing choices we make.

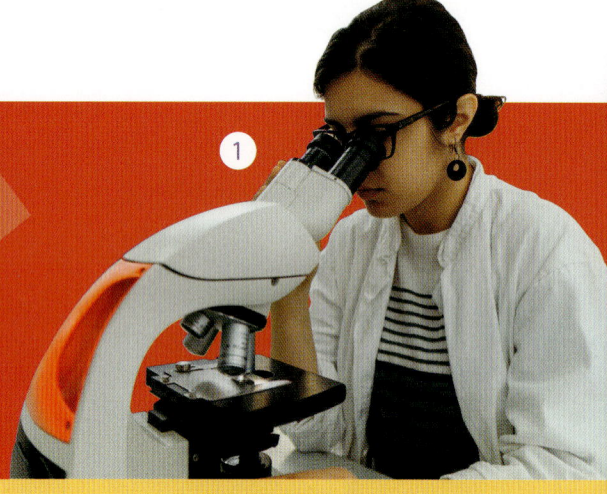

## Power dressing

Not convinced? Imagine turning up for an interview at a big city firm, in the jeans you've been wearing for the past three days and an old baggy t-shirt. Would you be successful in getting the job? Unlikely. Would you feel self-conscious about what you're wearing? Very likely. It seems that wearing smart clothes, such as a well-cut suit, could help you feel more confident. And when we're feeling confident we negotiate better, we respond better to questions and we put other people at ease.

## Breaking free

On the flip side, wearing fitted or tailored clothing is not what most of us would choose to wear when we are trying to be creative. Can you imagine writing the next great novel, or coming up with a great innovation, sat typing away in a £2000 designer suit? This is why many leading tech companies have an ultra-relaxed dress code and encourage casual clothing. Mark Zuckerberg isn't topping any best-dressed lists but his billions of dollars make up for it. Furthermore, many places of work have 'Casual Fridays' to encourage employees to let their hair down a bit and get creativity flowing.

## Uniform thinking

Wearing a uniform can make us feel part of something – provide us with a sense of belonging, but also one of duty. Many people argue that wearing school uniforms encourage us to work harder. Whilst this is not necessarily true, there is no doubt that when, for example, a firefighter puts on their helmet or a doctor a white coat it comes with a responsibility. So fundamentally, to dress the role is to start to live it.

### Glossary
**adage (n)** a well-known phrase that says something about life and human experience
**clique (n)** a small group of people who seem unfriendly to other people
**unconsciously (adv)** without realising or being aware of one's actions

C **READ FOR DETAIL** Read the article again. Complete each statement with one to three words from the article.

1 People should wear _____ when they're feeling low.
2 _____ could help people come up with new ideas.
3 People sometimes wear _____ clothing to fit in.
4 _____ may encourage people to make healthier choices.
5 People should wear _____ to feel more persuasive.
6 _____ may make people more careful at work.

D **SPEAK** Discuss in small groups.

1 What surprised you most about the blog post?
2 Do you think your own choice of clothes affects how you think and behave?

### Gym ready

It's not just work that clothing affects, but lifestyle as well. Professional and semi-professional athletes tend to stick rigidly to an 'athleisure' style. Their reasoning? They don't enjoy wearing formal clothes. And they want to be able to work out whenever they feel like it. And for many, having the clothes on reminds them to make healthier choices … to choose the fruit salad over the fruit cake.

### Pack Mentality

Have we really evolved that much away from our primal, tribal instincts? Visit any city centre at lunchtime on a Saturday and your answer will be probably not. The packs of roving teenagers are dressed in a pseudo uniform of branded clothing, like Ray-Bans and Hype T-shirts. We unconsciously imitate the clothing of people we have regard for. A shared sense of style builds rapport and helps you to instantly feel part of a clique. Maybe it's self-preservation, or maybe it's a hope that you will be infused with the qualities you so admire.

### Lift your mood

That our mood impacts on what we choose to wear will not come as a surprise. How many of us think about it the other way round? What we wear could affect how we are feeling for the better or worse. One of the best cures for when you're feeling down is to wear that cosy, bright yellow jumper. More people than you might think are great believers in wearing bright colours to boost positivity. It seems simple, but why not give it a shot next time you're having a bad day?

## GRAMMAR
Nominal clauses

A Read the sentences. Is the underlined part of each sentence the subject or the object?

1 They don't enjoy <u>wearing formal clothes</u>.
2 <u>Wearing a uniform</u> can make us feel part of something.

B Work in pairs. Underline the nominal clauses in sentences 1–6 from the article. Use the information in the box to help you. The first two have been done for you.

### Nominal clauses

Nominal clauses are clauses that work like nouns. They are very common as objects, but they are also possible as the subject, after a preposition or the verb *be*, and in the following ways.

a nominal *-ing* clause ___
b nominal *that* clause ___
c nominal question-clause ___
d nominal *to* + infinitive ___
e We often use a phrase like *the fact/idea that* or *the experience/problem of* to introduce a nominal clause and make it easier to understand. ___
f *That* clauses and *to* + infinitive can sound unnatural as the subject. We can use *it* as an empty subject instead. ___

1 Luke is upset <u>that he didn't pass</u>.
2 Lisa doesn't enjoy <u>watching horror films</u>.
3 It wasn't surprising that Tara came in first place.
4 The fact that the team won the league shows how good the manager is.
5 Where you go to university is your choice.
6 To tell a lie about something so important was wrong.

C **WORK IT OUT** Match sentences 1–6 in Exercise B with the rules (a–f) in the box.

D Go to the Grammar Hub on page 122.

E Complete the sentences so they are true for you. Then discuss in pairs.

1 What I like doing most of all in the evenings …
2 How a person is dressed …
3 Spending a lot of money on …

## SPEAKING

**DISCUSS** Work in groups. To what extent do you agree with the following statements? Give reasons for your answers.

- Wearing a uniform affects what grades you get at school.
- Buying expensive clothes is the best way to succeed in life.
- Spending lots of money on luxury goods makes people more generous.

## 1.1

### LISTENING

**A SPEAK** Work in pairs. Look at the infographic from a fashion magazine. What do you think the results would be in your country?

**B LISTEN FOR RECOMMENDATIONS** Listen to a conversation between two friends. What nine tips does Carly give Dan? Use the information in the box to help you.

> **Listening for recommendations**
>
> When listening for recommendations, pay attention to phrases like *it's a good idea to*, *it's always worth*, or *don't forget to*.
>
> Also listen for phrases that signal a shift from main points to examples (e.g. *for instance*, *let's say*) and those that move from examples to new main points (e.g. *more generally*, *that's an example of*).

**C LISTEN FOR DETAIL** Listen again. Choose the correct answers (a, b or c).

1 Why is Dan worried?
   a He doesn't know what to wear for his new job.
   b He thinks people won't respect him.
   c He won't earn enough to buy nice clothes.

2 What's good about the suit Dan wants to buy?
   a the price
   b the fit
   c the quality

3 Why did Dan wear baggy trousers for his job interview?
   a He knew the interviewers couldn't see them.
   b He wanted to create a good impression.
   c He didn't have any other trousers.

4 What should Dan do with his suit trousers?
   a mend them
   b sell them
   c bin them

5 According to Carly, what's good about ugly sales pages?
   a You can charge more money.
   b You appear inexperienced.
   c You can buy things cheaply.

6 Where does Carly say you can find good second-hand bargains?
   a posh parts of town
   b trendy neighbours
   c areas near universities

**D SPEAK** Work in small groups.

1 Which of Carly's tips do you already follow?
2 Would you try any of them in the future? Why/Why not?

## FASHION TRENDS
### in the UK according to our readers

**75%** of you only buy **BRANDED** sportswear

**45%** believe **QUALITY** is more important than **VALUE** for money

**IMAGE** is the first thing that **85%** of you notice about someone the first time you meet them

**65%** **THROW** ripped clothing away rather than **MENDING** it

**40%** of our readers think **FASHION** is more important than **COMFORT**

### VOCABULARY
Metaphors

**A SPEAK** Work in pairs. Look at the sentences. What do the underlined words and phrases mean?

1 a I'd love to come out tonight, but I'm on a tight budget. ___
  b They had some lovely suits, but they were all too tight. ___

2 a The dress was so finely stitched that it looked seamless. ___
  b It needs to be a seamless process for your customers. ___

3 a Instead of buying a cheap off-the-shelf suit, save up for a tailor-made suit. ___, ___
  b Don't use an off-the-shelf template for your company's website. We can design a tailor-made site to help you stand out from the competition. ___, ___

4 TRENDS

**B** Work in pairs. Decide whether the underlined words in Exercise A are literal (l) or metaphorical (m). Use the information in the box to help you.

> **Metaphors**
>
> A metaphor is a word or phrase that's used in a different context from its literal meaning. It's easier to understand a metaphor when you know the literal meaning. For example:
>
> Literal: *There is a breeze outside.* (= a light wind)
> Metaphorical: *It was a breeze! I got the job.* (= easy and pleasant)

**C** Complete the sentences with the correct form of the words in the box.

| catch | drain | peanut | run | snap | wind |

1 I'm getting quite _____ up about it.
2 You're throwing money down the _____.
3 It's much better in the long _____.
4 Then you'll have two suits in your wardrobe for _____.
5 Choose a template that _____ your eye.
6 All the best stuff will be _____ up immediately.

**D** Work in pairs. What is the metaphorical meaning of each sentence in Exercise C?

**E** Complete the questions with the correct form of a word from Exercises A or C.

1 When one person leaves a job and another person takes over, how can they make the transition as _____ as possible?
2 Are you the kind of person who plans for the long _____? Or do you tend to make snap decisions?
3 Have you ever bought anything that was _____ especially for you? Or do you always buy _____ products?
4 Which current trends really _____ you up?

**F SPEAK** Work in pairs. Discuss the questions in Exercise E.

## PRONUNCIATION
### Linking and intrusive /r/

**A** Work in pairs. Read the sentences below aloud. Draw a (‿) between any words that you think are connected by a /r/ sound.

1 I saw a nice suit yesterday for 40% off.
2 You're only saving money if you buy something you need.
3 I just wore a jacket from an old suit.
4 They had no idea I was wearing tracksuit trousers.
5 Are auction sites the best place to pick up cheap clothes?
6 Avoid shops in a trendy area or one with lots of students.
7 Many shop assistants are authorised to offer discounts.

1.2

**B** Listen to check. Then practise saying the sentences.

## SPEAKING HUB

**A PREPARE** Choose one of the following roles. Spend a few moments thinking about your character (e.g. your age, background, ambitions, the problems you face, etc).

- **Role 1: The fashion victim.** You always want the latest designer fashions, but you're worried you spend far too much.
- **Role 2: The reluctant shopper.** You hate shopping and don't care what you wear, but all your clothes are old and scruffy.
- **Role 3: The trendsetter.** You like to take risks and experiment with your clothes. Just one problem: you've run out of ideas!

**B DISCUSS** Work in groups of two or three. Roleplay a conversation between your characters. Ask your partners for more information about their situation. Offer each other (good or bad) fashion advice.

*I know it feels good to snap up a bargain, but in the long run, it's just money down the drain, don't you think?*

**C REFLECT** Report back to the class on the best and worst advice for each character.

○ Talk about style and fashion
○ Give fashion advice

## 1.2 Trendsetting

- Compare different trends
- Make a podcast or vlog

**G** — comparatives and superlatives
**P** — emphatic stress
**V** — experimenting with prefixes and suffixes
**S** — using contrasts to work out meaning

## READING

**A SPEAK** Work in pairs. Think of as many trends from the past five years as you can in one minute. Use the topics below to help you.

- technology
- music
- fashion
- culture

# THE LIFECYCLE OF A TREND

**B READ FOR MAIN IDEA** Read *The lifecycle of a trend* quickly. Match the paragraphs (1–7) with the topics (a–d). Some paragraphs cover more than one topic.

a  musical styles ___
b  music formats ___, ___, ___
c  games ___
d  human needs ___, ___, ___

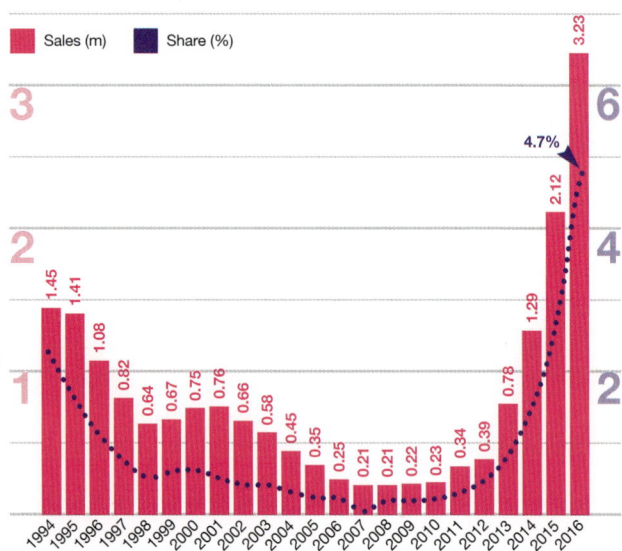

**Source:** British Phonographic Industry

**1** Technology trends are very simple at first sight: older technologies become <u>outdated</u> and <u>anachronistic</u>, to be replaced by **newer**, **funkier** technologies, until they are rendered <u>obsolete</u> with the next cycle. In this way, the vinyl records of the 1970s gave way to cassettes in the 1980s. By the 1990s, cassettes were <u>old hat</u> and CDs were <u>state-of-the-art</u>. By the 2000s, we all loved <u>novel</u> gadgets like MP3 players. But by the 2010s, we had cloud-based music streaming services like Spotify. Why limit yourself to the music you own, when you can stream every song ever recorded?

**2** But in 2016, the unexpected happened: sales of vinyl records in the UK outstripped digital music sales for the first time. The renewed interest in vinyl is a powerful reminder that trends don't always flow in a straight line from <u>fringe</u> products to mass-market <u>blockbusters</u>. It also reminds us to pay attention to the durability of trends over decades, not just the short-term ups and downs of **the latest** fads.

**3** These trends are **clearest** in the world of popular music, which seems to be on a 20-year cycle. In the 1980s, music from the 50s and 60s was cool, while 70s music was <u>naff</u>. By the 1990s, 70s music was enjoying a revival, but 80s music had become the height of uncool. After 2000, it was OK to like 80s music again but now 90s music was for losers. The 20-year cycle makes **rather more sense** when you remember that the average trendsetter is about 22 years old. They <u>feel sheepish about</u> the music they enjoyed when they were 12, but they can look back **a great deal more fondly** at the music from their early childhood.

**4** There's a key difference between a trend, a flash-in-the-pan and a fad. A flash-in-the-pan pops up suddenly, grabs everyone's attention, and then disappears again **almost as suddenly**. A few years ago, the whole world went crazy for a new smartphone app called 'Pokémon Go'. At one point, people were playing it everywhere you looked. But within a few months, almost everybody had abandoned it, leaving only a handful of <u>die-hard fans</u> to persevere with it.

**5** A fad, on the other hand, may be **a little more enduring**, but it too is doomed to disappear sooner or later because it serves no useful purpose. It may be <u>quirky</u> or amusing, but unless it fulfils a basic human need, like 'convenience', 'social status', 'self-expression' or 'security', it will never be **more than a gimmick**.

**6** In contrast, an <u>authentic</u> trend always fulfils one of **our very deepest** needs – something that's shared by every human that's ever lived. Of course, nobody really needs **a slightly thinner than usual phone** or every song ever recorded, but we do need things like relaxation, creative stimulation, self-confidence and a sense of belonging to a social group, which those products and services satisfy.

**7** This idea of basic human needs also goes some way towards explaining **by far the most curious** feature of the vinyl revival: almost half of buyers of vinyl records never actually listen to them according to a poll by ICM Unlimited! As long as we see vinyl as 'a music format' to fulfil our need for 'relaxation' and 'creative stimulation', this makes no sense. But don't forget, we also have a need to own beautiful physical objects to express our personality, and this is **every bit as important as** those other needs. And of course, the large-sleeved LPs **more than meet** that particular need, to **a lot greater an extent than** either <u>diminutive</u> CDs or <u>intangible</u> digital downloads.

### Glossary

**doom** (v) to make someone or something certain to fail, be destroyed, be extremely unhappy, etc
**durability** (n) the ability to continue to exist or work for a long time.
**outstrip** (v) to become larger than something else
**revival** (n) the process of becoming active, successful, or popular again

**C WORK OUT MEANING** Read the article carefully and answer the questions. Use the information in the box to help you.

### Using contrasts to work out meaning

It's often possible to work out the meaning of new words and phrases by looking for contrasts with known words and phrases. Look out for linking words (e.g. *while, but*) that signal a contrast.

1 Which underlined adjectives in paragraph 1 mean *old-fashioned*? Which mean *new*?
2 What do the two underlined words in paragraph 2 contrast?
3 What do the underlined words and phrases mean in paragraph 3?
4 What does the underlined phrase in paragraph 4 mean? What is it being contrasted with in the same sentence?
5 Which two verbs are being contrasted in the last sentence in paragraph 4?
6 Which of the underlined words in paragraphs 5 and 6 have a positive meaning? Which have a negative meaning?
7 What do the underlined adjectives in paragraph 7 mean? Which words in the same paragraph have the opposite meanings?

**D** Work in pairs. Compare your answers to Exercise C.

**E SPEAK** Work in pairs. Discuss the questions.
1 Do you agree that all successful trends are popular because they fulfill a basic human need?
2 Can you think of any examples or counterexamples to support your opinion?

## GRAMMAR
Comparatives and superlatives

**A** Are these statements true (T) or false (F)?
1 After a comparative adjective (e.g. *bigger*), we always need *than*.    T / F
2 We form the comparative and superlative of *-ly* adverbs (e.g. *quickly*) by changing *-y* to *-ier/-iest*.    T / F
3 We always need *the* before a superlative (e.g. *fastest*).    T / F

**B** Work in pairs. Justify your choices in Exercise A with examples in bold from the *The lifecycle of a trend*.
1 _____
2 _____
3 _____

**C WORK IT OUT** Complete the rules with an example in bold from the article.

### Advanced comparatives and superlatives

1 Some modifiers start with *a/an* (e.g. *a little*). When we use these together with *a/an* + noun, the second *a/an* goes after the comparative: _____
2 Only a few words (*anticipated / expected / hoped for / necessary / usual*) can come between *than* and a noun: _____
3 We can use the structure *more than* with a small number of verbs (*double, make up for, meet*): _____

**D** Go to the Grammar Hub on page 122.

**E SPEAK** Tell your partner about one of the following. Use comparative and superlative structures.
- a film that you enjoyed more than you thought you would
- a concert that you went to or an album you really love
- the most enjoyable holiday you've ever had

## SPEAKING

**DISCUSS** Work in pairs. Compare the following things. Use structures from this lesson.
1 fashion from 1 / 5 / 10 / 20 / 50 years ago
2 popular music from 5 / 10 / 20 / 30 years ago
3 technology now / 10 / 20 / 50 years ago
4 society now / 10 / 20 / 100 years ago

## LISTENING

**A SPEAK** Work in pairs. Discuss the questions.

1. What's the difference between the types of people in the box? Do you know any of these types of people?

   > blogger   influencer   podcaster   trendsetter   vlogger

2. Do you listen to any podcasts or watch any vlogs? If so, which ones?

**B LISTEN FOR GIST** Listen to a podcast about trendsetting. Which topics do the speakers give advice about?

- [ ] 1 making money
- [ ] 2 choosing a focus
- [ ] 3 using social media to build a community
- [ ] 4 the problem with perfection
- [ ] 5 designing your own website
- [ ] 6 learning from statistics
- [ ] 7 long-term planning
- [ ] 8 learning from mistakes

**C LISTEN FOR DETAIL** Listen again. Are the statements true (T) or false (F)? Correct the false statements.

1. Dora and Adam are in the same room. T / F
2. Dora regrets that she made so many mistakes. T / F
3. Hardly anyone watched Dora's videos at first. T / F
4. Dora releases a video at the same time every week. T / F
5. Dora replies to every comment on her videos. T / F
6. Dora sees herself as an overnight success. T / F
7. Adam is unsure about filming himself. T / F

**D SPEAK** Discuss in pairs.

1. Do you think the idea of an 'overnight success' is a myth?
2. Have you ever had a blog or vlog? If not, would you ever consider starting one? Why/Why not?

## VOCABULARY
Experimenting with prefixes and suffixes

**A** Complete Dora's advice using the words in the box.

> amateurish   biggish   disaster-prone
> hyper-influential   re-editing   super-lucky
> tech-savvy   unmute   user-friendly

### VLOG AWAY!

A lot of the vlogs on the web are very ¹_____. Stand out by editing and ²_____ until your vlog is as slick and professional as possible.

If you're not particularly ³_____, do some research into ⁴_____ software – one with clear instructions.

Look at some of the videos made by the most ⁵_____ vloggers and some with a ⁶_____ number of subscribers. Success isn't down to being ⁷_____, it's about hard work and perfecting the craft.

You don't have to be a ⁸_____ person to sometimes forget to ⁹_____ the mic. Remember not to be too hard on yourself. We all make mistakes, the important thing is to learn from them. You'll get more confident with experience.

8   TRENDS

**B** Complete the information in the box with examples from Exercise A. Use the information in the box to help you.

### Experimenting with prefixes and suffixes

1 Some prefixes (e.g. *un-*, *re-*) allow you to invent completely new verbs: _____ , _____
2 *Super-*, *hyper-* and *ultra-* all mean 'much more than usual': _____ , _____
3 You can add *-y* or *-ish* to nouns to invent new informal adjectives: *rubbishy*, *babyish*, _____
4 You can add *-ish* to an adjective or number to mean 'more or less': *twentyish*, *smallish*, _____
5 *Friendly*, *prone*, *proof*, *resistant* and *savvy* can be used as suffixes to make adjectives: *environmentally friendly*, *waterproof*, *heat-resistant*, _____ , _____ , _____

**C** Replace the underlined phrases in these extracts with a word with a prefix or suffix. You may need to change the word order in some sentences. Then listen to check.

1 You actually need to <u>forget all you learnt about</u> all those rules about perfection!
2 Whenever I have a <u>fairly good</u> idea for a podcast, then I try to make it within a few days.
3 You also need to be far more <u>aware of how to use social media</u>.
4 Well, there are plenty of people who post offensive comments <u>that are like spam</u>.
5 Your content would work much better as videos <u>that work well on smartphones</u>.
6 I really think you should <u>have a second think</u> and become a vlogger instead.
7 I feel <u>incredibly exhausted</u> just thinking about it.

**D** Go to the Vocabulary Hub on page 142.

**E** SPEAK Work in pairs. Think of examples of the following.
- websites that aren't very user-friendly / smartphone-friendly
- a person who's tech-savvy / fashion-savvy
- any objects you own that are waterproof or water-resistant
- any objects you own that are damage-prone

## PRONUNCIATION
### Emphatic stress

**A** Listen to the extracts from the recording. Underline the words that are stressed.

1 One of the most common mistakes that new vloggers and podcasters make is to expect everything to be perfect.
2 But after a while, it got a lot easier!
3 … if nobody cared after a year, I'd give up. And it did take a while to get noticed.
4 … you've found your niche and you've created some excellent content.
5 Every Wednesday at ten o'clock, there will be a new video on my channel.
6 I suppose in many people's eyes, I am an overnight success.
7 I felt awkward at first, too, but you do get used to it.
8 Dora Cho, thanks so much for joining me today.

**B** Work in pairs. Why did the speaker use emphatic stress in the extracts in Exercise A? Practise saying the sentences.

**C** Decide where to add emphatic stress in these sentences. Then listen to check.

1 That's one of the most popular vlogs on the web.
2 When you reach one million subscribers, it will be worth it!
3 Is it possible to be a trendsetter and an influencer?

## SPEAKING HUB

**A** PLAN Work in small groups. You are going to make a podcast or vlog episode about trends. Discuss the following questions.
- What will it be about?
- Why will anyone want to listen/watch?
- What topics could you cover?
- How will you add your own personalities?

**B** DISCUSS Share your initial ideas with the class. Ask your 'audience' what the next episodes should focus on. Try to engage with them to generate enthusiasm.

**C** PREPARE Plan an episode of your podcast/vlog. Don't simply write a script – you'll need to stay spontaneous.

**D** PRESENT Make your podcast/vlog. If you have recording equipment, e.g. a phone, you can use that. Otherwise, present your episode to the class.

- Compare different trends
- Make a podcast or vlog

# Café Hub

## 1.3 Diet and lifestyle
A – give it a go    S – using circumlocution

### ▶ Veganuary

**A** Work in pairs. You are going to watch a video titled *Veganuary*. What do you think *Veganuary* means?

**B** ▶ Watch the video and check your answers to Exercise A.

**C** ▶ Watch the video again. Complete the sentences with one word or a number.

1. There are now more choices for vegans when they eat out and at _____.
2. The food which Tabitha says she misses most is _____.
3. Tabitha initially became a vegan because of _____ reasons.
4. Many cafés sell a wider selection of products to appeal to _____.
5. Some people limit eating meat to one or two times a _____.
6. In the UK _____ people attempted *Veganuary*.

### Glossary
**boom (v)** to experience an increase in activity, interest or growth
**ethics (n)** a set of principles that people use to decide what is right and what is wrong
**mainstream (adj)** considered ordinary or normal and accepted or used by most people
**niche (n)** a specialised segment of the market for a particular kind of product or service

## AUTHENTIC ENGLISH

**A** Read the sentence from the video. What do you think the phrase in bold means?

*Health, ethics, there are just so many reasons, I think, to **give it a go**.*

**B** Read the information in the box to check your answer to Exercise A.

### give it a go
We use *give it a go* to express it's a good idea to attempt something you haven't done before. We also use *give it a try*, *give it a shot*, *have a go* and *have a stab* to express the same idea.

**C** Work in pairs. Respond to the sentences using *give it a go* or one of the other expressions from the box in Exercise B.

1. We're not sure whether to try skiing when we're in Switzerland.
   *Why not have a go and see if you like it?*
2. Sam would like to study French but he's always found languages difficult.
3. I've never travelled abroad alone before.
4. Nina's always been too shy to introduce herself to complete strangers.

**D SPEAK** Discuss three things you would like to start doing that you have never tried before.

# ▶ The big pitch

 SAM   MALCOLM   AMANDA   HARRY   EMILY

A ▶ Watch the video. Work in pairs. Discuss the questions.
1  Who is Sam and how does he spend his day?
2  What do the following people do?

Emily   Malcolm   Amanda   Harry

B ▶ Watch the video again. Complete the sentences with the best option.
1  Emily feels *confident about / unprepared for* her pitch.
2  Emily would like to *grow her current business / start a new sustainable business*.
3  Emily's yoga experience package will include *two / three* meals a day.
4  Emily's business will focus on *yoga and food / outdoor yoga*.
5  Emily thinks *she will make profits evenly every year / her profits will equal her costs in the first year*.

## SPEAKING SKILL

A  Work in pairs. Look at the example from the video. Why has Emily used this phrase?

> **Emily:** … Well, it's kind of like my yoga classes that I teach, but with the idea that you would be getting more than just exercise.

B  Look at the information in the box. Then underline examples of circumlocution in the sentences from the video.

### Using circumlocution

We often use circumlocution, the use of many words where fewer would do, in a deliberate attempt to be vague or evasive, when we are nervous or can't think of the exact word, or even to make an idea sound more impressive. Look at these other sentences from the video and underline examples of circumlocution.

1  I mean what I really want to do is to expand my business into something more sustainable, you know, a yoga retreat where people can stay for a few days.
2  Full body cleansing, you know the physiological withdrawal of toxins from the body.

C  Why do you think Amanda uses circumlocution in the sentences from Exercise B?

D  Work in pairs. Ask each other about the following things. When you answer try to be evasive or vague. Use the expressions from Exercise B to help you.
- your favourite café
- your diet
- your job or studies

## ◯ SPEAKING HUB

A  **PLAN**  You are going to make a short pitch for a business you would like to set up. Think of a business idea.

B  **PREPARE**  Make notes on what you are going to say. Consider the following points.
- product/service
- market
- USP (Unique Selling Point)
- profitability

C  **PRESENT**  Work in groups. Pitch your business idea.

*Well, I'd like to give running my own exercise boot camp a go.*

D  **REACT**  Once everyone in the group has pitched their idea, decide which is the best. Give reasons.

◯ Pitch your own business idea

▶ Turn to **page 156** to learn how to write a blog post about a trend.

# Unit 1 Review

## GRAMMAR

**A** Put the words into the correct order to make nominal clauses.

**A:** Why are you getting rid of those trousers? There's nothing wrong with them!

**B:** Well, the fact ¹**aren't / in the knees / holes / that / there** doesn't mean I can wear them for ever. These trousers are so last year!

**A:** Come on! ² **your clothes / people / think about / what** isn't important! What counts is ³**on / what's / inside / the**!

**B:** Exactly! But you know what they say: ⁴**on / smart / to look / outside / the** is to feel smart on the inside. And anyway, ⁵**fashion / gives / following** me a lot of pleasure.

**A:** Yeah, apart from the fact ⁶**you can afford / that you spend / more than**.

**B:** ⁷**much / I spend / How** is up to me!

**B** Choose the correct options (a, b, c or d) to complete each sentence.

1 This is the ___ worst film I've ever seen.
   a just
   b marginally
   c somewhat
   d absolute

2 There was a slightly larger than ___ crowd at the game.
   a anticipated
   b believed
   c hope for
   d previous

3 Some online shops are ___ as cheap as high-street stores.
   a by far
   b double
   c far and away
   d twice

4 My achievements are ___ as impressive as yours.
   a considerably
   b every bit
   c rather
   d significantly

5 The hotel offers ___ best views across the bay.
   a at least
   b fractionally
   c the very
   d dramatically

## VOCABULARY

**A** Match numbers (1–6) to letters (a–f) to form full sentences.

1 If Jon decides to come to the wedding,
2 If you get a new job in an office,
3 If celebrities dress in a stylish way,
4 If you wear creative and original clothes,
5 If you want to stay cool in the summer,
6 If you're going away for the weekend,

a wear light, baggy clothes.
b you'll fit in well here – everyone has a very unique style.
c pack at least four outfits.
d make sure he doesn't wear his usual scruffy clothes.
e check the company's dress code before you start.
f they often set a trend.

**B** Complete the words in the sentences. Some of the letters have been given to help you.

1 I can't afford to eat out again this week – I'm on a very __ __ g __ __ budget.
2 We offer a range of __ __ __-the-__ __ __ __ __ and __ a __ __ __ __-m __ __ __ __ suits for our customers.
3 I got really __ __ u __ __ up this morning when I couldn't find a parking space.
4 I know it seems expensive now, but it's worth it in the long __ __ __.
5 If we leave it too late to go to the sales, all the bargains will have been __ __ __ p __ __ __ up!
6 If you have the time to look, you can buy great clothes for p __ __ n __ __ __ in charity shops.
7 The exam was an absolute __ __ __ __ z __ – I'm sure I got full marks!

**C** Complete the advert using a prefix or suffix from the box with the words in brackets. Each prefix or suffix may be used more than once. Other changes may be necessary.

-ish  ultra-  -savvy  -prone  -y  -friendly  -proof

### TRENDY KID

Are you looking for an ¹_____ (*cool*) fashion gadget for an ²_____ (*accident*) child?
Our new unbreakable 'Trendy Kid' smartwatch is completely ³_____ (*child*).

No need to be ⁴_____ (*tech*)!
This watch uses the latest skeuomorphic design principles to make it as ⁵_____ (*user*) as possible.

Available in ⁶_____ (*flower*) pink or ⁷_____ (*mud*) brown.

Do you love the design but worry that you'll look too ⁸_____ (*child*) wearing a 'Trendy Kid' watch? Head over to our store for a huge range of on-trend adult smartwatches!

12 TRENDS

# 2 CREATIVITY

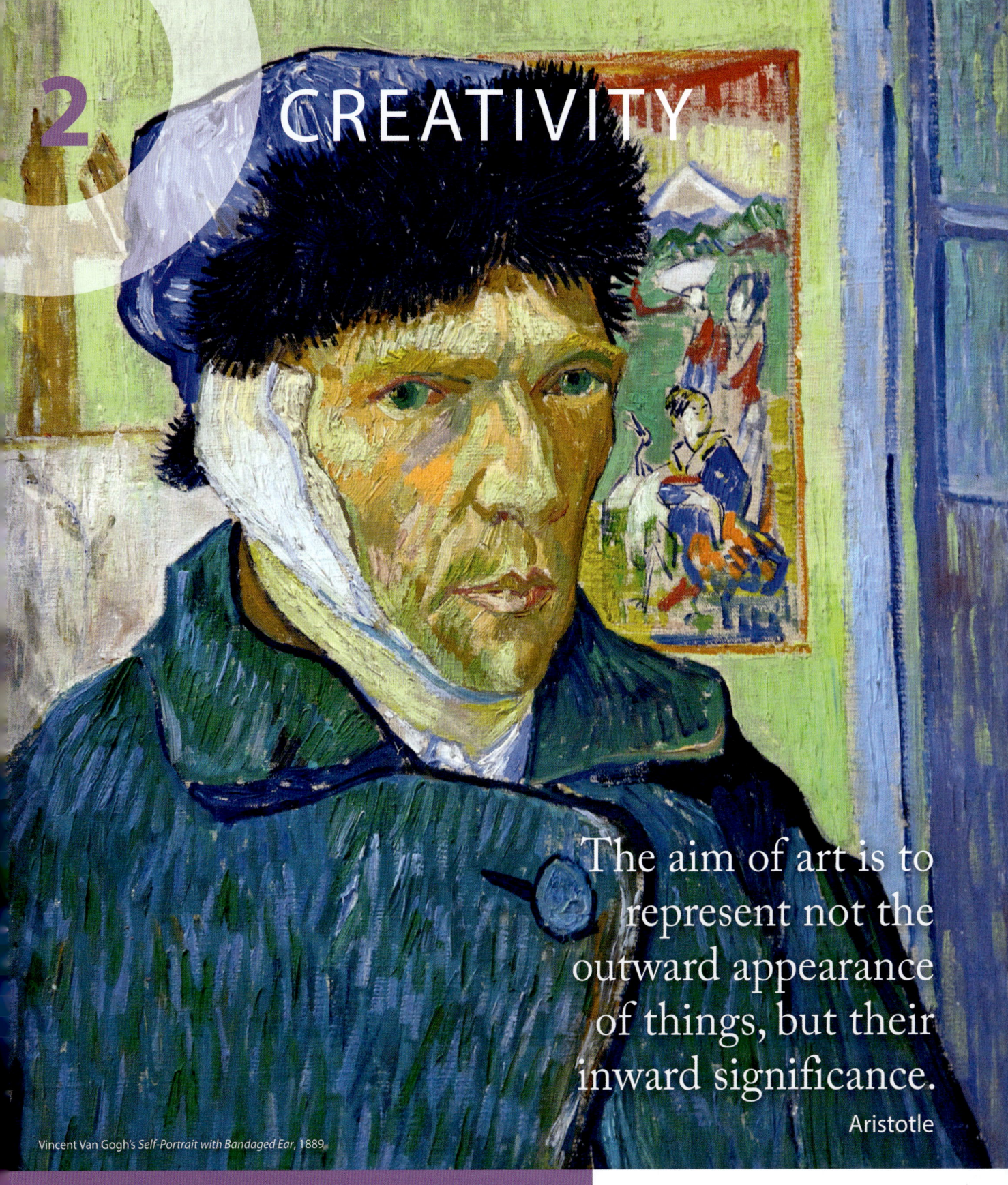

Vincent Van Gogh's *Self-Portrait with Bandaged Ear*, 1889

> The aim of art is to represent not the outward appearance of things, but their inward significance.
> — Aristotle

## OBJECTIVES

- give a presentation about art
- talk about creative projects
- talk about finding inspiration
- describe a life-changing moment
- discuss a work of art
- write a review

Work with a partner. Discuss the questions.

1 Look at the picture. What is your opinion of works of art like this?
2 What does Aristotle mean in the quote? Do you agree with him?
3 Is the main aim of art:
   - to tell a story
   - to celebrate an event
   - to express emotion
   - to create beauty
   - to persuade
   - to entertain?

# 2.1 The story behind it

- Give a presentation about art
- Talk about creative projects

**V** – describing art   **P** – contrastive stress   **G** – narrative tenses   **S** – anticipating content before listening

## VOCABULARY
Describing art

**A** **SPEAK** Work in pairs. Look at the pictures (a–e) and discuss the questions.
1 Do you know any of these works of art?
2 Which do you prefer? Why?

**B** Choose the correct adjectives to complete the comments (1–5).

**C** Go to the Vocabulary Hub on page 142.

**D** What art forms are being described in Exercise B?
1 _____   2 _____   3 _____   4 _____   5 _____

**E** **SPEAK** Think of an example of an art form from Exercise D. Describe it to your partner.

*I find this installation groundbreaking. It makes you think about space in a different way.*
*It's actually fairly …   It's not that …   It's somewhat …*

---

1 I think some famous works of art are **overrated / repetitive**. But that isn't the case here. The artist's use of light and shade in this composition was different from anything that had come before – it was truly **pretentious / groundbreaking**.

2 It was **hilarious / tedious**! I couldn't stop laughing. OK, the same jokes again and again becomes a bit **underrated / repetitive**, but the comic perfomances were **awesome / appalling**.

3 It's a very **unconventional / repetitive** piece. I can see why some people wouldn't want something so big and strange put up in a public space. They probably think it's a bit **acclaimed / pretentious**, as if the artist is trying too hard to be different.

4 Most people recognise this image. It's so **iconic / hilarious**, capturing the mood of the time it was taken. It's **thought-provoking / unconventional**, too – it really makes you consider the human story behind this historical event.

5 The risk with performances like this is if the songs are **appalling / iconic** then it's really not enjoyable. It just makes them really **tedious / awesome** – so long and slow. Fortunately the music, lighting and costumes in this show were really special. It was a truly **sensational / iconic** experience. I can see why it's been **overrated / acclaimed** by critics and audiences.

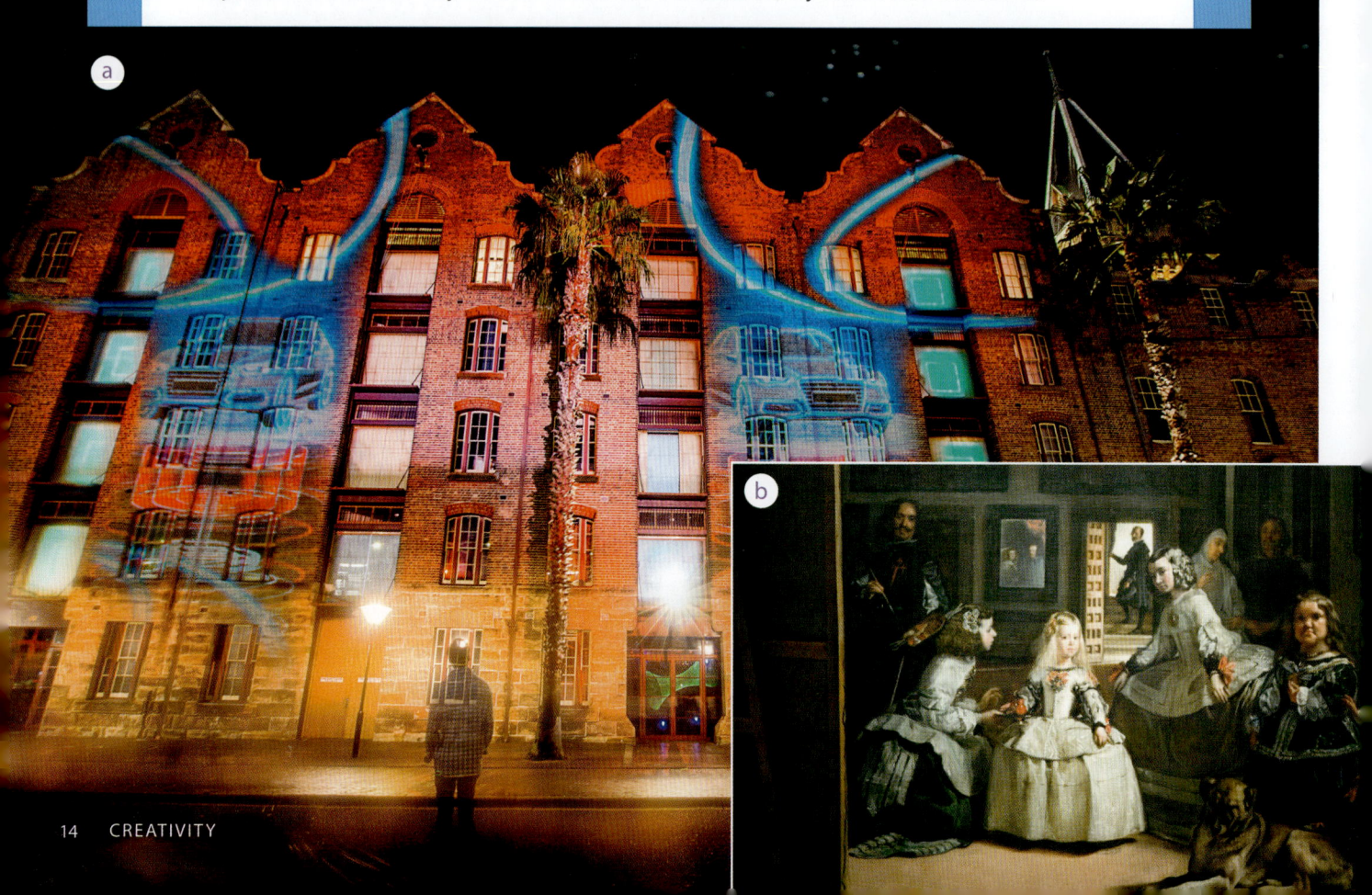

a

b

14   CREATIVITY

# LISTENING

**A** Work in pairs. Read a review of the radio programme *More than meets the eye*. Are there similar radio programmes in your country?

> ### More than meets the eye ★★★★★
> gives an analysis of one different piece of groundbreaking fine art each week. The guest speakers make these discussions unique and sometimes quite unconventional. They don't just have specialist knowledge of the artist, but also some personal connection to the pieces.

**B** **ANTICIPATE CONTENT** You're going to listen to an episode of *More than meets the eye* about picture b. Work in pairs and answer the questions below. Use the information in the box to help you.

> **Anticipating content before listening**
>
> You can use different types of information to predict what you will hear.
> - Read notes, reviews, handouts, etc.
> - Look at titles or images for clues about what the speaker will cover.
> - Use your own knowledge to predict topics or themes.
> - Use information to think of questions you expect to be answered.

1 What topics will be discussed in the programme?

2 What questions will be answered?

**C** **LISTEN FOR GIST** Listen to the programme and check your predictions in Exercise B.

**D** **LISTEN FOR DETAIL** Listen and write down the different ideas about who the main subject of the painting is.

1 _____
2 _____
3 _____

**E** **SPEAK** Work in pairs and discuss the questions.

1 Who do you think the subject of the painting is?
2 Why do you think the artist chose this composition?

# PRONUNCIATION
## Contrastive stress

**A** Listen to these extracts from the radio programme. Draw arrows to show whether the intonation rises (↗) or falls (↘).

1 Yes, we can see her entourage on the right (__), but to the left (__), we can see the artist himself, standing next to a gigantic canvas.

2 So, it's a portrait of the King and Queen (__), not the Infanta (__).

**B** Underline the words you think will be stressed and draw arrows to show where you think the intonation will rise (↗) or fall (↘). Then listen to check.

1 Actually, Mondrian wasn't American, he was Dutch.
2 Although I like his landscapes, his portraits are much better.
3 Why don't we watch a film instead of going to the gallery?
4 I don't think it's tedious. I just think it's overrated.
5 It was painted in 1656 – you said 1666.
6 **A:** You study art history, don't you?
  **B:** No, I study fine art, not art history.

**C** **SPEAK** Guess whether your partner likes these things or not. Respond to your partner's guesses. Use contrastive stress when appropriate.

> classical music   comic books   crime novels
> heavy metal   Hollywood movies   modern art   musicals
> science fiction films   soap operas

*A: You like Spiderman comics.*
*B: No, I like Batman not Spiderman.*

# SPEAKING

**A** Choose a work of art that you really like. It could be a painting, a sculpture, a photograph, a film, a book, a play, a poem or a song.

**B** **PLAN** Make notes so that you can talk about:
- information about the artist / writer / singer
- a description of the work of art
- your interpretation of the work of art
- the reasons why you like this work of art.

**C** **PRESENT** Give a short presentation to your partner about the work of art you have chosen.

**D** **DISCUSS** Ask your partner about the work of art they chose.

c

d

e

CREATIVITY 15

## 2.1

### READING

**A PREDICT** Look at the pictures in the article. What kind of place is this? Do you know anything about it?

**B SKIM** Read the box below about the Eden Project. Check your answers to Exercise A.

> The Eden Project is a spectacular tropical garden housed inside huge plastic bubbles within a crater the size of thirty football pitches.

**C READ FOR DETAIL** Read *How we made the Eden Project*. Put the events (a–h) in the correct order. Two events are not needed.

___ a They hired a lot of people to work on the project.
___ b They did lots of tests to make sure the building would be safe.
___ c They tried out some innovative techniques.
___ d They had to stop working until they found more money.
___ e They started working on designs without a specific location in mind.
___ f Tim Smit had the inspiration for the project.
___ g They found the ideal location.
___ h They conducted a feasibility study.

## How we made the Eden Project

### Tim Smit, *founder*

We started the construction with just £3000 in the bank. To persuade civil servants to part with public funds, you have to do a feasibility study and that's expensive. So we simply progressed on faith, and hope, promising ourselves that we'd never use the word *if* only *when*.

The idea for a huge horticultural expo had come to me as I worked on the Lost Gardens of Heligan. [1]I'd always loved the thought of a lost civilisation in a volcanic crater, and when I saw the lunar landscape of the old Cornish clay pits, [2]I realised they'd be the perfect site.

A friend put me in touch with an architecture firm. I hadn't received a penny in funding at that point, or even a site, just a belief that the idea of a lost world in a crater would appeal to anyone who's ever been 12. They thought the idea was mad, but it struck them as an adventure and they agreed to start work for nothing. Meanwhile, a construction firm put some money into the project in return for a share of the profits. Everyone was now suddenly highly motivated.

Our two horticultural directors recruited anyone they'd ever worked with and debated what to put in the buildings. I'd envisaged rainforest and Mediterranean areas, keen for it to be the greatest ever collection of plants useful to humans. But it was also a question of finding a balance between the wow factor and more meditative moments. So we have a giant waterfall along with a prairie that, in winter, is about the most boring thing you can see – then, for six weeks a year, it bursts into spectacular life.

### Glossary

**arch (n)** a structure with a curved top and straight sides that you can walk through
**camaraderie (n)** friendship and trust between people in a group
**crater (n)** a large round hole in the ground
**pioneer (n)** one of the first people to do something important
**pit (n)** a very large hole dug in the ground in order to obtain a particular substance or type of stone
**quarry (n)** a place where stone is dug out of the ground.

**D SCAN** Read the article again. What were the obstacles they had to overcome to build the Eden Project?

**E SPEAK** Work in pairs. Discuss the questions.
1 Why do you think people agreed to work on the project while funding was uncertain?
2 Why do you think this project succeeded?
3 Would you like to have worked on this project?
4 What other kinds of projects would you like to work on?

### Jolyon Brewis, *architect of Grimshaw Architects*

Most architects dream of creating a new world on a scale that eclipses all that's gone before. So, in the early days, when there was always the threat of construction being stopped because of lack of money, all the companies involved carried on regardless: we were so enthralled by the vision.

Our first designs were for different locations, including a tent-like structure for a hillside, then Smit discovered the china clay quarry at Bodelva. It had a romantic, lost world feel since it would be hidden from view until you were almost upon it. For a long while it all seemed a terrific gamble. Usually, the one thing an architect can rely on is solid ground, but since it was still a working quarry there was a lot of movement. What's more, to work out costings, we had to design our buildings right down to the last detail, even though no one knew if there'd even be enough money to buy the site.

³We'd been working on a series of snaking arches linked with glass, but while one of our design team ⁴was washing up, they realised that bubbles would have far more stability on the shifting soil. Building on such a huge scale involved untried technology: this was a leap into the unknown. Glass would have been too heavy so we pioneered 11-metre hexagonal pillows of inflated plastic. It had never been used so big before and we had no idea how it would behave. So we had to work through various disaster scenarios, such as what would happen if one deflated, then filled up with water and brought down the entire structure.

The worst moments were at the start when we ⁵hadn't been given the funding yet and some of the foundations ⁶got washed away during one of the wettest winters in memory. But there was a great feeling of camaraderie. We felt there was nothing we couldn't cope with.

## GRAMMAR
### Narrative tenses

**A** Match the underlined words (1–6) in the article with the tenses.

past simple ___   past perfect continuous ___
past continuous ___   past simple passive ___
past perfect simple ___   past perfect passive ___

**B WORK IT OUT** Complete the rules with the tenses in Exercise A.

| Narrative tenses |
|---|
| 1 When we tell a story, we use the _____ and _____ to explain the main events. |
| 2 We use the _____ and _____ to give background information for actions that were completed before the main events of the story. |
| 3 We use the _____ and _____ to give background information for actions that were in progress before the main events of the story. |

**C** Go to the Grammar Hub on page 124.

**D** Choose a sentence and continue the story. (It doesn't have to be a true story!)
1 I had been working for several hours when …
2 I had been planning to go to … for months, but …
3 I had just gone to bed when …
4 It had been raining all day, so …
5 I had been feeling unwell all day because …
6 I had already eaten a big breakfast, but …

### SPEAKING HUB

**A PREPARE** Think of an anecdote about an interesting project you worked on or a piece of work you have done. Use the ideas below to help you prepare what you are going to say.
- what was the project or piece of work
- what went well
- what went badly
- what would you do differently if you could do it again

**B PRESENT** Work in groups. Tell your anecdote about the project or piece of work.

**C DISCUSS** Listen to your classmates' anecdotes, react to what they say and ask questions.

**D REFLECT** Choose the best anecdotes.

○ Give a presentation about art
○ Talk about creative projects

CREATIVITY

# 2.2 Creative people

- Talk about finding inspiration
- Describe a life-changing moment

**V** – ideas and inspiration; compound adjectives
**G** – future in the past
**P** – questions for comment or criticism
**S** – inferring meaning

## VOCABULARY
### Ideas and inspiration

**A** Read the blog post *Sparking ideas*. Choose the correct definition (a or b) for the underlined phrases (1–10).

1. a find the right location
   b find the right mood
2. a abandon an idea
   b develop an idea
3. a working from nothing
   b working with no equipment
4. a steal someone's ideas
   b discuss something with someone
5. a get ideas from
   b paint a picture of
6. a escape a problem
   b help you to think of some ideas
7. a become very involved with something
   b are about to finish
8. a feel more energetic about
   b get a different view of
9. a find a good idea
   b am unable to progress
10. a think carefully
    b rely on your feelings

# SPARKING IDEAS

**Jasmine, artist**

'Some people are very practical about finding ideas. But not me. I need to ¹get into the right state of mind, whatever it takes. It means travelling miles to get away from everyone, working through the night or going for a walk – until I find inspiration or it finds me. Then I just ²run with an idea and see where it takes me.'

**Leo, dancer and choreographer**

'⁵I draw inspiration from other art – film, paintings, even books are great ways ⁶to jump start your creativity. They're not just sources of inspiration for my dance. When ⁷you immerse yourself in other art forms, you get the distance you need from your own work. You ⁸get a fresh perspective on it.'

**Michelle, director**

'³Working from a blank canvas, with no idea where you are going to start, can be really scary. So, … I call my mum! It's great ⁴to bounce ideas off someone. Even if you disagree, it can help you move forward.'

**Sam, playwright**

'Although writing is my job, when ⁹I hit a wall and just can't find the ideas, I start doodling cartoons, shapes. It really helps me to think. Then when the ideas start to come, ¹⁰you trust your instincts. You just know which ideas to use, which to combine and which to just forget.'

18 CREATIVITY

## 2.2

**B** Choose the correct phrases to complete the sentences.

1. I've just *got into the right state of mind / hit a wall* with this project. I've got no inspiration and can't get any further with it.
2. With art projects, you can't always know for certain you have the best idea. Sometimes you just have to *trust your instincts / work from a blank canvas*.
3. When you're feeling uninspired, talk to other people. *Bouncing ideas off someone / Running with an idea* can only help.
4. When there are no distractions and you are completely focused, you can truly *get a fresh perspective on / immerse yourself in* something.
5. We had no idea where we could begin with the design. We were *jump starting our creativity / working from a blank canvas*.

**C** SPEAK  Work in pairs. Do you ever have to be creative in your daily life? How do you come up with ideas?

## LISTENING

**A** LISTEN FOR MAIN IDEA  Listen to Mark and Lauren discussing an article about inspiration. What seven tips for getting inspiration do they discuss?

### SEVEN TIPS FOR GETTING INSPIRATION

1. _____
2. _____
3. _____
4. _____
5. _____
6. _____
7. _____

**B** LISTEN FOR DETAIL  Listen again. Which of the tips does Mark like?

**C** SPEAK  Work in pairs. Have you ever tried any of the ideas mentioned in Exercise A? Why/Why not?

## PRONUNCIATION
### Questions for comment or criticism

**A** Listen to the questions from the discussion. Draw arrows in the brackets to show whether the intonation rises (↗) or falls (↘) at the end of each sentence.

1. Isn't that a bit pretentious? ( )
2. Is he crazy? ( )
3. Why does she keep writing if it's terrible? ( )
4. Don't you think? ( )
5. Is she serious? ( )
6. How can you make something when you don't know what you're doing? ( )

**B** Choose the correct intonation for the questions. Then listen to check your answers.

1. **A:** Do you think it's sensible to schedule time for creativity?
   **B:** What's the point of that? (*rise / fall*) You can't be creative if you're not in the right state of mind.
2. **A:** Do you ever have creative ideas while you're dreaming?
   **B:** Yes, but I can never remember them. Isn't that frustrating? (*rise / fall*)
3. **A:** Do you find it easier to be creative when you're listening to music?
   **B:** Are you serious? (*rise / fall*) I can't think properly unless it's quiet.
4. **A:** Do you feel more creative early in the morning or late at night?
   **B:** Late at night. Definitely. Who feels creative first thing in the morning? (*rise / fall*)

**C** SPEAK  Ask your partner the questions in Exercise B. Try to use a question for comment or criticism in your answer.

## SPEAKING

**A** Look at the infographic. Think of an advantage and disadvantage for each suggestion.

**B** Work in pairs. Compare your ideas with your partner.

**C** Now decide which is the best suggestion for finding ideas. Talk for about one minute.

**D** DISCUSS  Work in pairs and discuss the questions.

1. Are you a creative person?
2. How important is the ability to be creative?
3. Do you think everyone should try to do something creative from time to time?

CREATIVITY

## 2.2

### VOCABULARY
Compound adjectives

**A** Complete the fame quiz.

#### ARE YOU CUT OUT FOR FAME?

**RATE YOURSELF ON A SCALE OF 1 to 5.**
1 = Strongly agree  5 = Strongly disagree

1. You would trade having privacy for being world famous.  1 2 3 4 5
2. You are very focused on one kind of career. You are not open-minded to other career choices.  1 2 3 4 5
3. You would describe yourself as a highly-motivated person.  1 2 3 4 5
4. You are thick skinned. You don't mind being criticised.  1 2 3 4 5
5. You would rather be self-employed than do part-time work for someone else for the same money.  1 2 3 4 5
6. You'd prefer to be paid less in a fun creative job than well paid and bored at work.  1 2 3 4 5
7. You can handle working long days and doing late-night shifts.  1 2 3 4 5

**B** Work in pairs. Turn to **page 149** of the **Communication Hub** to see what your answers say about you.

**C** Find eight compound adjectives in the quiz. Use the information in the box to help you.

> **Compound adjectives**
>
> Compound adjectives can be formed in several ways, including:
> - adjective + noun: *last-minute*
> - adjective + participle: *left-handed*
> - adverb + participle: *never-ending*
> - noun + adjective: *sun-dried*
> - noun + participle: *career-ending*
>
> We always hyphenate compound adjectives before a noun, but not after a noun. However, some compound adjectives are written as one word (e.g. *heartwarming*) or always hyphenated (e.g. *self-important*).

**D** Go to the **Vocabulary Hub** on **page 142**.

**E** **SPEAK** Work in pairs and discuss the questions. Use some of the adjectives in Exercise C.
1. Would you like to be famous?
2. What do you think are the good and bad points of being famous?

# CHANGE OF PLANS

Some people choose a career at a young age and stick with it. However, here are four famous people who ended up with very different careers from what they expected.

### CHARLIZE THERON

Charlize Theron, originally from South Africa, was to have been a ballerina. However, she suffered a career-ending injury to her knee that meant she had to abandon her childhood dream. Instead, she decided she would turn to acting. After finding it difficult to land speaking roles, she watched hours of television to try to pick up an American accent. But, the roles still didn't come and although she was getting modelling work, money was tight. One day she was trying to cash a cheque at the bank but the teller said he was not going to accept it. Theron started to argue with the teller, making a scene in the bank as she tried to explain that she was about to be thrown out of her apartment if she couldn't cash the cheque. Eventually a man in the line behind her came over to help resolve the situation and, after she had her money, he gave her his business card – he was an agent. A couple of months later, Theron had landed her first film role.

### ANDREA BOCELLI

World-famous opera singer Andrea Bocelli was supposed to have a very different career. Although he displayed a clear talent for music from an early age, his parents encouraged him to study law so that he would always have a steady income. Following his parents' advice, he attended law school and became a lawyer. However, he also continued with his music – playing in piano bars in the evenings to earn money for singing lessons. It was at one of these bars where he got the lucky break that was to launch his career. Zucchero, a famous Italian singer, heard him sing, and thought that he would be perfect for a demo he wanted to make. As a result of that meeting, Bocelli ending up going on tour with Zucchero. Bocelli even sang at Zucchero's birthday party – and was immediately signed up by an agent at the party. The agent knew he was going to be a big star – and she was right.

> **Glossary**
>
> **renovate** (v) to make something old look new again by repairing and improving it, especially a building
> **embroidery** (n) the activity of decorating cloth with coloured stitches

CREATIVITY

## READING

**A SPEAK** Look at the pictures of the people in the article *Change of plans*. What do you know about them?

**B READ FOR DETAIL** Read *Change of plans*. What do the four people's stories have in common?

**C INFER MEANING** Read the article again and answer the questions. Use the information in the box to help you.

### Inferring meaning
Writers do not always explain everything in detail. They sometimes provide readers with the facts and allow them to infer the meaning by drawing a conclusion from the available information.

1 Why was Charlize Theron unable to get speaking roles?

2 Does Andrea Bocelli still work as a lawyer?

3 What do we know about Harrison Ford's personality when he was younger?

4 How did Grandma Moses learn to paint?

**D SPEAK** Work in pairs and discuss the questions
1 Which was the most interesting story? Why?
2 Which person do you think was the luckiest?

### HARRISON FORD
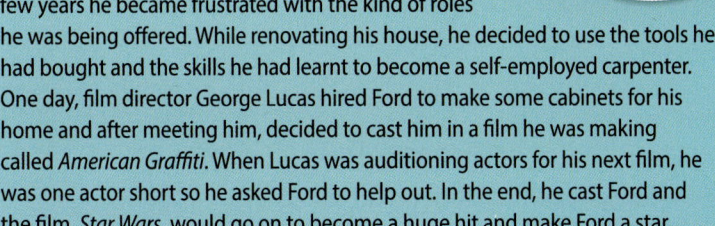

Harrison Ford first became interested in acting at the age of 18 because he thought <u>it would</u> be an easy way to get a good grade on his English course. He dropped out of college and moved to Hollywood in his early 20s. He managed to get some small acting jobs, but after a few years he became frustrated with the kind of roles he was being offered. While renovating his house, he decided to use the tools he had bought and the skills he had learnt to become a self-employed carpenter. One day, film director George Lucas hired Ford to make some cabinets for his home and after meeting him, decided to cast him in a film he was making called *American Graffiti*. When Lucas was auditioning actors for his next film, he was one actor short so he asked Ford to help out. In the end, he cast Ford and <u>the film, Star Wars, would go on to become a huge hit</u> and make Ford a star.

### GRANDMA MOSES

Grandma Moses (Anna Mary Robertson Moses) became a famous painter at the age of 80 – despite not having had any formal training. She was born in 1860 and raised on her parents' farm. She didn't attend school regularly, because she knew <u>she would be leaving home</u> to start working on another farm when she was 12. She married at 17, was widowed at 47, and retired at 76. In fact, she didn't start painting until she took it up as a hobby at the age of 78. She only started because <u>she was giving up embroidery</u> due to pain from arthritis. She painted rural scenes from her childhood, which she gave away or sold cheaply. However, one day an art collector saw her paintings in a local shop. He drove straight to her farm and asked to buy all the paintings she had, and, later that year, he exhibited some of her paintings at a show for new painters. This led to solo exhibitions, and soon <u>her shows would break</u> attendance records around the world. She died in 1961.

## GRAMMAR
Future in the past

**A WORK IT OUT** Look at the underlined phrases in the article. Then choose the correct words to complete the rules.

### Future in the past
1 When we talk about plans, intentions and predictions that we had in the past, we use *past / present* forms of the verbs we usually use to talk about the future.
2 We use *be + to + infinitive* for events that *came true / didn't come true* and *be + to + have + past participle* (or *be + supposed to + verb*) for events that *came true / didn't come true*.

**B** Go to the **Grammar Hub** on **page 124**.

**C** Write sentences using the future in the past to explain the situations (1–5). Then share your ideas with a partner.
1 You didn't get up early today.
2 You missed your train or bus this morning.
3 You didn't eat lunch yesterday.
4 You got lost in the city.
5 You went to see a film with a friend.

*I was going to get up early, but I forgot to set my alarm clock.*

## SPEAKING HUB

**A PLAN** Think of a time when a change of plans had a big effect on your life. Choose one of these situations or think of your own idea.
- You changed your mind about something.
- You suddenly had an unexpected opportunity.
- Something did not go as you had planned.
- Something good came out of a bad situation.

**B PREPARE** Make notes to prepare to talk about this event.

**C PRESENT** Tell your partner about what happened.

**D DISCUSS** Listen and ask your partner questions.

○– Talk about finding inspiration
○– Describe a life-changing moment

CREATIVITY 21

# Café Hub

## 2.3 Art and design
A – *nowhere* phrases  S – managing a discussion

### ▶ City design festival

a

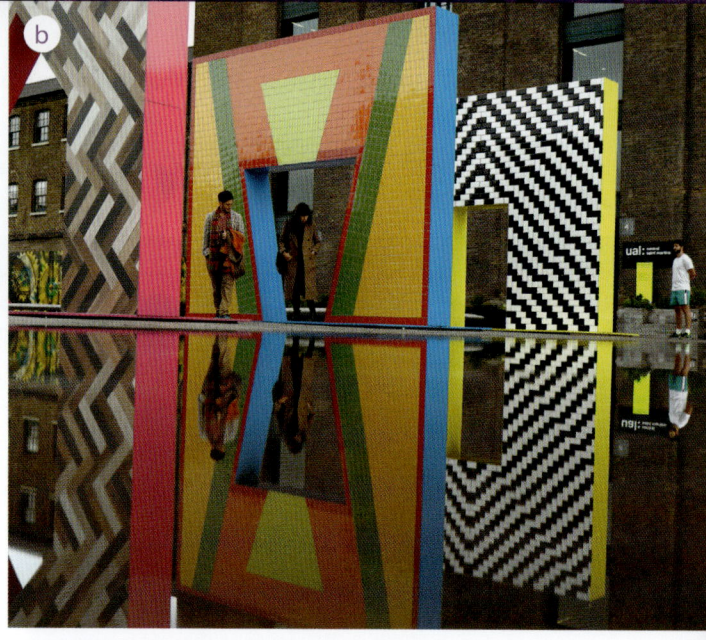
b

**A** Work in pairs. Look at the pictures (a and b) and discuss the questions.

1. Where are they?
2. What do you think they are?

**B** ▶ Watch the video and check your answers to Exercise A.

#### Glossary
**accessible (adj)** art, music, literature, etc, which is easy to understand and enjoy
**ceramic (adj)** made from clay baked at a high temperature so that it has become hard
**eccentricity (n)** the state of behaving in a strange and unusual way, sometimes in a humorous way
**installation (n)** a piece of art that consists of several objects or pictures arranged to produce a particular effect

**C** ▶ Watch the video again. Tick the things you see.

1. People walking inside an installation. ☐
2. A designer creating an installation. ☐
3. An indoor design exhibition. ☐
4. A man sitting at a table with a cup of coffee. ☐
5. Children playing on the installation. ☐
6. A person taking a photo of an installation. ☐
7. People walking through arches. ☐
8. A designer showing a group of people around an installation. ☐

**D** ▶ Watch the video again. Complete the sentences with the best option.

1. What Camille Walala loves most about an outdoor art installation is that it *makes art easier for people to understand and enjoy / allows her to be more creative*.
2. Camille has lived in London for *fifteen / twenty* years.
3. A woman says Camille Walala's installation looks like a *theme park / bouncy castle*.
4. Adam Nathaniel Furman says people think ceramics are something *found in your bathroom and kitchen / used to cover buildings*.
5. Ben Evans says *a minority / the majority* of London's design community have British passports.

## AUTHENTIC ENGLISH

**A** Work in pairs. Read the sentences from the video. Then choose the correct words to complete the information in the box.

*There's **nowhere quite like** it, especially when it comes to design.*

*I absolutely love London, it's like an eccentricity that you've got **nowhere else**.*

*There's **nowhere else** really in the UK where you can just walk down the street and see exciting things like this every day.*

#### *nowhere* phrases
We use *there's nowhere quite like*, *that you've got nowhere else* and *there's nowhere else where* to express that a place is *ordinary / unique*.
We have many other phrases with *nowhere* like: *nowhere on earth*, *... but nowhere more so than ...*, *out of nowhere*, *go nowhere*, *be going nowhere fast*, *in the middle of nowhere*, *nowhere near* and *nowhere to be found*.

**B** Write sentences using phrases with *nowhere* about these places.

1. Paris *There's nowhere on earth like Paris for culture.*
2. London _____
3. Dubai _____
4. New York _____
5. Italy _____
6. Brazil _____

**C** Work in pairs. Tell each other about some of your favourite places (countries, cities, restaurants, shops, museums, etc) and why they are unique.

## ▶ Art critics

SAM   MALCOLM   AMANDA   HARRY   EMILY

**A** Work in pairs. Discuss the questions.
1 Do you like modern art? Why/Why not?
2 What do you think about art criticism?

**B**  Watch the video and answer the questions.
1 What does Malcolm like about the painted paper?
2 What does each of the following people think the message of the painted paper is?
   - Amanda
   - Malcolm
   - male customer
3 Whose opinion is most popular amongst the three of them?
4 What misunderstanding has occurred?

## SPEAKING SKILL

**A** Work in pairs. Look at the underlined expression from the video and answer the questions.

> **Amanda:** The artist is clearly making a comment on …
> **Sam:** I think you're a bit confused …
> **Amanda:** Sam … <u>Can you let me finish?</u> Thanks. The artist is clearly making a statement on feelings of isolation …

1 What has happened in the exchange between Sam and Amanda?
2 Why do we use expressions like this when we're speaking?

Read the information in the box. Which of the ways of managing a discussion (1–5) are used in the exchange in Exercise A?

**B** Match the ways of managing a discussion (1–5) with the examples from the video (a–e) below.

### Managing a discussion

1 **Interrupting:** Say something to stop someone speaking so that you can speak instead.
2 **Taking the floor:** Signal that you are now going to join a debate or discussion.
3 **Returning to a point:** Indicate that you want to further discuss a point that you previously made.
4 **Stopping an interruption:** Tell the person who is trying to interrupt that you want to finish your point first.
5 **Pre-empting an interruption:** Anticipate that someone will interrupt you and briefly state all the points you want to cover before they cut in.

a Well that leads back to my point … without meaning there is no relationship.
b If I could just finish … my main point though is that it doesn't really matter what it is.
c I couldn't agree more … it does evoke some really quite intense emotions.
d I don't mean to cut you off, Amanda, but I think it's the exact opposite.
e And that's my point exactly. When you are using bold colours like this artist has, you are clearly trying to expose just how superficial those connections are.

**C** Work in small groups. Discuss one of the following topics. Use the strategies from Exercise B.
- Art in the past and now
- The greatest artist ever
- Different forms of art

## 🎤 SPEAKING HUB

**A PREPARE** You are going to talk about a work of art in a small group. Look at the picture on page 13. Think about what you want to say about the picture and art in general.

**B PRESENT** Work in small groups. Discuss the picture and present your views.

> A: *I usually tend to prefer landscapes rather than portraits …*
> B: *Can I just stop you there? … The style of painting is what makes it special.*
> A: *Exactly. What I was actually saying was that while I usually prefer landscapes, in this case …*

○─ Discuss a work of art

➤ Turn to **page 157** to learn how to write a review about a classic book or film.

# Unit 2 Review

## VOCABULARY

**A** Complete the conversations with the words in the box.

> groundbreaking   hilarious   repetitive
> sensational   tedious   unconventional

1. **A:** That was a really funny film. I was crying with laughter.
   **B:** Yes, it was _____.
2. **A:** I thought her performance was amazing.
   **B:** She was _____. She deserves an Oscar.
3. **A:** Have you read this book? I'm finding it pretty dull.
   **B:** Yeah, it's a bit _____, isn't it?
4. **A:** It was such an innovative musical. I loved it.
   **B:** Me, too. As you say, it was _____.
5. **A:** Shall we turn this off? It's just car chase after car chase.
   **B:** Yeah, it's kind of _____, isn't it?
6. **A:** Do you like her work? Her pieces are very unusual.
   **B:** She's _____, but I find her work exciting.

**B** Complete the sentences with the words in the box. Then choose which ideas help you feel most creative.

> bounce   draw   fresh   trust
> immerse   run   stimulate   hit

1. Take a break. _____ yourself in a TV show for 30 minutes.
2. _____ ideas around with your best friend. Ask them for a _____ perspective.
3. _____ inspiration from a piece of music.
4. Whenever you _____ a wall, go for a walk.
5. Drink coffee to _____ your creativity.
6. Don't think carefully – just _____ with an idea. _____ your instincts.

**C** Match numbers (1–8) to letters (a–h) to form full sentences. Then think of some jobs which match each sentence.

1. You need to be thick-
2. It's a well-
3. You need to be highly
4. Most people won't become world-
5. It's like being self-
6. There are a lot of late-
7. You have to be open-
8. It's a high-

a. night shifts, so you'll have an irregular sleeping pattern.
b. risk job, so it pays well.
c. employed, because you can work from home.
d. paid job.
e. minded, because things change all the time.
f. motivated, because it's competitive.
g. skinned to handle the criticism.
h. famous, but they still make a living.

## GRAMMAR

**A** Complete the text with the correct form of the verbs in brackets.

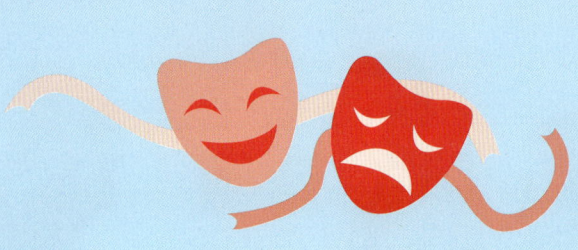

# My first role

When I was about ten, I ¹_____ (join) a drama group in a nearby town and they ²_____ (perform) a show every year. That year, we ³_____ (do) Peter Pan.

We ⁴_____ (rehearse) for weeks. I ⁵_____ (give) a pretty big role – I ⁶_____ (play) Michael, the smallest of the children Peter Pan ⁷_____ (bring) to Neverland. I ⁸_____ (remember) how nervous I ⁹_____ (be) when we ¹⁰_____ (peek) out from behind the curtain to see the people in the audience.

However, it was worth all the nerves when the audience ¹¹_____ (applaud) at the end. I ¹²_____ (feel) so proud – and I couldn't wait to start practising for the next show.

**B** Choose the correct option to complete the sentences.

1. The band did not know they *would have / were to be* the biggest selling rock group this decade.
2. Little did he know, it was this discovery that *was to change / is to have changed* the experiment completely.
3. This *was supposed to be / would be* a dream holiday, but it turned into a nightmare.
4. They *were to finish / be finished* in May, but the deadline was pushed back until June.
5. The motorway was *due / meant* to be completed by now.
6. Carlos had been *about / set* to go through airport security when he realised he didn't have his passport.

24  CREATIVITY

# 3 PROGRESS

If there is no struggle, there is no progress.
— Frederick Douglass

Blazing a trail at thirty thousand feet.

## OBJECTIVES

- make predictions about the future
- use persuasive language to sell something
- discuss progress and society
- evaluate costs and benefits
- discuss renewable energy
- write a persuasive email

Work with a partner. Discuss the questions.

1 Look at the picture. What does it say about progress? What other examples can you think of to illustrate the same idea?
2 Read the quote. What does Douglass mean?
3 How could you measure 'progress':
   - in your own life
   - in your city/country
   - in the world?

# 3.1 Progressive design

- Make predictions about the future
- Use persuasive language to sell something

- V — sustainability; forming verbs from adjectives
- P — sounding persuasive
- G — future structures
- S — listening to identify persuasive techniques

## VOCABULARY
### Sustainability

**A** Work in groups. Which of these sustainable / environmentally friendly solutions would most benefit your country?

- recycling
- biodegradable plastic
- electric vehicles
- beach clean-ups
- wind power

**B** Choose the correct words to complete these statements about sustainability.

1 We will *never / soon* run out of **renewable** energy sources like solar and wind power.
2 A sustainable building generates *less / more* electricity than it **consumes**.
3 To be carbon-**neutral**, you might *cut down / plant* some trees to **offset** the pollution caused by a plane journey.
4 A zero-**emission** factory causes no *air / water* pollution.
5 Over-exploitation of natural resources will *lead to / prevent* the **depletion** of those resources over time.
6 **Biodegradable** materials break down into *harmful / harmless* parts which don't **accumulate** in the environment.

**C** Go to the Vocabulary Hub on page 143.

**D SPEAK** Work in groups. Discuss the questions.

1 Can ordinary people be carbon-neutral/cause zero-emissions in the modern world?
2 Is it worth the effort? Can ordinary people make a difference?

## READING

**A SPEAK** Look at the pictures in the article. What might be special or unusual about the buildings?

**B READ FOR GIST** Read the article quickly. Match the names below with the pictures (a–c).

1 Aequorea ___
2 Nautilus Eco-Resort ___
3 The Lilypad ___

**C READ FOR DETAIL** Read the article again. Which project(s) from Exercise B does each statement apply to?

1 Scientists will work there.
2 It takes its shape from the natural world.
3 It will collect its own water.
4 It will use less energy than it generates.
5 The buildings will move up and down.
6 It will move from place to place.
7 It will hold tens of thousands of people.

**D SPEAK** Would you like to live or stay in any of these places? What would be the benefits and drawbacks?

a

## GRAMMAR
### Future structures

**A** Look at the underlined sections (1–10) in the article. What time do they refer to?

**B WORK IT OUT** Match the sections (1–10) with the rules in the box (a–f).

### Future structures

a We use the future continuous to describe a situation that will be in progress at a particular point in the future (___), or to emphasise that it will cover an extended period of time (___).
b We use the future perfect simple to describe changes that will be completed before a particular point in the future (___).
c We use the future perfect continuous to focus on the future results of an earlier future process, and/or to measure the length of time of that process (___).
d We can use a modal verb (e.g. *might*, *could*) instead of *will* in these structures (___).
e After words like *if*, *unless*, *when*, *while*, etc, future tenses (e.g. future continuous) usually become present tenses (e.g. present continuous) (___, ___).
f Other future structures include *be on the brink/verge of (doing)* (___) and *be about / due / set to (do)* (___, ___).

**C** Go to the Grammar Hub on page 126.

## SPEAKING

**SPEAK** Work in pairs. Ask and answer the questions about the times in the box.

> ten years from now    the end of this lesson
> this time next year

1 Where will you be? What will you be doing?
2 What will you have achieved? How will the world have changed?
3 How will you be feeling? Why?

26  PROGRESS

# ONE ARCHITECT'S VISION
## TO BRING US BACK FROM THE BRINK

The world of 2100 will look considerably different to the world of today. ¹By then, much of the ice around the north and south poles will have melted, according to the Intergovernmental Panel on Climate Change. ²Sea levels could well have risen by as much as 88 cm. ³Many of the world's low-lying islands and coastal regions will be disappearing – or will already have disappeared – beneath the rising tides. Millions of people will have lost their homes. In short, ⁴we're on the brink of witnessing irrevocable changes to our world.

A visionary Belgian architect, Vincent Callebaut, has an innovative answer to the problem of rising sea levels: The Lilypad, a futuristic-looking city that will drift around the world following ocean currents like a giant ship. If his plans come to fruition, ⁵this self-contained city is set to become home to around 50,000 climate refugees.

The Lilypad's design is inspired by the shape of the *Victoria amazonica* lilypad. At its centre will be a lake to catch, store and purify rain water, surrounded by three 'mountains'. Thanks to a series of renewable energy sources, this eco-city will produce more energy than it consumes. All its carbon dioxide and other waste will be recycled, making the Lilypad entirely zero-emission.

The Lilypad isn't Callebaut's only attempt to re-think the design of buildings and cities. Back in 2015, he revealed spectacular plans for the world's first underwater skyscrapers, called Aequorea, which will be 500 metres wide, have 250 floors and be capable of holding 20,000 people. These eco-friendly structures will be self-sufficient, as they'll produce all their own energy, heat, food and water. They'll also be made of 100% recycled plastic, collected from the world's oceans.

Each oceanscraper will have a jellyfish-like structure: the entrance will be located at the surface and then the structure will spiral down to depths of 1000 metres. Inside will be homes, offices and workshops, science laboratories, sea farms and fruit and vegetable gardens. Fresh drinking water will be produced using in-depth pressure to separate salt from seawater.

The Aequorea will be moored off the coast of Brazil, rather than in the open ocean. Residents will certainly be glad of the chance to visit the mainland and soak up some much-needed sunshine at the end of each working week – ⁶they'll have been breathing processed air and staring out into the deep, dark ocean all week, after all.

Mr Callebaut's latest project, the Nautilus Eco-Resort in the Philippines, takes its name and inspiration from a mollusc, the nautilus. The hotels themselves will also be shaped like seashells, which will rise and fall as they rotate around a central coil. Visitors can expect uninterrupted sunshine throughout the day as the towers follow the course of the sun. Some rooms will even disappear underground ⁷when they're not being used. But before you book your ticket, be warned that ⁸the resort isn't about to open any time soon – like most of Mr Callebaut's designs, it's still some way from actually being built.

The Nautilus Eco-Resort aims to be a 'zero-emission, zero-waste, zero-poverty' project, built entirely from reused or recycled materials from the islands. Visitors will also be actively involved with scientists, engineers and ecologists to ensure their experience encourages sustainable progress. So if you do decide to take a luxury holiday there, ⁹you won't be spending all your time lounging around by the pool. You'll also get some practical lessons on sustainability ¹⁰while you're collecting rubbish from the beach!

### Glossary

**brink (n)** the point in time when something very bad or very good is about to happen

**irrevocable (adj)** impossible to change or stop

**moor (v)** to stop a ship or boat from moving by fastening it to a place with ropes or by using an anchor

**sustainable (adj)** using methods that do not harm the environment

**visionary (adj)** original and showing a lot of imagination

## 3.1

### LISTENING

**A SPEAK** Work in pairs. Read *(Very) Smart Materials*. Discuss why each material mentioned might be useful.

> **Glossary**
> **smart materials (n)** technologically advanced materials with properties (e.g. colour, shape, magnetism, etc) that can change in response to stimuli such as light, temperature, pressure or moisture

# (VERY) SMART MATERIALS

### 1
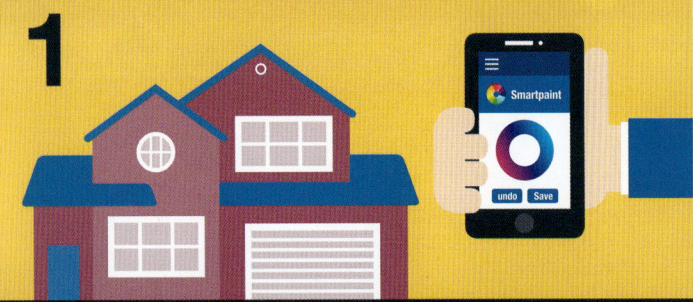
**COLOUR-CHANGING PAINT:**
The roof and walls of a building automatically change colour during the day, depending on the temperature.

### 3

**PIEZOELECTRIC SHOES:**
Walking in the shoes causes crystals in the soles to change shape, generating an electric current.

### 2
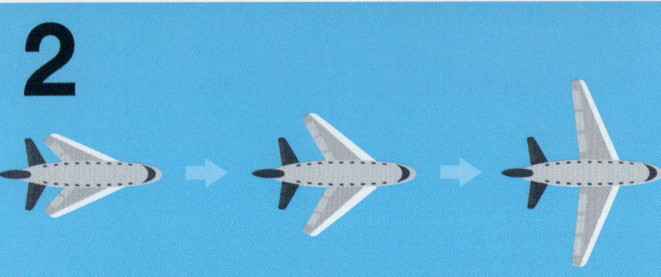
**SHAPE-CHANGING AEROPLANE WINGS:**
The wings detect the plane's height (using atmospheric pressure) and change shape automatically.

### 4

**SELF-REPAIRING RUBBER TYRES:**
The rubber contains tiny balls of glue. If the tyre is damaged, the balls open, glue is released and solidifies, and the holes are repaired.

---

**B LISTEN FOR DETAIL** Listen to a conversation about smart materials. Choose the correct options (a, b or c) to answer the questions.

1 What is the woman trying to do?
  a make friendly conversation
  b teach the man something
  c sell something

2 How does the hat work?
  a Its fibres change shape to control air flow.
  b It uses electricity to warm your head.
  c You can adjust its shape based on the weather.

3 What must the man do to keep the hat?
  a write a detailed report about his experiences of wearing it
  b pay £50
  c test it in the rain

4 Why does the woman phone her boss?
  a to ask for advice about the jacket
  b to persuade her boss to lower the price
  c to put the man under pressure to buy the jacket

**C LISTEN FOR TECHNIQUES** Listen again. Which persuasive techniques does the woman use for 1–6? Use the information in the box to help you.

> **Listening to identify persuasive techniques**
>
> People sometimes use tricks to persuade us to do things. When someone is trying to persuade you, listen out for these tricks.
>
> **Exaggeration:** listen for words like *absolutely* and *extremely*.
>
> **Leading questions:** listen for questions that 'push' you towards a particular answer, including question tags (e.g. *isn't it?*).
>
> **Personalisation:** listen for phrases like *if you imagine* and overuse of *you/your*.

1 cycling more often  _____
2 how the hat works  _____
3 testing the hat  _____
4 the problem and the solution  _____
5 the smart jacket  _____
6 paying for the jacket  _____

**D SPEAK** Work in pairs. Discuss the questions.

1 Is it acceptable to use techniques like these to persuade or manipulate other people? In what situations is it OK? When is it unfair?

2 What techniques do you use when you're trying to persuade someone?

## PRONUNCIATION
### Sounding persuasive

**A** Listen to the extracts which include the sentences below. How is the woman trying to sound persuasive? Use the information in the box to help you.

1 You just look like a very fit and sporty person.
2 Yeah, tell me about it!
3 Hmm, I know exactly what you mean.
4 I think you've got yourself an excellent deal there, sir. I can see you're a very smart negotiator!
5 You know what? Maybe I can help you out there.
6 But … hmm … maybe … I can offer you … a special price … to thank you for your help.

> **Sounding persuasive**
> a Speak fairly quietly (as if you're sharing a secret) and slowly, with lots of pauses (as if you're thinking of new ideas while speaking).
> b Start fast and then slow right down, placing extra stress on all positive words.
> c Use slightly exaggerated rising and falling intonation on key words to express emotions.

**B SPEAK** Work in pairs. Practise saying the sentences in Exercise A as persuasively as possible.

## VOCABULARY
### Forming verbs from adjectives

**A** Complete the extracts with the correct form of the verbs in the box.

> ensure   formalise   simplify   strengthen   tighten   warm

1 I bet you can't wait for the weather _____ up!
2 It's quite complicated technology, but I'll try _____ it for you.
3 The fibres in your hat respond to the cold temperature by _____ up.
4 That _____ there's no heat loss from your head.
5 As the hat gets wet, the water _____ the fibres.
6 I just need you to sign this form _____ our agreement.

**B** What adjective is each verb from Exercise A formed from?

**C** Use the affixes in the box to create verbs. The same affix is used for all words in each group. Other spelling changes may also be needed. One group doesn't require any change.

> -en   -ify   en-   -ise

| | | | |
|---|---|---|---|
| 1 | strong | long | short |
| 2 | final | visual | equal |
| 3 | empty | smooth | narrow |
| 4 | pure | solid | simple |
| 5 | danger | able | large |

**D** Complete the advice with the adjectives you formed in Exercise C. Sometimes more than one answer is possible.

> **How to be persuasive**
> 1 Don't just offer weak opinions. _____ your arguments with evidence and examples.
> 2 Help your potential customers to _____ themselves using your product.
> 3 Don't try to persuade everybody at the same time: _____ your focus to a small group of key people.
> 4 _____ complicated explanations to make them easier to understand.
> 5 _____ the decision-making process for your customers by removing any barriers that make their decisions harder.
> 6 Don't speak too quickly. Try to _____ the pauses between key words.

## SPEAKING HUB

**A PREPARE** Work in pairs. You are going to try to persuade somebody to buy a product made from smart materials. Choose one of the ideas from Listening Exercise A or use your own idea.

**B DISCUSS** Discuss how your product works and why it's useful.

**C PLAN** Plan a sales strategy using the persuasion techniques from Listening Exercise C.

**D PRESENT** Swap partners. Take turns to try to persuade your new partner to buy your product.

**E REFLECT** Share your experiences with the class. Would you buy your partner's product? Why/Why not?

○– Make predictions about the future
○– Use persuasive language to sell something

# 3.2 Better ... or worse?

- Discuss progress and society
- Evaluate costs and benefits

**P** – stress-shift words
**G** – negative inversion
**V** – verb–noun collocations
**S** – reading to determine costs and benefits

## LISTENING

**A SPEAK** Work in groups. Do you think life is generally getting better or worse for your generation?

**B LISTEN FOR MAIN IDEA** Listen to the first part of a radio show. Match the people (1–5) with the opinions (a–e).

1 Bob  ____
2 Mary ____
3 James ____
4 Callum ____
5 Sonia ____

a I'm more aware of bad things happening than I was.
b The earlier generation didn't have the same financial worries as we do.
c Everything was better when I was younger.
d Young people were more polite in the past.
e I feel bad when I compare myself with others.

**C SPEAK** Work in pairs and discuss the questions.

1 Do you agree with the interviewees' opinions?
2 What are some possible explanations for their opinions?

**D LISTEN FOR GIST** Listen to the second part of the radio show. Match the opinions (a–e) in Exercise B with the concepts (1–5).

1 the inequality paradox ____
2 the reminiscence bump ____
3 the them-and-us delusion ____
4 the invisible struggle phenomenon ____
5 the window-on-the-world effect ____

**E LISTEN FOR DETAIL** Listen to the second part again. Are these sentences true (T) or false (F)? Correct the false sentences.

1 Professor Martinelli believes that life is getting better everywhere. *T / F*
2 Declinism proves that things really are getting worse. *T / F*
3 When average levels of well-being improve, it can lead to a rise in declinism. *T / F*
4 People often have nostalgia for their youth. *T / F*
5 We tend to focus on good behaviour in groups that we don't belong to. *T / F*
6 Professor Martinelli's parents never worried about financial problems. *T / F*
7 Professor Martinelli is optimistic that people will try to prevent global tragedies. *T / F*

**F SPEAK** Work in pairs. Discuss the questions.

1 What are your experiences of the five concepts from the radio show?
2 Are you generally optimistic or pessimistic about the near future?

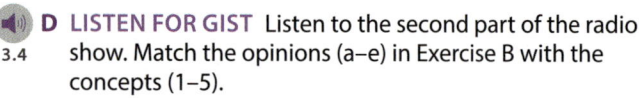

## PRONUNCIATION
Stress-shift words

**A** Listen to the sentences. Underline the stressed syllables in the words in bold.
1 Despite amazing **progress** in technology and sharp **increases** in living standards, many of us believe our quality of life has actually **decreased**!
2 Let's hear a few **extracts** from those interviews.
3 You feel like a **reject** from society.
4 It's almost as if we **rewrite** the events in our memories.
5 You've simply erased their negative **attributes** and bad **conduct** from your memory.
6 We tend to **attribute** other people's success to luck.
7 That's a major source of inter-generational **conflict**: young adults always **suspect** that earlier generations had it much easier!

**B** Underline the stressed syllables in the words in bold. Then listen and check.
1 Why are you always such a **rebel**? Why do you always **rebel** against everything I say?
2 I didn't think I'd like Thai food, but now I'm a **convert**. Your cooking has **converted** me!
3 You need to install an **upgrade** for your computer. When did you last **upgrade** it?
4 I deal with **imports** and **exports** in my job: I **import** raw materials and **export** finished products to customers.
5 I **frequent** this café during the summer, but I'm not really a **frequent** visitor during the rest of the year.

**C** Practise saying the sentences with the correct stress.

## GRAMMAR
Negative inversion

**A** Complete the extracts from the radio show with one word.
1 No sooner _____ an older person got on the bus than we all stood up.
2 Only after they'd all got off the bus _____ I finally sit down.
3 No way could I _____ afford a flat.
4 None of our neighbours had much money, and neither _____ we.
5 Not _____ did I have great friends, but we also did cool things all the time.
6 By no means _____ I suggesting that life is wonderful for everybody everywhere.
7 _____ in a million years **did it occur to me** that my parents were worried about money.

**B** **WORK IT OUT** Match the sentences (1–7) in Exercise A with the rules (a–d) in the box.

> **Negative inversion**
>
> When we want to emphasise a negative element of a sentence (e.g. *never*), we can move it to the beginning and swap the subject and auxiliary verb. This process is called inversion.
> a When there is no auxiliary verb, we add *do/does/did*. ___ ___ ___
> b Inversion with *could* is common after phrases like *only after* and *no way*. ___ ___
> c Inversion is very common in the structure *not only … but also*. ___
> d After *no sooner*, we need a *than*-clause. ___
>
> We don't use inversion when a negative word/phrase is the subject: *Not one person offered me a seat.* (NOT: ~~did offer~~)

**C** Go the **Grammar Hub** on **page 126**.

**D** Complete the sentences so they are true for you.
1 Under no circumstances would I …
2 Only rarely do I …
3 Not only do I think …

## SPEAKING

**A** **PREPARE** Work in pairs. Imagine you are on a radio interview about progress. Student A – read the information below. Student B – go to the **Communication Hub** on **page 154**.

**B** **SPEAK** Roleplay your interview.

Student A

> You're a radio interviewer. You believe that while people complain about the world today, overall it is actually getting better. Interview Student B about progress. Also give your view on the subject.
>
> Discuss the following areas.
> - the impact of technology
> - community
> - quality of life
> - cost of living
> - employment
> - the environment

PROGRESS

## 3.2

### READING

**A PREDICT** Work in pairs. Discuss the questions.

1 Look at the pictures and title of the article. What do you think 'voluntourism' might be?
2 What do you think attracts people to these kinds of activities?
3 Why might some voluntary work do more harm than good?

**B SKIM** Read *Voluntourism: more harm than good?* quickly and check your ideas in Exercise A.

**C READ FOR COSTS AND BENEFITS** Work in pairs. What are the deep costs and benefits of voluntourism? Use the information in the box to help you.

> **Reading to determine costs and benefits**
>
> When you read a for-and-against article, it's useful to distinguish between **surface-level** costs/benefits (e.g. obvious, short-term or unimportant ones) and **deep** costs/benefits (e.g. hidden, long-term or highly important ones). When deciding if you agree with the writer's opinion, focus mainly on the deep costs and benefits.

# VOLUNTOURISM
## more harm than good?

When Pippa Biddle was a teenager, she went on a school trip to Tanzania, where she and her classmates were tasked with building a library for an orphanage. Lacking even basic construction skills, they did their best and, remarkably, over the course of a week, the building started to take shape. Only later did Pippa learn the truth: every night, a group of professional builders had been carefully undoing and redoing the teenagers' work in order to make the construction structurally sound. The whole project was an illusion: the true purpose wasn't to get help on the building project, but to make the teenagers feel good about themselves.

Welcome to the world of voluntourism, where volunteering meets tourism. Unlike true volunteering, this is paid work – but it's the worker who pays for the privilege. On the surface, voluntourism is a win–win situation. The voluntourist seizes an opportunity to travel to an exotic country and work with real people in authentic locations, while the recipients get free help. But the reality, as Pippa's story brings home to us, is rather more complicated.

The main criticism of voluntourism is that it perpetuates the myth that people in some countries need help from wise and generous benefactors in richer countries. The reality, of course, is that these countries have plenty of kind-hearted experts of their own. But of course, most voluntourists aren't even experts: they're typically gap-year students looking for a quick adventure, with no valuable skills to offer. At best, their input is often a waste of time. At worst, it could do more harm than good, as with Pippa's building experience.

Even worse are stories of fake projects created merely to keep the volunteers busy, regardless of any inherent local need. For example, there are English-language schools in remote communities where the locals neither want nor need to study English.

It's hard to avoid the conclusion that voluntourism is nothing more than an ego-trip: a chance to pretend you're making the world a better place, so you can wow your friends back home with tales of your generosity, your suffering and your profound experience of 'finding yourself'.

But there's another side to voluntourism. While many people do sign up with naïve expectations, they often emerge from their experiences with a far deeper understanding. On their return home, they can spread a more positive and realistic image of the countries they visit, and counter rather than perpetuate stereotypes. Finally, many voluntourists go on to become committed life-long volunteers, with their new-found habit of helping others, whether globally or in their own communities.

It's also an oversimplification to claim that voluntourism is always harmful to local communities. Highly-skilled volunteers like doctors, scientists and engineers can indeed bring real benefits. The key is to do so in a spirit of cooperation and mutual respect with local experts, rather than following the 'watch me and learn' approach. Many voluntourism agencies can have a genuinely positive impact both on the volunteers and the communities they serve.

So if you're considering signing up as a voluntourist, seize the initiative and do some research beforehand. Be honest and realistic about your skills and expectations. Above all, never forget that the main beneficiary of your voluntourism adventure will probably be you. With the right mindset, this could well be the most important experience of your life.

**D READ FOR DETAIL** Work in pairs. Read the article again and discuss the questions.

1 Why did the builders work at night?
2 How did Pippa's building experience 'do more harm than good'?
3 What does the writer mean by 'the right mindset' in the last paragraph?

**E SPEAK** Work in groups. Do you think voluntourism does more harm than good? Would you consider doing it yourself?

## VOCABULARY
### Verb–noun collocations

**A** Choose a verb to complete each pair of verb–noun collocations. Then decide on the best collocation to complete each sentence. Use the information in the box to help you.

> **Verb–noun collocations**
>
> Verb–noun collocations are a good way to build vocabulary. Sometimes these include advanced verbs (e.g. *perpetuate*), but mostly they include very common verbs (e.g. *make, do, take*). Try to underline these as you read in English.

1 Unless you have valuable work experience you'll usually _____*do*_____ *your best* / *more harm than good*.
2 Volunteer organisations should always _____ the *time* / *shape* to train volunteers before a project.
3 A trained English teacher can _____ *benefits* / *home* to a host community.
4 It's vital that voluntourists _____ *the responsibility* / *the opportunity* to understand their host community before and during their visit.
5 Volunteer organisations should not _____ the *myth* / *problem* that their projects are just extended holidays.

**B** Go to the Vocabulary Hub on page 143.

**C SPEAK** Work in pairs. Do you agree with sentences 1–5 in Exercise A? Why/Why not?

## SPEAKING HUB

**A PREPARE** Work in pairs. Imagine you are going to volunteer abroad. Choose one of the following voluntary projects or use your own idea.
- working at an animal sanctuary
- planting trees
- teaching children
- cleaning up litter

**B PLAN** Create a list of surface-level and deep costs and benefits for:
- you and your partner
- who you are helping
- the world in general.

**C DISCUSS** Discuss whether the benefits outweigh the costs. How could the costs be reduced? How could the benefits be increased?

**D PRESENT** Present your plans to the class. Whose ideas would have the best chance of making the world a better place?

### Glossary
**beneficiary (n)** someone who gets an advantage from a situation
**illusion (n)** a false or wrong belief or idea
**mindset (n)** a way of thinking about things
**orphan (n)** a child whose parents have died
**perpetuate (v)** to make something such as a situation or process continue, especially one that is wrong, unfair or dangerous
**profound (adj)** used about very strong feelings
**recipient (n)** someone who receives something

- Discuss progress and society
- Evaluate costs and benefits

# Café Hub

## 3.3 Sustainability

**A** – the 'rule of three'  **S** – maintaining a conversation

## ▶ Seaweed farming

**A** Work in small groups. What is being shown in each picture (a–e)?

**B** ▶ Watch the video. Check your ideas to Exercise A and number pictures a–e in the order they appear.

**C** ▶ Watch the video again. Answer the questions.
1. What have scientists discovered about seaweed?
2. What can seaweed help us do?
3. What are the three countries mentioned in the video?
4. Is the presenter's tone generally positive, negative or neutral?

### Glossary

**allotment (n)** a small piece of land in town you can rent and use for growing vegetables
**harvest (v)** to pick and collect crops or plants
**seaweed (n)** a green or brown plant that grows in the sea

## AUTHENTIC ENGLISH

**A** Work in pairs. Read the sentence from the video and the information in the box. What three things doesn't seaweed need?

*This doesn't need lots of land space to grow it, it doesn't need awful artificial fertilisers, it doesn't need lots of fresh water.*

### The 'rule of three'

The 'rule of three' is a rhetorical device we use to express concepts more completely, emphasise our points and increase the memorability of our message. In the 'rule of three', we often repeat the same grammatical construction.

**B** Work in pairs. Complete the sentences using your own ideas and the 'rule of three'.

1. To succeed in life, you need to work hard, you need _to have passion_ and you need _to have a role model_.
2. I'm ready to start the day. My face is washed, my _____ and my _____.
3. Maria was the ideal employee – she was always on time, she always _____ and she _____.
4. The present government has ruined the economy, it _____ and it _____.
5. I told the shop assistant I wanted to exchange the item, _____ or _____.
6. I _____. You _____. The whole class _____.

**C** Compare your sentences with another pair.

**D** Work in small groups. Write sentences with the 'rule of three' to say what you need to do to learn a language successfully.

34 PROGRESS

3.3

## ▶ Fuelling the future

SAM  MALCOLM  AMANDA  HARRY  EMILY

**A** Work in pairs. Discuss the questions.

1. Do you prefer to use public transport or travel by car? Why?
2. What do you think about policies that ban or limit cars in city centres?

**B** ▶ Watch the video. Are these statements true (T) or false (F)? Correct the false sentences.

1. Malcolm has recently achieved a long-held ambition. T / F
2. Amanda understands the appeal of owning a sports car. T / F
3. Malcolm believes speed is the main positive of car ownership. T / F
4. Amanda says that all new vehicles will be banned from the UK by 2040. T / F
5. Amanda thinks that other feasible options besides petrol vehicles currently exist. T / F
6. Harry thinks alternative fuels will be the norm in the distant future. T / F
7. Malcolm is going to let Amanda test drive his car. T / F

## SPEAKING SKILL

**A** ▶ Watch the video again. Complete the sentences (1–6) from the video.

1. _____ coming out for a look at my new wheels?
2. I mean we don't really need them in the city. _____?
3. _____ Harry? You're a cool young guy ... you must like sports cars.
4. Just the other day we were discussing alternative fuels, _____?
5. That kind of thing, must be a long way off though, _____?
6. _____ Malcolm?

**B** Work in pairs. Look at your answers in Exercise A. What are the speakers doing in each sentence?

*1 Malcolm is asking Amanda to give her opinion.*

### Maintaining a conversation

**Inviting people to give their opinion or speak**

Ask a direct question (*Would you like to say something here, Andy?*) or invite someone to speak using a statement (*You haven't said anything yet, Maria.*)

**Noticing changes in attitude**

Respond to body language and facial expressions by asking questions or making statements. (*I can tell you don't agree with me.*)

**Question tags**

Add these to a statement to make it a question or to request agreement. (*I think we all pretty much agree on this, don't we?*)

**Asking questions to get agreement**

Ask people directly to agree with you in order to move conversations along. (*Am I right in thinking that's true?*)

**C** Work in pairs. Choose one of the topics below and try to maintain a conversation for four minutes without any long pauses.

- the environment
- a documentary you watched recently
- public transport in your country

## ○ SPEAKING HUB

**A PREPARE** Work in a small group. Think about the pros and cons of the sources of energy below.

- wind power
- tidal power
- fossil fuels
- nuclear power
- solar power

**B PLAN** You are going to discuss which of the energies would be the best for achieving a sustainable future with another group. Plan how you are going to achieve agreement within your group and get all the members of the group to give their opinion.

*A: What's your opinion?*
*B: Tidal power is too expensive compared to other renewable sources.*

**C DISCUSS** Join with another group to discuss the pros and cons of the sources of energy.

**D REFLECT** As a class decide which arguments were the most convincing and which of the energy sources are necessary for a sustainable future.

○– Discuss renewable energy

➤ Turn to **page 158** to learn how to write a persuasive email about sustainability.

# Unit 3 Review

## VOCABULARY

**A** Complete the leaflet with the words in the box. There are two extra words that you do not need to use.

> accumulate   biodegradable   consume   depletion
> emissions   exploitation   neutral   offset   renewable

### Want to live a more sustainable life?

**Here's how.**

1. Stop buying products wrapped in plastics, which _____ in the oceans. Choose products that use _____ packaging instead.

2. Cut down on the energy you _____, and use solar power, wind power or other _____ energy sources if possible.

3. Reduce your _____ of greenhouse gases by walking or cycling instead of driving.

4. Become carbon-_____ by planting trees to _____ the carbon you generate.

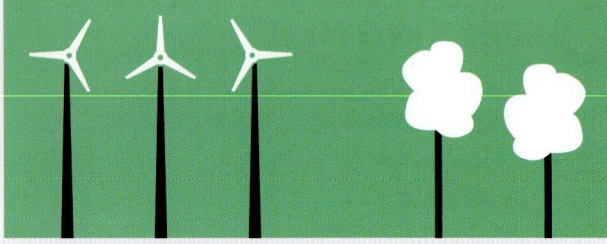

**B** Complete the sentences with the correct form of the word in brackets.

1. They want to _____ (*large*) our university by adding a new building.
2. The dirty water is _____ (*pure*) before being released into the sea.
3. If your dinner's cold, you can _____ (*warm*) it up in the microwave.
4. They're _____ (*strong*) the old bridge before it falls down.
5. We didn't bother to _____ (*formal*) our agreement – we trust each other.
6. Some screws are loose on this table. Can you _____ (*tight*) them up?
7. We were winning six-five, but the other team _____ (*equal*) in the last minute.

**C** Complete the conversation with one verb in each space.

A: I want to ¹_____ the world a better place, but I don't know how. Could you ²_____ me in the right direction?

B: The only thing that ³_____ to mind is voluntourism.

A: Good idea! I'll go for it.

B: Well, please don't ⁴_____ this personally, but you don't really have any skills to offer. They have strict rules about who they accept.

A: Really? Maybe they'll ⁵_____ an exception for me.

B: No, I think you need to ⁶_____ the time to research it carefully so you don't end up ⁷_____ more harm than good.

A: OK, thanks for the advice. I'll try to ⁸_____ it on board.

## GRAMMAR

**A** Find and correct the mistakes in four of the sentences.

1. Fifty years from now, the world will have been changing completely.
2. My life's about getting a lot more complicated.
3. We'll be seeing a lot more of each other when we're neighbours.
4. Call me again at ten – I might have finished by then.
5. I'm on the verge of resigning from my job.
6. Your eyes will hurt after you'll have been studying all night.
7. Prices setting to fall by 10% over the next year.

**B** Reorder the words to make sentences. The first word is given in bold.

1. **By** / you / do / I / should / means / believe / no / resign
   _____.

2. **Under** / be / opened / may / circumstances / no / this box
   _____.

3. **Not** / did / thanked / all the work / you / have / me / once / for / I
   _____.

4. **Only** / the waiter / our food / three times / we / bring / complained / had / after / did
   _____.

5. **No** / the washing / started / had / than / put out / sooner / it / I / to rain
   _____.

6. **No** / to college / ever / going back / I / way / consider / would
   _____.

7. **Not** / this hard / since / worked / students / we / have / I / were
   _____.

# 4 INTELLIGENCE

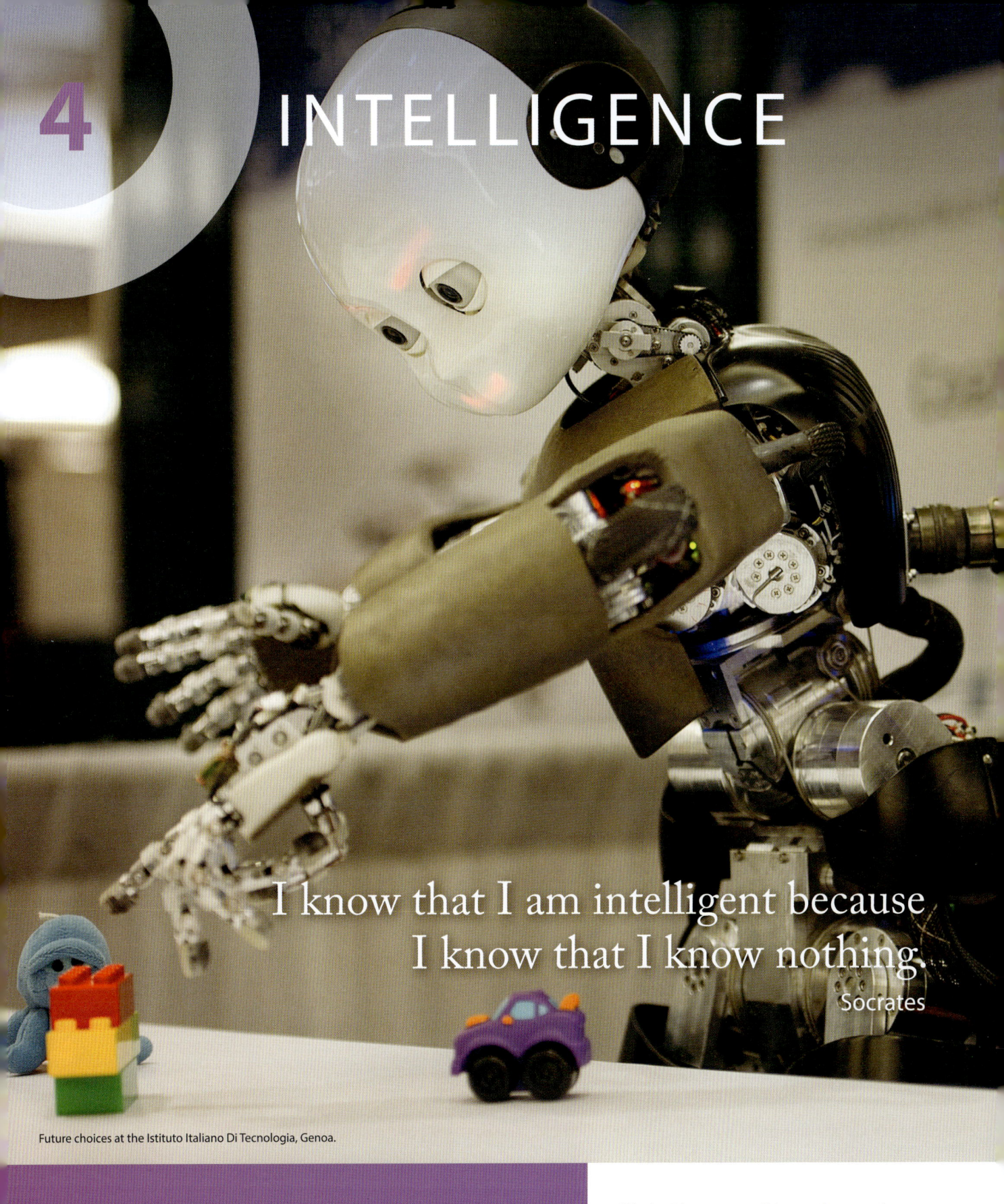

> I know that I am intelligent because I know that I know nothing.
> — Socrates

Future choices at the Istituto Italiano Di Tecnologia, Genoa.

## OBJECTIVES

- discuss improving the brain
- talk about future technology
- talk about regrets
- discuss intelligence
- recount events
- write a report

Work with a partner. Discuss the questions.

1 Look at the picture. How is it connected to the topic of intelligence?
2 Read the quote. What do you think Socrates means? Do you agree?
3 Would you rather be very intelligent, very strong or very attractive? Why?

# 4.1 Brain training

- Discuss improving the brain
- Talk about future technology

G – conditionals without *if*   V – conceptual metaphors   P – adding information   S – identifying logical fallacies

## LISTENING

**A** Work in pairs. Look at the brain teaser below. Do you know the answer? Go to the Communication Hub on page 149 for more brain teasers.

### TODAY'S BRAIN TEASER

David's mother had three children.

The first one was named April.

The second one was named May.

What was the name of the third child?

**B LISTEN FOR GIST** Listen to a radio discussion about ways to increase your brain power. What four methods of boosting brain power are discussed?

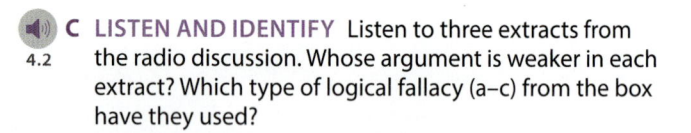

1 _____
2 _____
3 _____
4 _____

**C LISTEN AND IDENTIFY** Listen to three extracts from the radio discussion. Whose argument is weaker in each extract? Which type of logical fallacy (a–c) from the box have they used?

#### Identifying logical fallacies

a **Generalisation:** drawing a conclusion about a large group from a very small amount of data.

b **Anecdotal evidence:** using non-scientific personal experience as proof for something.

c **False cause:** claiming a relationship exists between two things when there is no evidence to support this.

1 Dr Carter / Amanda   ___
2 Dr Carter / Amanda   ___
3 Dr Carter / Amanda   ___

**D SPEAK** Work in pairs and discuss the questions.

1 Which of the methods that the speakers discussed do you think can really boost people's brainpower?
2 Do you agree with what Dr Carter said about Sudoku?
3 Why do you think findings have been inconclusive on some methods?

## PRONUNCIATION
Adding information

**A** Underline the part(s) of these sentences that provide additional information about something.

1 To answer the question, I'm joined today by two experts, Dr Ramona Carter, a leading neuroscientist, and Amanda Saraha, a life coach and the author of *How to be smarter*.

2 So for example, if you do a lot of Sudoku, the maths puzzle where you write the numbers in boxes, it's most likely that you will just become better at playing that game.

3 Recently, we've seen a lot of media stories about super foods, food that you should eat to boost your brain power.

**B** Listen to the sentences in Exercise A. Draw arrows where the intonation rises or falls.

**C SPEAK** Work in pairs. Give additional information about the underlined words.

1 I like to do some exercise before I start work in the mornings. (give more detail)
2 My friend is definitely one of the smartest people I know. (give more detail)
3 I try to do some meditation because it helps me relax. (define the word)

38  INTELLIGENCE

## VOCABULARY
### Conceptual metaphors

**A** Match the sentences (1–6) with the related conceptual metaphor (a–c). Use the information in the box to help you.

> **Conceptual metaphors**
>
> Conceptual metaphors help us to talk about abstract or complex ideas by comparing them with something else. For example, life is often compared with a journey, such as in sentences like this:
> *She had <u>reached a crossroads</u>. Should she go to university or continue with her job?* (= reached a point when she needed to make an important decision about her life)

1. I spent an hour doing Sudoku. ____
2. She shot down my arguments. ____
3. He has a really fiery temper. ____
4. After I had cooled down, I apologised. ____
5. I've invested a lot of time in brain training. ____
6. I couldn't defend my position. ____

a anger = heat
b argument = war
c time = money

**B** Read three sentences from the radio show. What do the underlined words and phrases mean?

1. Of course, everyone would like to be more intelligent, but is it really possible? And if so, how can we make ourselves <u>brighter</u>?
2. A team from Cambridge actually tried to <u>shed some light on</u> the impact of brain training games.
3. As Dr Carter says, we may still be <u>in the dark</u> about the science behind it, but I personally believe that the food we eat has a huge effect on every aspect of our lives.

**C SPEAK** Identify the conceptual metaphor being used in the questions. Then discuss the questions in pairs.

1. Do you think brain training is a waste of time?
2. What's a good strategy to convince people to buy brain-training products?
3. Do you think intelligent people are usually more hot-tempered?
4. Are you able to stay cool in an argument?

## SPEAKING

**A** Look at the adverts. Which products would you try? Which would you avoid? Why?

### BRAIN WAVE
Drawing on the latest research, *Brain Wave* keeps you focused by providing regular stimulation in the form of a small electrical shock. Scientifically proven to boost performance – 73% of users agree that it has helped them to think more clearly.

### Brain Juice
Are you sick of feeling tired and run down? Then it's time to supercharge your brain with the next generation energy drink. Packed full of ingredients to boost your confidence, focus and mood. *Brain Juice* will help you outshine the competition and start living life to your full potential.

### SMARTER PHONE
Technology is dimming your intellect, so our new *Smarter Phone* has stripped out all the features that are making you lazy. No calculator, no map, no spell checker or auto-complete. It's time to turn off the technology and switch on your brain. Guaranteed results.

**B PRESENT** Work in groups. Think of a product or service that you could sell to people who wanted to boost their brain power. Present the product to the class. Which product is the most popular?

**C DISCUSS** Work in pairs and discuss the questions.

1. Do you believe that it's really possible to make yourself smarter?
2. Should companies be allowed to sell products like the ones in Exercise A? Why/Why not?

INTELLIGENCE

## 4.1

### READING

**A SPEAK** Work in pairs. If you could significantly boost your intelligence overnight, would you do it? Why/Why not?

**B PREDICT** Work in pairs. Look at *Brain augmentation: The key to super intelligence*. In your own words, explain to your partner what you think the article is about.

**C READ FOR MAIN IDEA** Read the article and complete the table.

|   | Method of augmentation | Examples of benefits |
|---|---|---|
| 1 |  |  |
| 2 |  |  |
| 3 |  |  |

**D READ FOR DETAIL** Read the article again and answer the questions.

1 When do scientists predict highly sophisticated robots will be a common sight?
2 How has technology been used to help blind people?
3 What did scientists learn from the research with epilepsy patients?
4 What potential dangers of brain augmentation does the article mention?

**E SPEAK** Work in pairs and discuss the questions.

1 What was the most surprising thing that you learnt from the article?
2 Do you think that the government should control this kind of augmentation?

# BRAIN AUGMENTATION:
## The key to super intelligence

How far would you go to enhance your own intelligence? Would you implant a chip into your brain? For many scientists around the world, the answer appears to be *yes*. Brain augmentation, enhancing the intelligence of human brains with implants, is a growing area of interest as some predict that super-intelligent cyborgs will be a normal part of everyday life within the next 10 to 20 years.

In fact, experts believe that there are three main approaches to brain augmentation: interfacing with the brain, stimulating the brain and enhancing the brain with implants.

Suppose that a computer could interface with a brain, it could record information, store it, and even use this information for some other purpose – such as sharing it with others. In theory, if people's brains were linked through the internet, they could benefit from each others' knowledge.

Another way of augmenting the brain is by stimulating it in some way – typically with electricity. One goal of stimulation is to produce artificial sensations, such as the sensation of touch or vision. In this case, the main motivation comes from a desire to help repair the brains of people with neurological conditions. For example, in the last couple of years, scientists from *Second Sight* have been able to partially restore the sight of some blind people by implanting a chip into their retinas that sends signals to the brain from a camera. Although these people cannot see, the stimulation of the brain creates pictures in their mind. At the moment these are just black and white, pixelated images, but assuming that the technology continues to improve, this could be the beginning of a permanent cure for blindness.

Another goal of stimulating the brain is to improve its function and its capabilities. A recent study led by Dong Song of the University of Southern California looked at the effects of stimulating the brain on memory. Researchers worked with twenty volunteers who were having electrodes implanted into their brains to treat epilepsy. Researchers examined the effects of stimulating the brain through these electrodes during tests that involved either the volunteers' short-term memory or working memory and found that the right kind of stimulation improved short-term memory by 15% and working memory by 25%. Interestingly, unless the right kind of stimulation was provided, the volunteers' memory was actually worse. So, there is clearly a lot of work to be done to understand the right kind of stimulation to provide.

INTELLIGENCE

## GRAMMAR
Conditionals without *if*

**A** Underline conditional sentences in the article with the same meaning as sentences (1–6).

1 If a computer could connect to a brain, it could download information and make it available to others. (Paragraph 3)
2 If the technology gets better, it could lead to a cure for blindness. (Paragraph 4)
3 If robots decided to fight against humans, we would have to be clever enough to take them on. (Paragraph 6)
4 If people created successful brain-augmentation implants, we would need to think about the moral implications. (Paragraph 7)
5 If you ask many people about what's happening right now, they will tell you they don't know anything about it. (Paragraph 8)
6 If the government had not allowed this work into augmentation, we would not be developing innovations to assist people with vision problems. (Paragraph 8)

**B** Choose the correct words to complete the rules (a–c). Then look at the example sentences you found in Exercise A to complete the rules (d–f).

### Conditionals without *if*

We can use inversions to talk about hypothetical situations in formal or literary English:

a *Had*: We use *had* + subject + *infinitive / past participle / verb*.
b *Should*: We use *should* + subject + *infinitive / past participle / verb*.
c *Were*: We use *were* + subject + *infinitive / past participle / verb*.

We can use other words instead of *if*:

d Verbs: *imagine*, _____
e Present participles: _____, *presuming, providing, supposing*
  • Past participles: *provided*
f We can also make a conditional sentence by starting with an imperative and joining the clauses with _____.

**C** Go to the **Grammar Hub** on **page 128**.

**D** Change the start of these sentences to make conditionals without *if*. Complete the sentences with your own opinions.

1 If people were able to upload information into their brains, …
2 If we ignore the potential danger of AI, …
3 If brain implants were only affordable for the super-rich, …
4 If I were to be offered a brain-boosting implant, …

**E** Compare your sentences with your partner. Do you agree with your partner's opinions?

## SPEAKING HUB

Work in pairs. Student A – go to the **Communication Hub** on **page 150**. Student B – go to the **Communication Hub** on **page 152**. Describe the situations to your partner. Discuss what you would do.

---

The final approach to augmentation is the most radical, because it involves merging man and machine. The biggest impact is likely to be from implanting a chip into your brain. Bryan Johnson, founder and CEO of neuroscience company Kernel, believes that these chips could be used to help us learn faster, enhance our memories, and provide us with a cognitive boost. *Space X* and *Tesla* are also working on technology to boost the human brain through the company Neuralink. One concern raised is that humans are able to enhance their intelligence, because, should AI turn against humans in the future, we would need to be smart enough to fight back.

Of course, were brain-boosting implants to be successfully developed, they would raise several difficult ethical questions. Would changing people's brains change their personalities? If someone had an implant fitted, would they be at risk of being hacked? Could these super intelligent cyborgs be a danger to the rest of us?

Ask many people about what's happening right now in this field and they will tell you they are completely in the dark. Unfortunately that includes the government, who many feel should be doing more to regulate the technology and ensure that it really is safe. However, had the government banned this kind of research, the technology to help blind people would not be under development.

### Glossary

**cyborg (n)** a creature in science fiction stories that is part human and part machine
**electrode (n)** a small metal or carbon object inside an electrical cell or a battery that electricity flows through. There are two electrodes, one positive and one negative.
**neurological (adj)** relating to your nervous system or to the diseases that affect it
**retina (n)** the part at the back of your eye that sends light signals to your brain, where they are changed into images

○ Discuss improving the brain
○ Talk about future technology

## 4.2 Thinking and thought

- Talk about regrets
- Discuss intelligence

G— wishes and regrets
P— adding information or changing the topic
V— science and research; thinking
S— identifying different writing styles

## READING

**A SPEAK** Read *No need to be embarrassed?* Discuss the following questions.
1 Have any of the situations described happened to you?
2 Which stories do you think are the most and least embarrassing?

**B** Read *The positive side of embarrassment*. What do scientists think is the purpose of embarrassment?

**C READ TO IDENTIFY** Who is each text written for? What is the purpose of each text?

Text 1 _____
Text 2 _____

**D** Read both texts again. Find examples of the writing styles (a–e) in the box. Use the information in the box to help you.

---
**Identifying different writing styles**

Texts written for a general audience usually use:
a shorter, simpler sentences (including sentences that start with *and*, *but* and *so*)
b idiomatic language (contractions, phrasal verbs, idioms).

Academic papers and articles:
c are objective not personal (no *I*, *you* or *we*, no emotional adjectives)
d use longer, more complex sentences
e use formal language (no contractions or phrasal verbs, but academic vocabulary).

---

**E SPEAK** Work in pairs. Do you agree that displaying embarrassment can make a positive impression on others?

# NO NEED TO BE EMBARRASSED?

### Glossary
**buddy** (n) (American English) friend
**consolation** (n) something that makes you feel less unhappy or disappointed
**cringeworthy** (adj) something that makes you feel embarrassed or ashamed

**PAUL**

**CAROLINE**

**GIANNI**

**Psychologists believe that embarrassment should actually be viewed as a positive thing. When we blush or stammer in embarrassment, we are showing that we know that <u>we shouldn't have said or done something</u> and that we don't normally do this kind of thing. In other words, showing we are embarrassed is a kind of non-verbal apology.**

Well that's all well and good, but when you're caught red-faced, I don't think that would be any consolation. In light of this research, I thought I'd do a bit of my own. Now I'm no stranger to embarrassment, but a quick survey revealed embarrassing work stories far worse than mine. Here are some of your most cringeworthy moments.

❝ Can you even begin to imagine what it's like to walk into a glass door at full speed? Must be painful, right? Now add to that the mortification that it was in front of your new boss. If I hadn't been trying to impress her with my walking-while-emailing skills – like I was a hot-shot political aide on an American TV show – I might have noticed the door. But the humiliation doesn't stop there. All of my co-workers were sat around a conference table on the other side of that glass door. <u>I would have loved to make a good impression</u>. But all I ended up with was wounded pride … and a broken nose. ❞

❝ Generally speaking I'm a pretty confident person. I'm great at putting people at ease and keeping conversation going. <u>I just wish I wasn't so absent-minded</u>. Over the years it has caused me infinite amounts of awkwardness. But never more so than just last month. An important client was flying in from Vancouver for an even more important meeting. So I offered to pick them up from the airport. The only problem was by the time he came through the arrivals gate, I had completely forgotten where I'd parked my car. We spent the next two hours wandering aimlessly around various car parks in the pouring rain. <u>I wish I'd never offered to give him a lift</u> … and I bet he does, too! ❞

❝ This happened five years ago but to this very day the memory still haunts me! The CEO where I used to work sent a (very smug) company-wide email congratulating *himself* on record profit margins. In response I wrote a very rude message making fun of the CEO to my office buddy … or so I thought. <u>If only I hadn't been in such a rush</u> to have lunch, I might have noticed that I had hit *reply to all* instead of *reply* … those two little words make a huge difference. My email was sent to every employee in London and Boston. It was only when I came back from lunch and everyone was sniggering that it clicked what had happened. I just wanted the ground to swallow me up. ❞

INTELLIGENCE

# The positive side of embarrassment

The outward signs of embarrassment are well known, and include blushing, gazing downward, turning away and face touching. However, researchers have been attempting to identify the evolutionary purpose of embarrassment.

Several researchers have postulated that embarrassment may help to signal whether humans are willing to develop long-term bonds with each other. For example, Lewis (2008) believes that embarrassment is when an individual makes a negative evaluation of their actions, thoughts or feelings because they feel they have not behaved according to social standards.

Feinberg, Willer, Keltner and Dacher (2012) **hypothesised** that embarrassment served several important social functions and **conducted** several **experiments** to test this hypothesis.

In one experiment, **participants** were asked to tell an embarrassing story and then complete a questionnaire that looked at their tendency to be kind. The **findings** indicated that people who showed more embarrassment were more likely to be kinder people. The researchers **concluded** that these people were more 'pro-social' – that is they wanted to be part of the group and not behave in a way that was counter to the social **norms** of the group.

In another experiment, participants witnessed an interaction between a researcher and someone that they thought was another participant (but was actually an actor). The researcher praised the fake participant's performance on a test, and the fake participant either expressed embarrassment or pride. The participants who saw the actor look embarrassed were more likely to think he was trustworthy and want to interact with him. This experiment **demonstrated** that people are more likely to have a positive perception of someone who shows embarrassment. The researchers **speculated** that this was because this person is showing a desire to fit in with the group.

From examining the findings of studies such as these, it appears that the evolutionary purpose of embarrassment was to help identify individuals who would be likely to cooperate with the group. So although embarrassment is widely thought of as a negative emotion, displaying embarrassment most likely makes a positive impression on others.

## VOCABULARY
Science and research

**A** Match the words in bold from the second text with the meanings (1–9).

1. do (an experiment, a study) _____
2. standard behaviour _____
3. suggest a theory _____
4. guess _____
5. people taking part in a study or experiment _____
6. results _____
7. test _____
8. decide _____
9. show _____

**B** Go to the Vocabulary Hub on page 143.

**C** **SPEAK** Work in pairs and discuss the questions.

1. Would you like to be a participant in a psychology study?
2. Think of an experiment you've heard about. What did it hypothesise? What were the findings?
3. Is it ethical to conduct a study where you make people feel embarrassed?

## GRAMMAR
Wishes and regrets

**A** **WORK IT OUT** Look at the underlined sentences in *No need to be embarrassed?* Then choose the correct words to complete the rules.

### Wishes and regrets

1. We use *wish* or *if only* + **present** / **past** simple to wish that the present was different.
2. We use *wish* or *if only* + **present** / **past** perfect to wish that the past was different.
3. We can use *should (not)* or *ought (not) to* + *have* + *past participle* or *been* + **present** / **past** participle to talk about regrets.
4. We can use *would* + *love* or *prefer* or *hate* + **to have** / **have** + *(not) past participle* to talk about regrets.

**B** Go to the Grammar Hub on page 128.

**C** Complete the sentences so they are true for you.

1. If only I could …
2. I wish I were …
3. I would have loved to …

## SPEAKING

**A** **PREPARE** Think of a time when you did something you regret. You can use the list of ideas on page 150 of the Communication Hub or your own ideas. What happened? What do you wish had happened differently?

**B** **DISCUSS** Tell your partner about what happened. Listen to your partner and ask questions.

## 4.2

### LISTENING

**A SPEAK** Work in pairs. Look at the pictures. Discuss which of the following gives people the biggest advantage in life. Give reasons for your choice.

- Money
- Intelligence
- Supportive family
- Good health

**B LISTEN FOR MAIN IDEA** You are going to listen to part of a debate about whether being highly intelligent gives people an advantage in life. What are the speaker's three main points?

1 _____
2 _____
3 _____

**C LISTEN FOR SPECIFIC INFORMATION** Listen again and answer the questions.

1 What is the 'nutty professor' stereotype?
2 What mistakes do intelligent people often make at social events?
3 What do intelligent people sometimes do to preserve their reputation?

**D SPEAK** Work in pairs. Can you think of any counter-arguments or challenges to the three points in Exercise B? Present them to your partner. Use the phrases below to help you.

> First of all, the speaker claimed that … but …
> In addition, the speaker stated that …
> The speaker also mentioned the fact that …

**E SPEAK** Work in pairs and discuss the questions.

1 Do you know any intelligent people who behave in the ways that the speaker described?
2 Do you think the speaker has a convincing argument? Why/Why not?
3 The speaker says that intelligence and happiness don't necessarily come together. Do you agree?

### VOCABULARY
Thinking

**A** Complete the questions (1–8) with the correct form of a word or phrase in the box.

> absent-minded   common sense   curious
> eccentric   eureka moment   overthink
> troubleshoot   wishful thinking

1 Are you good at _____ or do you find it difficult to find and fix problems and faults?
2 Do you sometimes think about the same thing over and over again? Are you _____ things?
3 Do you solve problems with sudden bursts of inspiration, like an _____?
4 Do you like to take things apart? Are you _____ about how things work?
5 Do you make time in the day to organise work? Or does it seem like _____ _____ to sit down and plan things?
6 Do you forget where you leave things? Are you _____?
7 Are you a practical person? Or do you lack _____?
8 Would you describe yourself as fairly conventional and similar to most people? Or are you a bit _____?

**B** Go to the Vocabulary Hub on page 144.

**C SPEAK** Work in pairs. Ask and answer the questions in Exercise A. Then decide if your partner is a genius.

## PRONUNCIATION
Adding information or changing the topic

**A** Listen again to the beginning of the debate. Draw arrows to show whether the intonation is rising (↗), falling (↘) or fall-rising (↘↗) at the end of the underlined words/phrases.

> Thank you very much. It's an honour to speak against the motion tonight. ¹Right, (__) it's easy to see why so many people believe being intelligent makes your life better. ²After all, (__) we see intelligent people thriving at school. We see them getting onto the university courses they want. We see them graduating with good academic qualifications. And ³on top of that, (__) we see the importance the world gives to qualifications.
>
> So, it may seem strange for me to stand here and argue that intelligent people aren't necessarily at an advantage in life. ⁴However, (__) that is exactly what I'll do. ⁵In fact, (__) there are several clear disadvantages in having a superior intellect.

**B** SPEAK Work in pairs. Read the dialogues, focusing on the intonation of the underlined words and phrases. Then continue them with your own ideas.

1 **A:** I read that highly-intelligent people often like to spend time alone.
   **B:** On top of that, they find it really hard to make friends.

2 **A:** Are you going to watch the debate on intelligence on TV tonight?
   **B:** Yes, I'm planning to. By the way, do you want to go to a debate?

3 **A:** Einstein has been voted the most intelligent person ever.
   **B:** Really? Incidentally, how did you do on your exam?

## SPEAKING HUB

**A** PREPARE Work in groups. Read the motion below and decide whether you will argue for or against it.

**Motion:** Highly intelligent people should be educated separately.

**Order of debate**
1 Presentation in support of the motion.
2 Challenge to this presentation.
3 Presentation against the motion.
4 Challenge to this presentation.

**B** PLAN Decide on the roles each team member will have. Brainstorm arguments to support your position. Try to anticipate the arguments the other team will make, and prepare counter-arguments to them.

**C** DISCUSS Hold the debate. Follow the order given in Exercise A.

**D** REFLECT Discuss the following questions:
- How successful was the debate?
- What was your real opinion about the motion?
- Is it difficult to argue for a point of view you don't really agree with?

○— Talk about regrets
○— Discuss intelligence

# Café Hub

## 4.3 Life-changing tech
A – *straight out of*   S – recounting events

## ▶ Sound and vision

a

b

**A** Work in pairs. Look at pictures a and b and discuss the questions.
1. In picture a, is each half of the circle the same shade of red?
2. In picture b, are the rectangles the same shade of blue?

Turn to **page 154** to check your answers.

**B** 🔊 4.6 Listen to three short pieces of music. What colours do they make you think of? Why? Turn to **page 153** to check your answers.

**C** ▶ Watch the video about an artist. Complete the sentence with the best option.

Neil Haribsson has …
1. partial colour blindness in which it is difficult to distinguish between blue and yellow, violet and red, and blue and green.
2. slight colour blindness in which it is difficult to distinguish between red, green, brown and orange.
3. total colour blindness in which colours are seen as black and white.

### Glossary
**implant (v)** to put an organ, group of cells, or device into the body in a medical operation
**sensor (n)** a piece of equipment that reacts to physical changes such as the amount of heat or light that exists somewhere
**skull (n)** the bony case which contains the brain

**D** ▶ Watch the video again. Complete the summary.

Neil Harbisson, an ¹_____, has never been able to see colour. He was ²_____ about colour because people always refer to it. He wanted to be able to ³_____ colour rather than to alter his sight. A team of doctors and ⁴_____ helped him create an electronic device. This is made up of a colour sensor and a ⁵_____. The sensor picks up ⁶_____ frequencies and the chip ⁷_____ the frequency into a sound. Each colour creates a different ⁸_____.

## AUTHENTIC ENGLISH

**A** Read the sentence from the video and the information in the box. Why do you think Neil's electronic device is compared to something from science fiction?

*With the help of a team of engineers and doctors he created something **straight out of** science fiction.*

### straight out of
You use *straight out of* to say that something is similar in type to something else. This structure is often used to compare the thing we are describing to an imagined or fictional scenario.

**B** Work in pairs. Complete the sentences in an interesting way.
1. The scenery in Ireland is stunning – straight out of _____a travel brochure_____.
2. The band are really like *The Beatles*. They sound like something straight out of _____.
3. Himari saw snow for the first time that winter. It was like something straight out of _____.
4. The village has spectacular old buildings, a beautiful lake and no roads. It's straight out of _____.
5. My bag had been stolen, it was pouring with rain and I couldn't speak the language. It was straight out of _____.
6. The climb to the summit was long and difficult. It was like something straight out of _____.

**C** Join with another pair. Compare your answers to Exercise B.

# ▶ Hearing colours

SAM   MALCOLM   AMANDA   HARRY   EMILY

**A** Work in pairs. Discuss the following questions.
1 What gadgets or devices do you use?
2 Are there any new gadgets or devices you want to buy?
3 Have you ever been to a technology fair or exhibition? Why/Why not?

**B** ▶ Watch the video. Are these sentences true (T), false (F) or not given (NG)?
1 Harry is off sick from work. T / F / NG
2 The café was very busy in the morning. T / F / NG
3 Emily was about to leave the Tech Fair when a woman approached her. T / F / NG
4 The device looked like headphones. T / F / NG
5 The first thing that Emily saw on the screen was a red square. T / F / NG
6 Emily agrees that Sam should go to the Tech Fair. T / F / NG

## SPEAKING SKILL

**A** Work in pairs. Put the following sentences from the video in the order they are spoken.

- [ ] Well, I was at this big Health Tech Fair earlier today, right?
- [ ] But hang on, I'll get to that.
- [ ] Tell me about it. I've had a bit of a strange one myself.
- [ ] [The woman] asked me to step inside a large box. So I did.
- [ ] [I'm] thinking about heading out when all of the sudden, this woman stops me.
- [ ] Overall it was a strange but unforgettable experience.
- [ ] I was just about to ask her what it was when she slammed the door on me!
- [ ] So I'm standing there saying 'Excuse me … what's going on' and thinking what on earth have I got myself into.

**B** Match the sentences from the video (1–8) with the strategies (a–d) in the box.

### Recounting events
We often recount events. To do this effectively we use a number of strategies.
a signalling the start of a story. For example, ___
b giving the background to a story. For example, ___
c evaluating parts of a story. For example, ___, ___
d sequencing events in a story. For example, ___, ___, ___, ___

## ◯ SPEAKING HUB

**A PLAN** You are going to tell an interesting anecdote to a partner. You can choose one of the following topics or use your own idea.
- a strange coincidence
- a great event
- an unforgettable trip

**B PREPARE** Make notes on how you are going to sequence the events in your anecdote.

**C DISCUSS** Work in pairs. Tell your anecdote. Change roles.

*So I'm thinking to myself this is like something straight out of a Hollywood movie.*

**D REFLECT** Work with a new partner and retell them your previous partner's anecdote.

◯─ Recount events
➤ Turn to page 159 to learn how to write a report about a study.

# Unit 4 Review

## VOCABULARY

**A** Identify the conceptual metaphor in each sentence. Do you agree with the sentences?

1. If you're not learning something, you're wasting your time.
2. Don't show that you're bright or people will expect big things.
3. Always keep moving, but never go backwards.
4. Invest in your friendships above all else.
5. If you want to win an argument, attack first and attack hard.
6. Keep people in the dark about your goals until you succeed.

**B** Replace the underlined words in the article with the words in the box. You may need to change the tense of the words.

> conclude   conduct   demonstrate   experiment   findings
> hypothesise   participants   speculate   the norm

### Pavlovian responses

One of the most famous psychological ¹studies was ²done by Ivan Pavlov, where the ³subjects were dogs. Pavlov observed that all dogs naturally salivated whenever they saw food, so he ⁴decided this was not a behaviour they had to learn.

However, he noticed that his dogs also salivated when his assistant, who often fed the dogs, walked into the room. Pavlov ⁵guessed that the dogs had learnt to associate his assistant with food.

He ⁶theorised that the dogs could learn to associate a stimulus with food and would salivate when exposed to this stimulus even when no food was present. He rang a bell whenever he fed his dogs, so that this became ⁷typical for them.

After several sessions, he rang the bell when no food was present and his dogs salivated. His ⁸results ⁹showed that dogs could learn an automatic response to a stimulus.

**C** Match the sentences (1–8) with the sentences (a–h) that have the same meanings.

1. You're great at troubleshooting.
2. You often overthink things.
3. You can be a little absent-minded.
4. You've got no common sense.
5. You're a little eccentric.
6. You often engage in wishful thinking.
7. You're naturally curious about everything.
8. You often have eureka moments.

a. You don't have conventional tastes.
b. You have sudden instances of inspiration.
c. You like learning about things and how they work.
d. You are pretty forgetful.
e. You're not always realistic when you think about future events or situations.
f. You have a tendency to spend too much time considering an issue.
g. You don't understand how to do basic things.
h. You're good at analysing and solving problems.

## GRAMMAR

**A** Rewrite the beginning of the sentences using the words in brackets. Then complete the sentences with your own ideas.

1. If all vehicles were automated … (*Were*)
2. If companies started selling robots to do the housework … (*Should*)
3. If schools employed robot teachers … (*Imagine*)
4. If humans could marry robots … (*Supposing*)
5. If factories hadn't started using robots … (*Had*)
6. If robots develop conscious thought … (*Suppose*)

**B** Choose the correct words to complete the sentences.

1. Jim wishes he *is* / *were* better at sports.
2. If only I *can* / *could* speak three languages.
3. She would love *have* / *to have* a better memory.
4. Tina and Bill wish they *could save* / *had saved* more money as they can't afford their mortgage this month.
5. We should *not eat* / *not have eaten* so much junk food when we were younger.
6. If only I *have* / *had* travelled more.
7. My brother ought to *spend* / *have spent* more time with our parents while they were visiting.
8. I wish I *can* / *could* cook.

# 5 GAMES

> We do not stop playing because we grow old; we grow old because we stop playing.
> — Benjamin Franklin

Generation games – a grandma and granddaughter play.

## OBJECTIVES

- discuss problem-solving tasks
- discuss gaming and game design
- identify generalisations
- discuss ideas for solving a challenge
- plan a fundraising event
- write a formal report

Work with a partner. Discuss the questions.

1 Look at the picture and read the quote. Why do you think people stop playing games? How does this make us 'grow old'?
2 What games did you like when you were younger? Did you stop playing these games? Why?
3 What games do you like now? Will you keep playing these games when you are older? Will you start any new games?

# 5.1 21st century games

- Discuss problem-solving tasks
- Discuss gaming and game design

**G** – the passive  **V** – competition and cooperation  **P** – expressing disbelief  **S** – understanding colloquial asides

## LISTENING

**A SPEAK** Read about escape rooms. Do they exist in your country? Are they popular? Why/Why not?

**B LISTEN FOR GIST** Listen to a conversation between three friends, Lin, Joe and Olga, in an escape room. The conversation is in three parts. Answer the same three questions after each part.
1 Which objects from the pictures did they mention for the first time?
2 Which problem(s) are they trying to solve in this part?
3 What do you think will happen next?

### ESCAPE ROOMS

An escape room is a game where a group of people try to escape from a locked room, for example by finding hidden objects, solving clues and working as a team. The idea came from TV shows and computer games with similar problem-solving activities. Escape rooms started in Japan in 2007 and quickly spread around the world. They are popular with children (as venues for birthday parties) and adults (for team-building exercises). There are now over 2800 escape room venues worldwide.

**C LISTEN FOR DETAIL** Listen to the whole conversation again. Choose the correct options (a, b or c) to answer the questions.

1 Apart from the metal bar, why can't they get the key out?
   a The cylinder is too deep to reach the bottom.
   b They're worried about breaking the cylinder.
   c The cylinder is too narrow for their arms.
2 How many of the friends have read the instructions?
   a one
   b two
   c three
3 Why can't they use the vase to transfer the oil?
   a It's full of water.
   b It's too big.
   c It can't be moved.
4 Why didn't they notice the message before?
   a The room was too bright.
   b They didn't look in the right direction.
   c They couldn't open the drawer.
5 Why does Joe want to keep playing?
   a He's having too much fun.
   b He's sure they've found all the clues.
   c He thinks people will laugh at him.
6 Why was the towel necessary?
   a Because they needed an accurate measurement.
   b Because the ball was too slippery to hold.
   c Because they needed to weigh it on the scales.

Labels: vase, metal bar, measuring cylinder, bath towel, chest of drawers, combination lock, jug of cooking oil, glass ball, sugar cubes, cork, screws, electric scales

50 GAMES

**D SPEAK** Work in pairs and discuss the questions.

1. How could they have escaped more quickly?
2. Do you think you would have solved all the puzzles?
3. How long would it have taken you to escape from the room?

## GRAMMAR
The passive

**A** Look at these sentences from the conversation. Complete the second sentence so that it is in the passive.

1. OK, so they've locked us in.
   OK, so, <u>we've been locked in.</u>
2. Somebody's probably listening to us right now!
   _____ right now!
3. Somebody must have written it in luminous paint.
   _____ in luminous paint.
4. They should have given us more clues.
   _____ more clues.
5. If we give up now, my friends will make fun of me for weeks.
   If we give up now, _____ for weeks.
6. I can't think when somebody's shouting at me!
   I can't think when _____!

**B** Match the sentences (1–5) with the rules (a–d).

> **The passive**
>
> a In the structure *make sb do sth*, you need to add *to* in the passive (e.g. ___).
> b You can make the passive from *-ing* forms (e.g. ___) and *to* + infinitives (e.g. ___).
> c The *get*-passive (*get* + past participle) is rather informal. Use it to describe unexpected/unwanted events (e.g. ___). It's also useful for distinguishing actions (e.g. *to get married*) from states (e.g. *to be married*).
> d Use the causative passive (*have/get* + something + past participle) to focus on the person who organises/pays for a service (e.g. ___) or is the victim of a crime (e.g. *I had my car stolen*).
>
> 1 We'll <u>get thrown out</u> if anything <u>gets broken</u>!
> 2 I don't remember <u>being given</u> any instructions.
> 3 We <u>were made to sign</u> a form at the reception desk.
> 4 I reckon the cylinder needs <u>to be filled</u> with water.
> 5 You need to <u>get your eyes tested</u>!

**C** Go to the **Grammar Hub** on **page 130**.

**D SPEAK** Work in pairs. Ask and answer questions about these topics.

- a way you like/don't like being treated
- a time when you were made to do something
- something you've had done recently/you need to get done soon
- a time when you got lost/stuck/delayed, etc

A: *I hate being treated like a child.*
B: *Really? When do you get treated like that? Who by?*

## PRONUNCIATION
Expressing disbelief

🔊 **A** Match the extracts from the conversation (1–7) with
5.2  the responses (a–g). Then listen to check.

1. It's at the bottom of this measuring cylinder.
2. Try pulling it really hard.
3. I wondered what that form was.
4. Shall we give up?
5. Something metal? Aha! Two screws.
6. You did it! We're free!
7. There's something in the jug!

a Screws? What are we supposed to do with them?
b Didn't you read it?
c Give up? No way!
d Seriously? That's cheating!
e Yeah right! There's nothing there apart from the oil.
f Really? That was easy!
g Are you joking? We still need to remove the metal bar.

🔊 **B** Listen and decide in which sentence (a or b) the
5.3  speaker is expressing disbelief.

1 ___   2 ___   3 ___   4 ___

**C SPEAK** Work in pairs. Take turns to talk about something surprising you did this month. Express disbelief at your partner's statements.

A: *I volunteered to teach in India.*
B: *Really? India? No way!*

## SPEAKING

**DISCUSS** Work in small groups. Imagine the room you're in now is an escape room. What clues might help you to escape? Where might those clues be hidden? Express disbelief at each other's suggestions.

GAMES 51

## 5.1

### READING

**A SKIM** Look at the picture and the title of the blog post. What do you think urban games are? Skim the blog post to check.

**B READ FOR GIST** Read the blog post. Which game (a–d) …

1. isn't only played in cities? ___
2. teaches you about a place while you play? ___
3. has more viewers than live players? ___
4. has players who stand out from the crowd? ___
5. can be confusing to play? ___
6. takes advantage of a weakness in technology? ___

a  Hidden Bonds
b  Geocaching
c  Pac Manhattan
d  Poznan Beyond Time

# URBAN GAMES
## TURN CITIES INTO PLAYGROUNDS

**Glossary**

**encapsulate** (v) to express something in a short clear form that gives the most important facts or ideas
**gobble** (v) to eat something quickly and often noisily

It's 6 am and I'm sitting on Trafalgar Square, feeling apprehensive. ¹What on Earth have I let myself in for? The square is virtually empty but I have the distinct feeling I'm being watched by thousands of curious eyes. I receive an SMS: 'Follow the man with the striped umbrella. Don't let him see you.' I spot the man in the distance, jump to my feet and set off in hot pursuit, heart pounding.

I'm playing *Hidden Bonds*, one of the new generation of urban games that are taking off in cities around the world. Urban games encapsulate the best elements of computer games and transfer them to the real world, adding social and physical dimensions to activities that would otherwise involve sitting alone for hours in a darkened room – ²something I'm all too familiar with!

Urban games originated from a game called *Geocaching*, which uses GPS devices to create virtual treasure hunts. Players are given the GPS coordinates of special boxes called caches, which could be hidden anywhere in the world. Part of the challenge comes from the limitations of GPS, which is only accurate to within a dozen or so metres, so you need to use your eyes. After locating a cache, you win the prize inside – but you must replace it with an appropriate prize for the next player. ³Sounds amazing, right? … If you're into trudging round muddy fields disorientated and in the middle of nowhere!

One of the best-known modern urban games is *Pac Manhattan*, a version of the arcade game *Pac Man*, played out on the bustling, grid-like streets of New York. ⁴How cool is that? Players dressed up as brightly-coloured characters from the game race around city blocks, gobbling up virtual 'dots' as they go – and trying to **outmanoeuvre rival** players to avoid being caught.

Luckily, some urban games are played at a more moderate pace. Visitors to Poznan in Poland can choose from a range of treasure-hunt games to explore the city, while solving clues about the city's cultural heritage and history. For example, in *Poznan Beyond Time*, players embark on a time-travelling adventure to save the world. All you need is a printed game sheet … and some good walking shoes – ⁵as I learnt to my cost!

Then there are games played out for an online audience – which brings me back to *Hidden Bonds*. It's quite complicated, but in a nutshell, there are four teams, each represented by five 'agents' on the streets of London. The objective is to **cooperate** with your **allies** to **overcome** rival agents, by sending a Bluetooth message to their phone before they can send one to yours. Problem is, the agents have no idea who the other agents are and who's just a normal passer-by, which can lead to some embarrassing moments, ⁶I can tell you! The agents receive instructions on their mobile phones from 'spymasters', who **coordinate** the players' movements based on the votes of hundreds of 'team members' watching the game live online. The team with the last remaining agent **prevails**.

At a rough estimate, I'd say I've played *Hidden Bonds* as an online team member about 50 times – ⁷yeah, sad, I know. **Collaborating** with hundreds of strangers is surprisingly satisfying, but playing live is altogether more exhilarating, especially when you come face-to-face with a rival agent. I managed to catch four opponents before getting caught myself mid-afternoon. Only later did I realise that I'd walked over 20 kilometres in the process! ⁸Pretty impressive, right? I'd do it again tomorrow if I could, but there's a seven-month waiting list to participate again as an agent. ⁹Just my luck, huh?

**C UNDERSTAND ASIDES** Look at the asides (1–9) underlined in the blog post. Then answer the questions (a–f). Use the information in the box to help you.

> **Understanding colloquial asides**
>
> Colloquial asides are informal phrases that comment on other information in the text (e.g. *Not bad, huh?*). They often take the form of questions or exclamations and they make a text feel more chatty, personal and friendly.
>
> Asides can reveal the writer's personality and attitudes. However, watch out for irony, where the writer means the opposite of what they've written.

Which aside(s) …

a express(es) genuine enthusiasm? _____
b is/are likely to be irony? _____
c suggest(s) the writer feels guilty about their lifestyle? _____
d show(s) how the writer felt at the beginning? _____
e suggest(s) the writer often describes frustrations in their blog posts? _____
f hint(s) at problems the writer experienced while playing? _____

**D SPEAK** Work in pairs and discuss the questions.

1 Which games from the blog post would you like to play? Why?
2 Which would you not want to play? Why?
3 Can you think of any dangers or weaknesses of urban games?
4 Why do you think games like this have become more popular?

## VOCABULARY
Competition and cooperation

**A** Match the words in bold in the blog post with the definitions.

1 _____ (v) working in partnership
2 _____ (n) people on the same side as you
3 _____ (v) wins (e.g. after a long contest)
4 _____ (v) organise people working together
5 _____ (v) beat another player or solve a problem
6 _____ (n) a person competing against you
7 _____ (v) help/support others

**B** Go to the Vocabulary Hub on page 144.

**C SPEAK** Work in groups and discuss the questions.

1 Do you prefer games that involve overcoming rivals or cooperating with allies? Think of examples.
2 Think of examples of sports or games where you have to outsmart, outmanoeuvre, outplay or outrun your opponents.

## ⓞ SPEAKING HUB

**A PLAN** Work in pairs. Create an urban game for your town/city. Use ideas from the blog post and your own ideas.

**B DISCUSS** Present your ideas to another pair. Ask and answer questions about how your game ideas will work in practice.

**C PREPARE** Choose one game idea to develop more fully as a group. Write some simple rules or instructions for your game.

**D PRESENT** Present your ideas to the class. Which games would you most like to play? Why?

○ Discuss problem-solving tasks
○ Discuss gaming and game design

# 5.2 Serious gaming

- **Identify generalisations**
- **Discuss ideas for solving a challenge**

**G** – passive reporting structures
**V** – reporting verbs; motivation and manipulation
**P** – -ate words
**S** – distinguishing generalisations from preferred solutions

## LISTENING

**A SPEAK** Work in pairs. Read *The Food Truck problem*. Discuss two or three possible solutions.

**B** Work in small groups. You are going to think of a solution for three more puzzles. Go to the Communication Hub on page 151.

**C LISTEN FOR SOLUTIONS** Listen to the presentation on Game Theory. What are the correct answers to the puzzles? Use the information in the box to help you.

5.4

> **Distinguishing generalisations from preferred solutions**
>
> A speaker often presents their preferred solution to a problem or puzzle, alongside obvious but problematic solutions or generalisations. Often the generalisation is discussed first, before the speaker's preferred solution.
>
> Use the following techniques to distinguish the preferred solution.
>
> - Pay attention to the order in which the speaker presents solutions. Preferred solutions may be presented later.
> - Listen for phrases that signal a generalisation (e.g. *it seems obvious, you might expect, according to conventional wisdom*).
> - Listen for solutions presented with questioning intonation. This may indicate the speaker does not believe this is the correct answer.
> - Listen for attitude words like adverbs which can show that the speaker has a sceptical or cautious attitude to a solution (e.g. *presumably, allegedly*).

**D LISTEN FOR DETAIL** Listen again. Are these sentences true (T) or false (F)? Correct the false sentences.

5.4

1. In puzzle A neither participant is likely to win any money. **T / F**
2. Game Theory uses scientific models to find solutions. **T / F**
3. The favourite in talent shows is rarely eliminated in reality. **T / F**
4. The food truck owner at C has no good reason to move. **T / F**
5. The new network would double the amount of traffic. **T / F**

## PRONUNCIATION
### -ate words

**A** The suffix *-ate* has two pronunciations. Listen to the extracts from the presentation on Game Theory. Complete the table with the words in the box.

5.5

accurate   appropriate   complicated
cooperate   eliminated   fascinating

| /eɪt/ | /ət/ |
|---|---|
| | |
| | |
| | |
| | |

**B SPEAK** Work in groups. Discuss the following questions.

- Do you prefer games where you have to cooperate with others rather than compete individually?
- What is the most fascinating sporting event you've ever watched?
- Do you prefer playing simple or complicated games?

## PUZZLE C: THE FOOD TRUCK PROBLEM

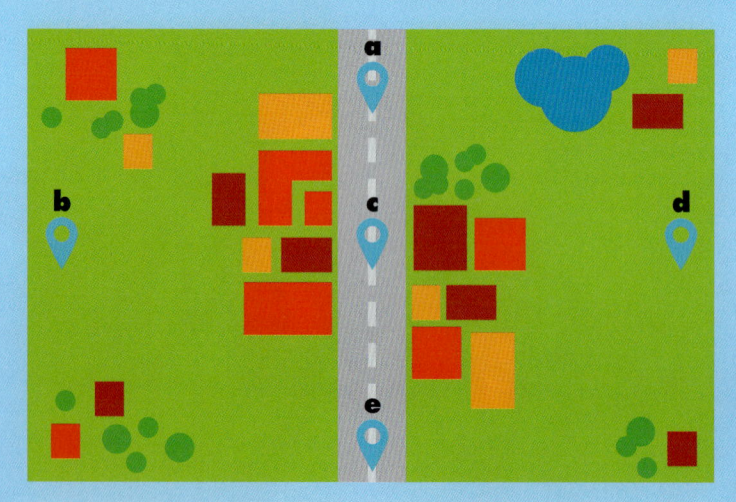

You decide to open a food truck business. There's already one other food truck in town, which always parks in the town centre (point C). Where's the best place to park your food truck? You can negotiate with the other food truck owner, if you wish.

54 GAMES

## VOCABULARY
### Reporting verbs

**A** Replace the underlined words in each sentence with the correct form of the verbs in the box.

> acknowledge   assert   conclude
> imply   instruct   urge

1 If you share the money, you're <u>saying indirectly</u> that you're willing to cooperate.
2 It's important to <u>say (although it makes my argument weaker)</u> that this strategy doesn't always work.
3 You might <u>decide after thinking carefully</u> that voting for her would be a waste.
4 So I'd <u>strongly advise</u> you to resist the temptation to vote tactically.
5 You should <u>give instructions to</u> the other truck to move to point D.
6 She can simply <u>state as a fact</u> that she's staying in her prime spot.

**B** Go to the **Vocabulary Hub** on **page 144**.

**C SPEAK** Complete the sentences with your own ideas. Then discuss your sentences with a partner.

- I firmly believe that …
- I'm not sure whether …
- I'm brilliant at …
- Perhaps if I'd done … I might not have …
- You really must …

**D** Swap partners and report what your previous partner said using reporting verbs.

## GRAMMAR
### Passive reporting structures

**A** Complete the sentences so they mean the same as the passive sentences with *It*.

1 **It** can be assumed that your opponent is having the same thoughts.
   Your opponent can be _____ having the same thoughts.
2 **It** is said that Game Theory is one of the hardest branches of mathematics.
   Game Theory is _____ one of the hardest branches of mathematics.
3 **It**'s rumoured that sports coaches have been experimenting with Game Theory.
   Sports coaches _____ have been experimenting with Game Theory.
4 **It**'s expected that she'll win by a landslide.
   _____ to win by a landslide.
5 **It**'s reported that this type of thing has happened many times in real life.
   This type of thing _____ happened many times in real life.

**B WORK IT OUT** Complete the rules about passive reporting structures with information from Exercise A.

> **Passive reporting structures**
>
> Reporting verbs can be used with passive structures when we want to introduce a widely held opinion or fact. There are two main ways of doing this.
>
> - _____ + passive + _____ clause
> - _____ + passive + *to* + infinitive
>
> Some verbs commonly used with these structures are:
> _____, _____, _____, _____ and _____.

**C** Go to the **Grammar Hub** on **page 130**.

**D SPEAK** Work in pairs and discuss the questions.

1 When is it useful to use the passive voice to report speech/thoughts?
2 Why do you think 'to rumour' has no active voice form?
3 What's the advantage of using the structure with *to* + infinitive?

## SPEAKING

**DISCUSS** Work in pairs to think of examples of how Game Theory might be used in sport, business, etc. Use the structure with *to* + infinitive to report generalisations, expectations and assumptions.

*The best time to make an investment is assumed to be when the price is low, but if everyone has the same idea at the same time, then …*

## 5.2

### READING

**A SPEAK** What tricks do smartphone games use to keep people playing again and again? Try to think of other situations where these tricks are used.

**B SKIM** Read *Gamification: treading the line between motivation and manipulation*. Are any situations from Exercise A mentioned?

**C READ FOR DETAIL** Read the article again. According to the article, are these sentences true (T) or false (F)? Correct the false sentences.

1 Many companies are not yet aware of the potential of gamification. T / F
2 Virtual prizes can still be highly motivating. T / F
3 The majority of people are aware that gamification has been used on them at some point. T / F
4 The major benefit of gamification for charities is that it increases financial donations. T / F
5 Gamification is used to help people recover from injuries. T / F
6 A brand new interactive show is being developed by a production company. T / F
7 Gamification sometimes encourages people to behave in a way that isn't right. T / F
8 The personality of workers may affect how motivating gamification techniques are. T / F

**D** Work in pairs. Look at the two quotes from Christabel Maware and Lisa Tanaka in the article. Which speaker do you agree with most? Why?

### VOCABULARY
Motivation and manipulation

**A** Match numbers (1–7) with letters (a–g) to form full sentences. Then check by looking for the underlined phrases in the article.

1 As a result of marketing tricks, customers **went**
2 Getting the university place I wanted **spurred**
3 People don't mind working hard if you can **tap**
4 If people know *why* they're doing something, they'll be more **inclined** …
5 Gamification can make people **act against** …
6 We offered virtual prizes to **coax** …
7 The online shop is designed to **steer** people …

a **to** spend time doing it properly.
b people **into** giving us their data.
c **me on** to study harder for the exams.
d **towards** the most expensive products.
e **nuts for** the new product.
f their best interests.
g **into** their natural desire to do a good job.

**B** Look at the complete sentences in Exercise A. Decide whether the phrases in bold are related to motivation or manipulation.

**C** Go to the **Vocabulary Hub** on **page 145**.

**D SPEAK** Work in pairs. Think of examples from your own experience of each verb in Exercise A. Tell your partner your examples.

*My friend tried to coax me into editing her dissertation for her.*

### SPEAKING HUB

**A PREPARE** Work in small groups. Choose one of the following challenges, or a similar idea, to solve with your group.
- How to motivate children to read/write more
- How to encourage people to pick up litter

**B PLAN** Discuss ideas for solving your challenge, using Game Theory and/or gamification techniques.

**C PRESENT** Present your challenge and solution to the class. Ask and answer questions about how it will work in practice.

**D REFLECT** Discuss with the class. Which solutions have a chance of becoming popular? Could they make money?

# GAMIFICATION
## treading the line between MOTIVATION and MANIPULATION

Hitting the treadmill before work, ploughing through deadlines, and finding time to study in the evenings. Perhaps these aren't the sort of activities you'd necessarily associate with fun. Yet a glut of apps, websites and online communities that place game-like experiences right at the centre of motivation might give you pause for thought. None of this is news for many commercial and public organisations which are already **tapping into** gamification – the application of elements from gameplay psychology to everyday tasks.

Gamification is about more than creating new games for non-gaming contexts. At its heart lies an understanding of the powerful principles that underlie gameplay, the elements that make it so compelling to so many: gratification, competition and rewards. Games increase engagement. Giving people rewards even virtual ones releases dopamine, the feel-good hormone. This leads them to associate that activity or behaviour with positive emotions. And that's often enough to **spur them on** to repeat it.

The applications of this are diverse: **steering commuters towards** the stairs over the escalator on the Odenplan subway in Sweden by turning them into a giant piano staircase or promoting good learning habits and classroom behaviour by giving students 'experience points'. It's highly likely you've experienced gamification yourself, although you probably didn't realise it.

So how can this benefit us? Gamification has made inroads into both the not-for-profit and health sectors. For charities, its greatest potential lies not in fundraising but in fostering a sense of community. If volunteers feel part of an engaged community, they are more **inclined to** stay. Furthermore, they can be incentivised to recruit others or blog about a cause through rewards.

Gamification can also be integrated directly into grassroots campaigning. Hopelab's Zamzee, a physical activity programme for families, uses child engagement with technology to improve health. It guides younger users towards doing more physical activity through an activity sensor and a 'physical points' reward system. More specialised healthcare like physical rehabilitation is using and trialling similar approaches. The Medical Interactive Recovery System (Mira) uses a camera to track a patient's physiotherapy movements and translate them into actions within a video game.

As well as bringing fun to areas where it might be wanting, gamification promises to take fun to the next level in traditional entertainment. Younger and more technologically-savvy viewers may crave an immersive experience, being able to participate in a TV show rather than simply view it. Well, now they can have both their needs for compelling stories and recognition or rewards for their gaming achievements, met at the same time. For example, the popular sci-fi TV show, *Defiance,* by Universal Cable Productions, allowed viewers to shape the plot of television episodes through their actions in an accompanying game.

Some are cautious about gamification, precisely because of its power and how widely it is being used. 'If it can help change our behaviour, it can also manipulate us to **act against** our best interests', warns technology lecturer and game designer Christabel Maware. 'I can see it being used quite cynically to exploit consumers and employees.' Some companies and organisations have already been called out. For example, a ride-sharing app was criticised for supposedly encouraging drivers to drive further without breaks.

And even where gamification is encouraging 'healthy' competition or making a mundane but necessary work task more appealing, there are concerns around work freedom and surveillance. While leader boards and badges can keep us motivated, having our performance and potentially complex interactions monitored, graded and immediately reported back on by machines sounds more dystopian. 'Quite simply, not everyone is going to **go nuts for** badges at work', says Recruitment Manager for AdTech Analytics. For workers who are more introverted or prefer to work privately, this kind of surveillance might be unwelcome and demotivating.

As Lisa Tanaka, founder and CEO of creative agency Gamified International puts it, 'On balance gamification can bring some very positive benefits to many sectors. This stuff works, our brains really are hard-wired for rewards and fun is addictive. We're already being **coaxed into** doing all kinds of things. But with such a powerful tool, there's a pressing need now for companies to be socially responsible in how they use it.'

### Glossary
**crave** (v) to want something very much and in a way that is very hard to control
**incentivise** (v) to give someone a reason for wanting to do something
**grassroots** (adj) relating to or involving ordinary people, especially in politics
**plough** (v) to finish something that takes a long time and is difficult or boring
**recognition** (n) praise, respect or admiration

- Identify generalisations
- Discuss ideas for solving a challenge

# Café Hub

## 5.3 Win or lose

A – ellipsis   S – building relationships

## ▶ Would you risk it?

**A** Work in pairs. What do you think is happening in the pictures (a and b) from the video?

**B** ▶ 00.00–01.00 Watch the first part of a video about an experiment. Answer the questions.

1 What happens if the coin lands on heads?
2 What happens if the coin lands on tails?

### Glossary

**flip** (v) to turn over quickly or to make something turn over
**heads** (n) the side of a coin that has a picture of a head on it
**scenario** (n) a situation that could possibly happen
**tails** (n) the side of a coin that does not have a picture of a person on it

**C** ▶ 01.00–01.30 Watch the second part of the video. Choose the best option (a, b or c) to complete the sentence.

In this situation most people …
a take a risk and maybe win an extra ten pounds or nothing.
b choose the safe option and take fifteen pounds.
c risk it for the chance to win an extra five pounds.

**D** ▶ 01.30–02.20 Work in pairs. Watch the third part of the video and complete the sentences with the correct option.

1 In the second scenario you are given *ten / twenty* pounds.
2 You have to choose to accept a safe loss of *five / ten* pounds or take a risk.
3 You flip a coin. If it comes up heads, you don't lose anything, but if it comes up tails, you lose *five / ten* pounds.

**E** ▶ 02.20–03.27 Watch the last part of the video. What do most people do in the second scenario? Why?

## AUTHENTIC ENGLISH

**A** Work in pairs. Read the sentence from the video and the information in the box. What word has been left out of the sentence?

*Would you choose the safe option and get an extra five pounds or take a risk and maybe win an extra ten or nothing?*

### Ellipsis

Ellipsis is the practice of leaving a word or words out of a sentence when they are not necessary for understanding it. In spoken English, unstressed words are often left out at the beginning of sentences if the meaning remains clear.

**B** Work in pairs. Match the questions (1–6) with the replies (a–f). Then cross out any words which can be omitted from each question and reply.

1 Did you enjoy your holiday?
2 Are you ready yet?
3 Is your dad any better?
4 Are you coming out with us tonight?
5 Did you have any luck with the tickets for the Beyoncé concert?
6 I'm sorry, are you talking to me?

a I'm almost ready. I'm just putting on my make-up.
b Yes, I was asking if you're doing anything nice at the weekend.
c Yes, thanks. He should be out at the weekend.
d No, they were all sold out. It's a shame, really.
e I'm afraid, I can't. I've got to work late.
f It was absolutely amazing! I've just got back, actually.

**C** Work in pairs. Take it turns to ask each other short questions from Exercise B and reply with your own short answers.

## ▶ How sure are you?

SAM   MALCOLM   AMANDA   HARRY   EMILY

**A** Work in pairs. Look at the picture.
1 What board games are popular in your country?
2 Do you ever play them?

**B** ▶ Watch the video. Answer the questions.
1 If Sam and Amanda go in an anti-clockwise direction, which category do they land on?
2 Why does Amanda think Geography is the better option?
3 How does Sam feel about Amanda's strategy?
4 How does Malcolm indicate the correct answer to Sam and Amanda?
5 How does Amanda suggest making the game more interesting?
6 Why doesn't Emily want to take the risk?
7 What's the question Emily and Harry have to answer?
8 What's Malcolm's answer? Is he correct?

## SPEAKING SKILL

**A** Work in pairs. Look at the underlined expression from the video and answer the questions.
1 What is Harry doing?
2 Why do we do this when we're speaking?

> **Sam:** Don't you think it's better to play it safe and go for your strongest categories first … you know … try and build up a lead?
> **Harry:** <u>That sounds like a solid strategy to me.</u>

**B** Look at the information in the box. Decide which strategy (a or b) is being used in the exchanges (1–4) from the video.

### Building relationships
We can build relationships using the following strategies.
a Agreeing with the other person by tagging on to what they have said.
b Relating to what the other person has said by evaluating or commenting.

1 **Sam:** I'm thinking we should go for Geography.
   **Amanda:** Totally … I absolutely hate Geography … it's better to try and get it out of the way earlier.
2 **Emily:** Ah, good – this is quite hard, I think.
   **Sam:** That is quite tricky.
3 **Sam:** OK, it can only be one of two countries …
   **Amanda:** … either Finland or Norway.
4 **Emily:** I mean sport hardly looks like it would be Malcolm's strongest category.
   **Harry:** I guess not but he is smart.

**C** Work in small groups. Give your opinions on one of the following topics. Use the strategies from Exercise B to build a positive rapport.
- your favourite board game
- your favourite type of film
- your favourite type of book

## ○ SPEAKING HUB

**A PLAN** Work in small groups. You are going to plan a fundraising event for a local charity. Decide on one of the following.

| a dinner | a board game evening | a yoga class |
| a bake off | a fashion show | a quiz |

**B PREPARE** Individually think about the preparations for the event. Consider the following points.
- space
- logistics
- timing
- cost

**C PRESENT** Work in small groups. Decide on a course of action for the event. Try to build up positive relationships and create a consensus.

> A: We could hold a banquet dinner at the town hall.
> B: Great idea! It could go on all evening.

○— Plan a fundraising event

➤ Turn to page 160 to learn how to write a formal report about gamification.

GAMES 59

# Unit 5 Review

## VOCABULARY

**A** Complete the instructions with the correct form of a word in the box.

> ally   collaborate   cooperate   coordinate   prevail   rival

### Bike clash

The game involves outmanoeuvring players on ¹_____ teams by racing around the city on bikes. Each team has four players, who ²_____ with each other, and a 'boss', who ³_____ their movements. By ⁴_____ with their ⁵_____, players solve puzzles to identify the times and locations of 'clashes', where they try to ⁶_____ their rivals. When a clash begins, the team with the most players wins a 'trophy'. Any teams that have been outnumbered lose a player. At the end, the team with the most trophies ⁷_____.

**B** Choose the correct word to complete each sentence.
1. Shops are often laid out to *discourage / steer / trigger* customers towards expensive items.
2. Salespeople try to manipulate us by *coaxing / dissuading / exploiting* us into spending more than we intended.
3. Loyalty cards can make people *act / spur / tempt* against their best interests.
4. My sister *spurred / influenced / dissuaded* me on to enter the race.
5. I wasn't *exploited / inclined / influenced* to go, but you've persuaded me.
6. Advertising can *tap / tempt / influence* into people's emotional needs.

**C** Complete the definitions with the words in the box.

> discourage   dissuade   exploit   influence
> manipulate   motivate   tempt   trigger

1. If you _____ somebody, you encourage them to want to do something.
2. If you _____ somebody, you use tricks to convince them do something.
3. If you _____ somebody from doing something, you persuade them not to do it.
4. If you _____ somebody from doing something, you encourage them not to do it.
5. If you _____ somebody, you take advantage of their kindness or naivety.
6. If you _____ somebody, you offer them something that's hard to resist.
7. If you _____ somebody's behaviour, you change it, perhaps without the person noticing.
8. If your actions _____ a response, they cause it to happen automatically.

## GRAMMAR

**A** Rewrite the sentences so they start or end with the words in brackets.
1. Somebody must have moved my car. (*my*)
   _____.
2. You can always rely on Leo. (*Leo*)
   _____.
3. I'm worried about somebody seeing me. (*seen*)
   _____.
4. They made us leave our phones outside. (*we*)
   _____.
5. Somebody's going to fix my car. (*I'm*)
   _____.
6. It was nice of them to invite us. (*invited*)
   _____.
7. How did somebody break the vase? (*broken*)
   _____?

**B** Put the words into the correct order to make sentences.
1. good / considered / my proposal / be / to / enough / wasn't
   _____.
2. to / anyone / to the party / expected / hardly / was / come
   _____.
3. have / reported / is / hundreds of complaints / received / to / the company
   _____.
4. going / at / been / alleged / have / the time / to / the driver / is / too fast
   _____.
5. planning / is / a new hospital / to build / rumoured / to / the city council / be
   _____.
6. been / the kidnappers / have / is / the letter / by / to / believed / written
   _____.

GAMES

# 6 DISCOVERIES

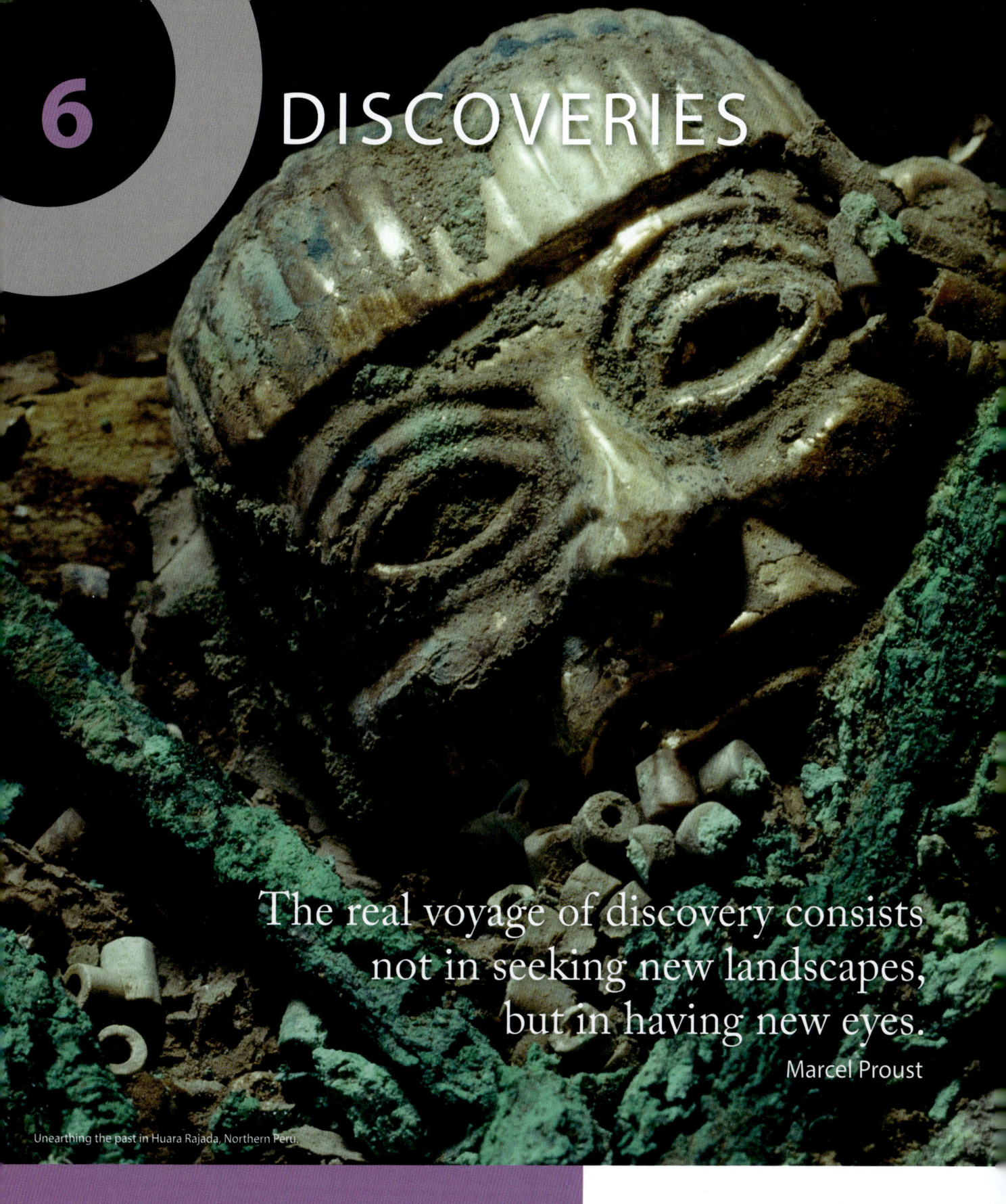

The real voyage of discovery consists not in seeking new landscapes, but in having new eyes.

Marcel Proust

Unearthing the past in Huara Rajada, Northern Peru.

## OBJECTIVES

- speculate and make deductions about the past
- plan an amazing journey
- discuss rewarding jobs
- give a presentation about someone you admire
- plan and perform an interview
- write an expository essay

Work with a partner. Discuss the questions.

1 Look at the picture. What do discoveries like this tell us? Are they important? Why/Why not?

2 Read the quote. What does Proust mean? Do you agree?

3 What do you think has been the greatest discovery ever? Give reasons for your answer.

# 6.1 Challenging journeys

- Speculate and make deductions about the past
- Plan an amazing journey

**V** — journeys and adventures; three-part phrasal verbs
**P** — showing your attitude
**G** — past modals of speculation and deduction
**S** — prediction strategies for reading

## READING

**A SPEAK** Work in pairs. Do you know any famous explorers? What did they do?

**B PREDICT** Look at the title and the pictures in the article. Read the information in the box and answer questions a and b.

### Prediction strategies for reading

Use the prediction cycle to help you predict the content of a text:

- Make predictions about the content of the text.
  - a What information will be included?
  - b What questions will it answer?
- Read part of the text to find out if your predictions were correct or not.
  - c Were your predictions correct?
  - d What information supported or challenged your predictions?

**C SKIM** Read *The disappearance of Percy Fawcett*. Answer questions c and d in the box in Exercise B.

**D READ FOR DETAIL** Complete the table with evidence for and against each theory in the article.

| | For |
|---|---|
| 1 | |
| 2 | |
| 3 | |

| | Against |
|---|---|
| 1 | |
| 2 | |
| 3 | |

**E SPEAK** Work in groups. Which theory do you think is the most likely explanation for what happened? Why?

## THE DISAPPEARANCE OF PERCY FAWCETT

In the age of **long-haul** flights and travel **off the beaten track**, many now consider themselves seasoned **globetrotters**. However, there was a time when travelling to the far corners of the world was both dangerous and rare.

This was true in January 1925 when accomplished British explorer Percy Fawcett **embarked on** his latest expedition, hoping to find an ancient city in the jungle, the Lost City of Z.

Despite previous failed attempts to find it, he was still convinced that a large city that was 'more ancient than the oldest Egyptian discoveries' lay **at the heart of** the Amazon. On 20th April, his group departed from the Brazilian city of Cuiabá and headed for the jungle.

On 29th May, Fawcett sent a letter to his wife telling her that they were about to enter **uncharted territory**. They were never heard from again.

So what happened to Fawcett and his party? This remains one of the world's greatest unsolved mysteries and has inspired a lot of speculation. Here are three possible explanations.

### 1 THEY WERE KILLED BY INDIGENOUS PEOPLE

Some people believe that Fawcett and his companions must have been killed by an indigenous tribe. While journalist David Grann was retracing Fawcett's journey in 2005, he met with a tribe called the Kalapalo. They told him that they had heard stories from their grandparents about explorers coming to their territory and ignoring warnings not to walk through territory belonging to another tribe because this tribe were hostile to intruders. The Kalapalo tribe believe that it is highly likely Fawcett and his companions were killed by this other tribe. However, no bones have ever been found.

62 DISCOVERIES

## 2 THEY DIED OF NATURAL CAUSES: EXHAUSTION, STARVATION OR ILLNESS

According to Henry Costin, a man who accompanied Fawcett on several of his previous expeditions, <u>Fawcett was always friendly and respectful towards the tribes he met, so he can't have been killed by them.</u>

Costin believed that <u>there was a distinct possibility, given the scale of the expedition and the **impenetrable** terrain, that Fawcett and his companions died from exhaustion, or lack of food when their **provisions** ran out.</u> Alternatively, given that several explorers at the time died from tropical diseases, <u>they may well have succumbed to illness in the jungle.</u>

## 3 THEY STAYED IN THE JUNGLE

After studying Fawcett's private papers, television director Misha Williams came up with an alternative theory. She believed that <u>Fawcett had become disillusioned with life in Europe and may have decided to establish a commune in the jungle and live a simpler life.</u>

However, many people point out that this theory doesn't make a lot of sense, because <u>Fawcett had a wife and two children, so he couldn't have deliberately abandoned them.</u> Similarly, <u>he could have found the Lost City of Z and decided to stay.</u> In recent years, archaeological discoveries have shown that Fawcett might have been right after all.

Researchers have found the ruins of huge cities in the Amazon that may well have been home to thousands of people. Did he finally find what he was looking for?

### Glossary

**disillusioned (adj)** disappointed because you have discovered that someone or something is not as good as you had believed
**starvation (n)** a situation in which a person or animal suffers or dies because they do not have enough to eat
**succumb (v)** to become very sick or to die from a disease
**intruder (n)** someone who enters a place where they are not allowed to go
**retrace (v)** to go along the same path or route that someone else has gone along previously
**seasoned (adj)** experienced in a particular activity or job

## VOCABULARY
### Journeys and adventures

**A** Scan the article again. Complete the definitions with the words in bold.

1 _____ (n) supply of food, drink, equipment, etc for a journey
2 _____ (adj) impossible to move through or enter
3 _____ (v) begin
4 _____ (n phr) places not covered by maps
5 _____ (n) middle of
6 _____ (n) frequent international travellers
7 _____ (adj) long distance
8 _____ (phr) away from frequently visited places

**B** Go to the Vocabulary Hub on page 145.

**C** SPEAK Work in pairs. Tell your partner about an adventurous journey you've been on or heard about.

## GRAMMAR
### Past modals of speculation and deduction

**A** Look at the underlined sentences in the article. Complete the rules with the words in the box.

> adjective   adverb   can't/couldn't
> could/might/may   may well   must

### Past modals of speculation and deduction

1 We use _____ + *have* + past participle for things we believe logically happened.
2 We use _____ + *have* + past participle for things we think are likely to have happened.
3 We use _____ + *have* + past participle for things we think possibly happened.
4 We use _____ + *have* + past participle to say something was not logically possible.
5 We can use phrases that start with *There's a/an* + _____ + noun + (*that*) … to speculate.
6 We can use phrases that start with *It's* + _____ + adjective (*that*) … to speculate.

**B** Go to the Grammar Hub on page 132.

**C** SPEAK Work in pairs. Discuss these theories about Percy Fawcett's disappearance.

1 They were attacked by wild animals.
2 Rival explorers killed them.
3 They were killed by a natural disaster.
4 They decided to join one of the tribes.

## SPEAKING

**A** DISCUSS Work in small groups. Group A – go to the Communication Hub on page 153. Group B – go to the Communication Hub on page 155.

**B** PRESENT Work with someone from the other group. Tell them about the historical mystery you read about.

DISCOVERIES

## 6.1

### VOCABULARY
Three-part phrasal verbs

**A** Work in pairs. Read *Seven reasons to go travelling*. Discuss which you think is the best reason to go travelling.

**B** Find nine three-part phrasal verbs in the article. Use the information in the box to help you.

1 _____
2 _____
3 _____
4 _____
5 _____
6 _____
7 _____
8 _____
9 _____

---
**Three-part phrasal verbs**

Phrasal verbs are common in informal English.

Most phrasal verbs only have two parts (for example, *sit down, turn up*). However, there are also three-part phrasal verbs which contain a verb + a particle + a preposition (for example, *look up to*).

---

**C** Choose the correct options to complete the rules. Use the examples in Exercise B to help you decide.

1 Most three-part phrasal verbs are *separable / inseparable*.
2 The particle and the preposition *can / can't* be separated.
3 Some three-part phrasal verbs can take an object after the *verb / particle*.

**D** Complete the sentences with a three-part phrasal verb from Exercise B. Use the hint in brackets to help you.

1 It's important to _____ (*research*) a place before you visit it.
2 If you _____ (*experience*) problems on a trip, it makes it more of an adventure.
3 _____ (*moving away from*) the crowds is more interesting than going sightseeing.
4 I don't think I _____ (*be interested in*) travelling to another country by myself.
5 I _____ (*remember*) my childhood holidays with fondness.
6 Travel is a great way to help people to _____ (*stop thinking about*) work or study.
7 You should always _____ (*review and practise*) your language skills before a trip.
8 You should always pack in advance rather than only _____ (*eventually do*) it the night before you leave.

**E** Work in pairs. Discuss whether you agree or disagree with the sentences in Exercise D.

**F** SPEAK Work in small groups. Which reasons from the article do you think are the most worthwhile? Why? Think of three more reasons to go travelling.

## Seven reasons
### TO GO TRAVELLING

① Because you are up for an adventure. Challenge yourself with something that pushes you outside your comfort zone. See how you react when you come up against obstacles.

② Because you want to find out about the world. You can read about different countries and cultures, but nothing compares to being there and seeing it for yourself.

③ Because you want to learn the language. If you really want to brush up on your language skills, you need to travel to where the language is spoken.

④ Because you want to learn about yourself. Getting away from home and work means you have time to reflect on your life and decide if you want to make any changes.

⑤ Because you need to recharge your batteries. If you find it hard to keep yourself away from work, travelling can help you switch off from all the things you need to do and get some well-earned rest.

⑥ Because you want to celebrate a special occasion with friends or family. Travel can create precious memories that you can look back on together.

⑦ Because you always wanted to. Don't keep putting it off or you'll never get round to it!

## LISTENING

**A PREDICT** Work in pairs. You are going to listen to a discussion about travel challenges on a radio programme. What do you think a travel challenge is?

**B LISTEN FOR GIST** Listen to the radio programme. Answer the following questions.
6.1

1 What is a travel challenge?

2 How many examples of travel challenges does Kyle give?

3 What reasons other than to be different does Kyle give for people doing these challenges?

4 What does the presenter think you need to do a trip like Adam Leyton's?

5 What does Kyle admire about Daniel Tunnard?

6 What is Kyle's most vital piece of advice for someone doing a travel challenge?

**C LISTEN FOR DETAIL** Listen again. What is the significance of the following numbers?
6.1

1 24 _____     5 41 _____
2 12 _____     6 140 _____
3 22 _____     7 14 _____
4 900 _____    8 55 _____

**D SPEAK** Work in pairs. Discuss the questions.

1 Do you agree that these kinds of travel challenges are becoming more popular?
2 Which of the three travel challenges sounds the most interesting to you?
3 Would you donate money to help someone pay for their trip?
4 Would you rather go on a normal holiday or try a travel challenge?

## PRONUNCIATION
Showing your attitude

**A** Listen to these extracts from the radio programme.
6.2 Match each extract (1–4) with the speaker's attitudes to what they say (a–d).

a certain that what they say is true ___
b believes what they say is a generalisation or approximation ___
c believes that what they say is an important point ___
d unsure that something is true ___

**B** Work in pairs. Draw arrows to predict whether the intonation
6.3 rises (↗), falls (↘) or fall-rises (↘↗) on the underlined attitude words. Then listen to check.

1 Allegedly, (___) you need to be very careful backpacking in some areas of that country.
2 On the whole, (___) I think it's better to travel alone than with a group of friends.
3 The question is, (___) have you got the luxury of taking time out from work.
4 Surely, (___) it can't be that much fun visiting a lot of countries in a short space of time.

**C SPEAK** Work in pairs. Discuss the questions using words, phrases and intonation to show your attitude.

1 Which countries would you like to visit and why?
2 Should people travel more within their own countries before they go abroad?
3 Do you think taking time out to go travelling can help your career?

## SPEAKING HUB

**A PREPARE** Work in small groups. You have entered a competition to win sponsorship for a trip abroad. To win, you must come up with an original travel challenge. Think of an idea to enter into the competition and prepare to present this idea to your class. Think about:

- how you will travel.
- where you will travel.
- what your goal will be.
- what the budget will be.
- how you will publicise the trip.

**B PRESENT** Present your idea to the class. Listen to the other groups' ideas.

**C DISCUSS** Vote on the most interesting idea.

○─ Speculate and make deductions about the past
○─ Plan an amazing journey

## 6.2 Inquisitive minds

- Discuss rewarding jobs
- Give a presentation about someone you admire

**G** -ing and infinitive forms
**V** binomial expressions
**P** pauses and pitch in presentations
**S** taking notes while listening

## READING

**A SPEAK** Work in pairs. Rank the following qualities in order of how important they are in journalism. Give reasons for your answer.

___ passion  ___ courage
___ curiosity  ___ determination
___ integrity

**B READ FOR MAIN IDEA** Read *Chase down your story*. What is the purpose of the article?

1 To give advice to journalism students.
2 To share life lessons which the writer has learnt from journalism.
3 To evaluate the importance of journalism in the 21st century.

**C READ FOR DETAIL** Read the article again. Match the questions (1–6) with the sections (a–d). Sections may be chosen more than once.

Which section of the article …

1 acknowledges a misconception the writer had? ___
2 highlights the difference between news in the past compared to now? ___
3 mentions an event which changed the writer's approach to learning? ___
4 describes a characteristic which the writer admires? ___
5 emphasises the importance of personal experience? ___
6 mentions discovering lessons by accident when looking for help? ___

**D SPEAK** Work in pairs. Discuss the questions.

1 Which do you think is the most useful piece of advice? Which do you think is the least useful? Why?
2 Have you ever learnt anything from work or study that you could apply to your personal life?

# Chase down your story

## a Finding stories

Ever wondered how journalists find the stories worth telling? Over my first year at a bona fide national newspaper, I learnt the hard way that getting the 'scoop' – being the first to report an exciting or important newsworthy story – was easier said than done. So I asked some of my more experienced colleagues to pass on their tricks of the trade. But what I soon discovered was that their advice could be applied not only to my job, but also to my personal life.

## b Be curious

As journalists, we're paid to be curious. The number one suggestion I got was to have an inquisitive mind: figure out what matters, and which stories will inspire, move or make us laugh. It is not enough to report facts these days. But if something sparks your curiosity, the chances are other people will be interested, too.

There was the time I met a woman who mentioned she was thinking about moving to a remote Pacific island for a year. A whole year away from family, friends … the internet! I had so many questions – and it was no surprise it made a great story, too.

In every conversation I have now, I think about what I can ask and what I can learn. Everybody has something they can teach you. It also helps to ask yourself questions about your own life: Why am I doing what I'm doing? What do I hope to achieve?

## c Local is global

Writers have a great imagination. But, as I learnt from my colleagues, that can sometimes have a downside. It can keep us looking towards the horizon, craving uncharted territory. Fresh out of university, I pictured myself jetting off to parts unknown to break the next big story. While there is much to be said for this, articles don't need to be exotic or even big news to catch a reader's attention. More often than not, we find that we write best when we write what we know. This second lesson is perhaps one of the hardest to learn as a new writer.

DISCOVERIES

## GRAMMAR
### -ing and infinitive forms

**A** Choose the correct form of the verbs to complete the sentences.

1 She was thinking about *moving / to move* to a remote Pacific island for a year.
2 It is time to acknowledge how vital it is *staying / to stay* on course.
3 It's all too easy for details *slipping / to slip* through the cracks.
4 Articles don't need to be exotic *catching / to catch* a reader's attention.
5 It is not enough *reporting / to report* facts these days.
6 Ever wondered how journalists find the stories worth *telling / to tell*?

**B** Scan the article again and check your answers to Exercise A.

**C** Match the examples in Exercise A to the rules in the box.

| -ing and infinitive forms |
|---|
| We use the *-ing* form: |
| a after prepositions _____ |
| b after expressions such as *it's no good …, it's not worth …, there's no point in …, have a good time/difficulty/fun/problems …* _____ |
| We use *to* + infinitive: |
| c after adjectives _____ |
| d after nouns _____ |
| e after quantifiers _____ |
| f after the word *time* _____ |

**D** Go to the Grammar Hub on page 132.

## SPEAKING

Work in pairs. Look at the pictures of people with different jobs below.

**Student A:** Compare the two pictures. Say what qualities and skills people need for these jobs and why people choose to do these jobs.

**Student B:** Which job would you most like to do and why?

---

Most of the greatest reporters have cut their teeth reporting on local news, whether that's uncovering home-grown corruption and injustice or just telling human-interest stories. What I've come to realise is that these stories often have a global reach because we have the same emotions, interests and concerns the world over. This has led me to believe – that whilst we must not be inward looking – appreciating what is right in front of us can be just as rewarding as looking further afield.

### d Follow up

We are living in a world that is always on, where consumers can access massive amounts of content and expect instant gratification. In comparison to only five or ten years ago, we are so concerned with the beginning of the story that the middle and end have fallen by the wayside. It's all too easy for details to slip through the cracks and for stories, which should be huge, to be all but forgotten by the next news cycle.

And here lies the last tip, get to the conclusion of your story. Don't get distracted. Many of the finest journalists in history were renowned for their tenacity – their innate ability to chase down the facts in the face of seemingly indomitable odds.

This is a quality to aspire to in life. It is time to acknowledge how vital it is to stay on course, not to allow yourself to be side-tracked by modern distractions and the illusion of endless choice. See things through to their conclusion: whether that's the project you're working on or the sport you're learning. And it applies to people too – valuing and caring for the friends and networks you have is as important as growing them.

| Glossary |
|---|
| **cut your teeth on sth (phr)** to get your first experience in a particular job by doing something |
| **tenacity (n)** the behaviour of being very determined and unwilling to stop when trying to achieve something |

DISCOVERIES

## 6.2

### LISTENING

**A PREDICT** Work in pairs. Look at the infographic of events in a famous inventor's life. Can you guess who it is?

**B** Read the information in the box and look at the notes table.

---

**Taking notes while listening**

When you need to take effective notes, you can use the Cornell system. It involves the following five stages:

**Stage 1 Notes:** Write notes in the note-taking column. Focus on main ideas. Use bullet points and abbreviations.

**Stage 2 Questions:** Write questions about your notes in the column on the left. (e.g. *Is this still true today?, What does inhalation mean?*)

**Stage 3 Summarise:** Read your notes and questions. Then write a summary of what you learnt.

**Stage 4 Reflect:** Think about what you have written. (e.g. *Overall, do you agree with the speaker?*)

**Stage 5 Review and recall:** Review your notes. Cover the second column and answer the questions in the first.

---

**C LISTEN TO MAKE NOTES** Listen to a presentation about an inventor. Follow the method in Stage 1 in the box. Make notes in the table as you listen.

| Questions | Notes |
|---|---|
|  |  |
| Summary |  |

**D REFLECT** Read your notes. Follow Stage 2 in the box. Write questions in the table.

**E SUMMARISE** Follow Stage 3 from the box. Write a summary of your notes in the table. Use the questions in the box to help you.

**F REVIEW** Compare your notes and questions with your partner. Are they similar? Can your partner answer any of your questions?

**G SPEAK** Work in pairs. If you were an inventor what type of invention would you focus on?

- inventions that save lives
- everyday products that fix common problems
- niche products for rich people

# AN INVENTIVE LIFE

One of the first African-American inventors to gain fame.

Invented a hair-straightening oil.

Designed a safety hood which he used when rescuing 32 workers from an explosion.

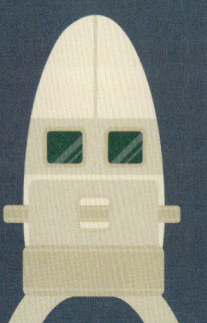

Came up with the idea of the orange caution light on traffic lights.

Ran for city council.

DISCOVERIES

## VOCABULARY
Binomial expressions

**A** Match the binomials in bold (1–10) with their definitions (a–j). Use the information in the box to help you.

> **Binomial expressions**
>
> A binomial expression is two words (nouns, verbs, adjectives or adverbs) joined by words like *and*, *or*, *but*, *by* and *to*.
> The two words can:
> - be antonyms (*give and take*)
> - be synonyms (*peace and quiet*)
> - use the same word twice (*back to back*)
> - use words that start with the same sound (*black and blue*)
> - use words that sound similar (*here and there*).
>
> When a binomial expression is a compound adjective used before a noun it is generally hyphenated (a *happy-go-lucky* person).

1 In my opinion, he's **far and away** one of America's greatest inventors.
2 He was soon selling it **far and wide**.
3 It was truly a **life-or-death** situation.
4 Morgan and his brother Frank raced to the scene and went in **side by side**.
5 They soon re-emerged **safe and sound** with survivors.
6 Morgan's fame began to spread **slowly but surely**.
7 **By and large**, in the early 1920s, American roads were dangerous places.
8 **Time after time** there were stories of injuries and fatalities in traffic accidents.
9 But he also put his **heart and soul** into the community.
10 While his life was a classic **rags-to-riches** story.

a generally
b all of one's energy and passion
c repeatedly
d by a very large amount
e next to each other
f from poor to wealthy
g unharmed and not in danger
h in many different places
i potentially fatal
j gradually

**B** Go to the **Vocabulary Hub** on **page 145**.

**C** **SPEAK** Work in pairs. Complete the sentences with your own ideas. Then share your ideas with your partner.

1 _____ is **far and away** the greatest invention.
2 I always put my **heart and soul** into _____.
3 When I was younger, I couldn't _____. Then **slowly but surely**, I learnt how.

## PRONUNCIATION
Pauses and pitch in presentations

**A** Listen to the first part of the presentation again and mark any pauses with (/).
6.5

> Today, I'd like to talk about someone who I particularly admire. In my opinion, he's far and away one of America's greatest inventors. His innovations have fixed everyday problems but also probably saved thousands of lives. In addition, he was one of the first African-American inventors to gain public recognition for his work. His name was Garrett Morgan and he was a prolific inventor and entrepreneur who lived between 1877 and 1963. And while you may not all know his name, you're likely to have experienced his innovations.
>
> One of Morgan's early successes was actually an accident. He was repairing a sewing machine in his shop when he noticed that some oil he was using had straightened the hairs on a cloth.

**B** Work in pairs. Turn to the **audioscript** on **page 172** and practise reading the presentation about Garrett Morgan. Focus on pauses and pitch.

## ○ SPEAKING HUB

**A** **THINK** You are going to give a presentation about someone you admire. Choose someone who made a big difference to the world by:
- leading social change
- challenging the status quo
- inventing or discovering something important.

**B** **PREPARE** Write a short presentation to tell your classmates about this person. Focus on:
- the life of the person you are talking about
- the main achievements of the person you are talking about
- a big problem the person solved.

**C** **PRESENT** Give your presentation.

**D** **DISCUSS** Listen to your classmates' presentations. Which of the people do you want to learn more about? Why?

○– Discuss rewarding jobs
○– **Give a presentation about someone you admire**

# Café Hub

## 6.3 World of knowledge
**A** – engaging listeners   **S** – conducting an interview

## ▶ Connecting with nature

**A** Work in pairs. Look at the pictures (a–c) and discuss these questions.
1. What are they?
2. How might they be connected?

**B** ▶ Watch the video. Check your answers to Exercise A.

### Glossary
**assemble (v)** to build something by joining parts together
**countless (adj)** very many
**tangled (adj)** twisted into an untidy mass
**vaporise (v)** to turn from a solid or liquid state into gas

**C** ▶ Watch the video again. Are the sentences true (T) or false (F) according to the video? Correct the false sentences.

1. An oak tree is made up of only carbon, nitrogen, oxygen and hydrogen. **T / F**
2. The carbon atom in the acorn was created inside a star billions of years ago. **T / F**
3. The carbon atom in the acorn has formed part of the earth for two billion years. **T / F**
4. The carbon atom in the acorn got into some ancient oak tree through the action of photosynthesis. **T / F**
5. In billions of years, when the sun dies and the earth is vaporised, all atoms will die. **T / F**

**D** ▶ Watch the video again. Complete the sentences.

1. When atoms react and _____ they make up everything in the Universe.
2. Many different types of plants, trees and animals make up the _____ of a woodland.
3. When you understand that everything is made of atoms, a woodland doesn't seem such a _____ place.
4. An atom in an acorn has spent many years in _____.
5. Life is only a _____ home of the atoms that make up the universe.

## AUTHENTIC ENGLISH

**A** Work in pairs. Read the sentence from the video and the information in the box. Which device has been used to engage listeners?

*So life is just a temporary home for the immortal elements that build up the universe.*

### Engaging listeners
Brian Cox is a very engaging speaker. He uses a number of strategies to engage listeners.
- Summarising information, for example, *So, when you look at it like that it's really not that complicated at all.*
- Repetition of certain words such as *billions* to emphasise a point.
- Dynamic words such as *thrown back out* and *vaporise*.

**B** Go to the transcript on **page 154**. Underline examples of the strategies from the box that Brian Cox uses to engage listeners.

**C** Write a short speech on a topic that you're passionate about. Use strategies to engage your listeners.

**D** Work in pairs. Read your speech to your partner. Try to be as engaging and passionate as possible.

# ▶ Getting answers

SAM  MALCOLM  AMANDA  HARRY  EMILY

**A** Work in pairs. Discuss the questions.

1 Do you ever watch documentaries about science? Why/Why not?
2 Should we try to make science more accessible than it is now?
3 Are there any cons to simplifying science for a wider audience?
4 What is Malcolm doing?

**B** ▶ Watch the video. Were any of the things you discussed in Exercise A mentioned?

**C** ▶ Watch the video again. Complete the sentences with one to three words.

1 Amanda is interviewing Veronica about _____.
2 Malcolm tells Sam that Veronica is one of the country's _____.
3 Veronica says she saw Brian Cox _____.
4 Since being inspired by Brian Cox, Veronica has been _____.
5 Malcolm comments that Veronica's book is at the top of the _____.

## SPEAKING SKILL

**A** Work in pairs. Complete the line from the video. Why has Amanda asked her question in this way?

> Professor Matos, _____ respond to accusations that your book is under-researched?

**B** Look at the information in the box. Match the questions (1–5) with the types (a–e).

### Conducting an interview

a **Direct questions** are asked in order to make a point about a situation or to point out something for consideration. For example, ___
b **Indirect questions** are used when we want to be more polite. We use an introductory phrase followed by the question itself in a positive sentence structure. For example, ___
c **Negative questions** can ask for confirmation of our opinions or make invitations or suggestions. For example, ___
d **Tag questions** can either be 'real' questions where we want to know the answer or simply ask for agreement when we already know the answer. For example, ___
e **Rhetorical questions** are often statements given in question format in order to make a point about a situation. For example, ___

1 Why don't you go over and introduce yourself?
2 It builds on some of the theories set out by Professor Brian Cox, doesn't it?
3 I hope you don't mind me asking, why did you decide to write a book?
4 Can I quote you on that?
5 Did I dumb down the science a bit for the masses?

**C** Work in pairs. Think of one more example for each of the question types (1–5) in Exercise B.

## ○ SPEAKING HUB

**A** **PLAN** Work in pairs. Student A: Imagine you are a journalist for a website. Look at the bullet points and prepare a list of questions to ask Veronica Matos.

Student B: Imagine you are Veronica Matos. You are going to be interviewed. Plan what you are going to say using the bullet points.

- when you first became interested in science
- your book
- your future career plans
- advice to young people

**B** **DISCUSS** Work in pairs. Perform your roleplay.

*A: What advice would you give to teenagers who want a career in science?*
*B: Decide early which area of science you want to work in. There are hundreds and hundreds of different career paths.*

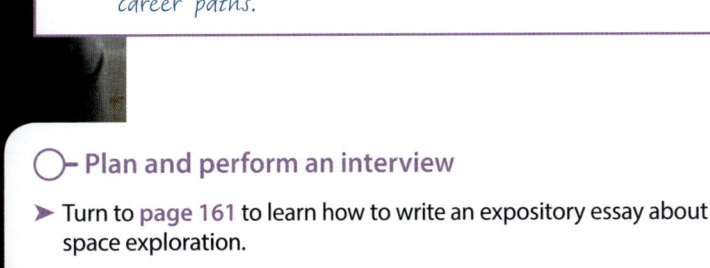

○─ Plan and perform an interview

➤ Turn to **page 161** to learn how to write an expository essay about space exploration.

# Unit 6 Review

## VOCABULARY

**A** Choose the correct words to complete the sentences.

1. Airlines keep introducing new long-haul flights to tempt today's *globetrotters / distance travellers*.
2. You *embargo / embark* from Santiago, Chile, to fly direct to Easter Island.
3. Fourteen of the world's highest *summits / culminations* are in the Himalayas.
4. It takes several hours of trekking through *ragged terraces / impenetrable terrain* to reach Waimea.
5. Manaus is the closest city to the *heart / heat* of the Amazon.
6. Siberia still has a lot of *unchartered / uncharted* territory.
7. You can quickly get off the beaten *track / road* in the outback in Australia.

**B** Complete the three-part phrasal verbs with the correct preposition.

1. I use language learning apps to **brush up** _____ my vocabulary.
2. I'd like to **find out** _____ volunteering.
3. Playing video games helps me **switch off** _____ the stress of the day.
4. I often **look back** _____ the holidays I took with my parents as a child.
5. I keep meaning to visit my grandparents, but I never **get round** _____ it.
6. I **am up** _____ a camping trip.
7. Whenever I suggest somewhere to go, my family **come up** _____ objections.
8. I don't like staycations. I want to **get away** _____ the area where I live for a holiday.

**C** Match numbers (1–10) to letters (a–j) to form full sentences.

1. I looked far and
2. She amazes me time after
3. Slowly but
4. She's far and
5. He always puts his heart and
6. They always work side by
7. It was a matter of life
8. It's a real rags-to-
9. By and
10. She returned safe and

a. surely he taught himself how to do it.
b. riches story, because he was born into a very poor family.
c. soul into everything he does.
d. wide, but I couldn't find it.
e. large, I don't read biographies, but his story was fascinating.
f. time with her ideas.
g. away the most important scientist working today.
h. side, which is really sweet.
i. sound from her adventures.
j. or death at one point, but he survived.

## GRAMMAR

**A** Complete the text using *can't have, could have, couldn't have, may/might well have, might have, must have* and the verbs in brackets.

In 1900, three men mysteriously disappeared from the lighthouse where they were working on a remote island in Scotland. Initially, newspapers contained implausible explanations such as that they ¹_____ (kill) by ghosts or they ²_____ (capture) by foreign spies. However, a later investigation concluded that they ³_____ (not abduct), because there were no signs of a struggle.

The investigation found a lot of damage had been done to one of the landing stages and that the kind of damage indicated that this ⁴_____ (cause) by large waves during a storm. Therefore, it's possible that the men were securing boxes on the landing stage in bad weather and the investigators believed that they ⁵_____ (sweep) into the sea by strong waves. Normally, one man should have stayed behind to man the lighthouse, but he ⁶_____ (go) to the landing stage to warn his colleagues of the approaching waves.

**B** Choose the correct words to complete the sentences. Then decide if you agree or disagree with each sentence.

1. In my country, schools have problems *encouraging / to encourage* children to study science.
2. It's not worth *studying / to study* the arts at school because it's not useful for work.
3. It's impossible *making / to make* history interesting for school children.
4. It's time *introducing / to introduce* more practical subjects into the school curriculum.
5. Schools need to teach computer programming *helping / to help* students get jobs in the future.

# 7 EXTREMES

> Courage is resistance to fear, mastery of fear – not absence of fear.
> 
> Mark Twain

Stepping over the abyss in Mondsee, Austria.

## OBJECTIVES

- describe reactions to extreme experiences
- describe extreme situations and achievements
- discuss extreme jobs
- deal with difficult interview questions
- tell a story about an exciting journey
- write a cover letter

Work with a partner. Discuss the questions.

1. Look at the picture. Why do people put themselves in extreme situations? When do you think this is a positive thing? When is it negative?
2. Look at the quote. How can we resist fear? Is it possible to master fear? Think of examples.
3. Do you prefer extreme experiences or safe/predictable ones? Why? What does it depend on?

EXTREMES 73

# 7.1 Beyond the limits

- Describe reactions to extreme experiences
- Describe extreme situations and achievements

**G** – *it* clefting    **V** – feelings    **P** – intonation in question tags    **S** – identifying causation

## READING

**A PREDICT** Work in pairs. Look at the picture. Discuss the questions.

1. What do you think the story is going to be about?
2. Have you ever been somewhere like this? If so, how did you feel? If not, how do you think you would feel?
3. Why do you think some people choose to put themselves in dangerous situations?

**B SKIM** Read *Into the abyss*. What different emotions does the writer go through on their journey? Were any the same as your answers to Exercise A?

**C READ FOR DETAIL** Read *Into the abyss* again. Six sentences have been removed from the story. Choose from the sentences (a–g) the one which fits each gap. There is one extra sentence which you do not need to use.

a It was his lack of words that finally allowed me to shake off the morning's nerves.
b It was myself who I was really trying to convince.
c It was that murky half-light, before the night gives in to the dawn, which I now watched.
d It is hard to describe moments like these.
e It is in situations like this that it occurs to me how often I put my life in the hands of complete strangers.
f It was reaching the summit that was my ultimate goal.
g It was just as Batsal disappeared over a rise that I lost my footing.

**D INFER MEANING** Work in pairs. Decide which of the words in bold from the story match the meanings (1–5).

1. _____ (n) fear of something bad that might happen or that is going to happen
2. _____ (n) a feeling of sadness and of being without hope
3. _____ (n) a feeling of extreme excitement and happiness
4. _____ (adj) relaxed and pleasant because shared with friends or friendly people
5. _____ (adj) very serious, and not smiling or friendly

**E SPEAK** Work in groups. Think of a time when you felt one of the emotions from Exercise D. Tell your group about your experience. Mention the following points.

- when you felt this way
- the reason(s) for feeling the emotion

## GRAMMAR
*it* clefting

**A** Find a sentence in Reading Exercise C that means the same as the one below. What is different about the version in the article? What is the focus in each sentence? Use the information in the box to help you.

*I was really trying to convince myself.*

> **it clefting**
> We can use *it* clefting to focus attention on part of a sentence (e.g. the subject, an object, a time clause, a *because*-clause, *to* + infinitive, etc).
> My ultimate goal was reaching the summit. → It was reaching the summit that was my ultimate goal.

**B** Rewrite the remaining sentences in Reading Exercise C so they don't use *it* clefting.

a _____
b *I was really trying to convince myself.*
c _____
d _____
e _____
f *My ultimate goal was reaching the summit.*
g _____

**C** Go to the **Grammar Hub** on **page 134**.

**D SPEAK** Work in pairs and complete the sentences so they are true for you.

1. It was because I wanted to … that I …
2. It's not … that's important …
3. It wasn't until …

## SPEAKING

**DISCUSS** Work in pairs. Can you think of a time when you felt a mix of emotions? Use the questions to help you.

1. What was the situation?
2. How did you feel?
3. What happened?

# INTO THE ABYSS

¹___ I had arrived early at the café and now sat waiting at a formica table, tentatively sipping the strongest coffee I had ever tasted. The bitterness was cloying, my hands shaking, but a 6 am start meant that rocket fuel was what I needed. The front door burst open, my coffee spilling across the table. The light struggling through the smeared glass door was blocked out by the silhouette of a man. He paused there in the doorway for a second. Though I couldn't see his face, I knew he was watching me.

He crossed the café in two strides. A weathered face forced itself into a half smile. 'Carla?' 'Yes. Batsal?'. A curt nod and then, 'If we are going, we go now, before the weather turns.'

I shouldered my pack and we set off down the pot-holed street beneath the shuttered-up houses and the tangle of electricity cables dangling menacingly low above us. 'Where is everyone?' He gestured a few metres ahead where a teenage boy was struggling to kick-start a motorbike, way past its prime, into life. The boy, who was almost certainly Batsal's son, glanced at me shyly and stepped aside as his father took hold of the bike. With a swift movement the engine roared. Batsal jerked his head at the seat behind him.

We were off. Hurtling down the road and then out towards the distant mountains. ²___ I've been conned, ripped off and outright robbed during my travels even by friendly-faced guides. Batsal was different though … I found his **dour** demeanour weirdly reassuring. ³___

Perhaps I was feeling too calm as we set off on foot up a narrow trail. My mind didn't dwell on the terrifying exposure of the route or the crevasses that seemed to plunge down into the depths of the earth. Instead I let my gaze calmly return to the untouched snow of the peaks which glistened in the low sun. We climbed in **companionable** silence for an hour or so. Up and over some boulders the size of cars.

⁴___ A small lapse in concentration. I found myself on my back skidding towards the edge. The boulder felt smooth. I watched in panic as my hands and feet flailed, trying to get purchase on something, anything. My legs were disappearing into the abyss. I thought of my family. Then time slowed, my focus narrowed and I gripped the rock. As I held on I found myself in a place I'd never been, somewhere between **dread** and calm.

A searing pain jolted through me as I was yanked by my arm. I twisted my neck to see Batsal retreating up the boulder, dragging me behind him like a rag doll. He pulled me to my feet. The question in his eyes. 'I can carry on,' I replied. ⁵___ And my shoulder throbbed in protest.

We scrambled upwards for five more hours over loose shale. The air was thinning out – every breath was laboured. But something of that strange calmness remained. When we reached a ledge, we stopped. I looked again over at the peaks that seemed no closer than they had at sunrise. 'OK, but let me see it properly before we turn back.' With one last effort I pulled myself up onto the ridge above the ledge and looked out over the perfect vista. ⁶___ The sheer **exhilaration** but also **melancholy** of a journey's end. After ten minutes, we began our descent. My heart thumping.

### Glossary

**gesture (v)** a movement that communicates a feeling or instruction
**skid (v)** to slide across the ground in an uncontrolled way
**weathered (adj)** appearance changed because of the effects of wind, rain, etc

## 7.1

## VOCABULARY
### Feelings

**A** Match the quotes (1–10) with the adjectives in the box. How do the people feel?

> courageous   devastated   disgusted   frustrated   grumpy
> humbled   hysterical   indifferent   resilient   superior

1 'I feel bad because there's nothing I can do about my situation.' _____
2 'I was overwhelmed by our local community's kindness and generosity.' _____
3 'I lost control of my emotions and started shaking and crying.' _____
4 'I feel terrible because I've lost all hope.' _____
5 'When I'm in a bad mood, I'm not very nice to other people.' _____
6 'You can do what you like. I really don't mind.' _____
7 'When other people do stupid things, it makes me feel better about myself!' _____
8 'I know it's dangerous, but I won't let my fear stop me.' _____
9 'When things go wrong, I just have to pick myself up and carry on.' _____
10 'I'm so angry! It makes me feel sick.' _____

**B** Go to the Vocabulary Hub on page 146.

**C** SPEAK Work in pairs. Think of examples of situations where people feel the ten emotions in Exercise A. Share your ideas with the class.

## LISTENING

**A** SPEAK Work in pairs and discuss the questions.
1 What morning TV programmes are there in your country?
2 What type of news stories are discussed on them?

**B** LISTEN FOR SPECIFIC INFORMATION Listen to part of a TV programme, *the Breakfast Show*. Decide if the statements are true (T), false (F) or not given (NG).
1 Arjun didn't see the accident happening. ___
2 The other driver helped Arjun to move the car. ___
3 The car that Arjun lifted weighed over 1500 kg. ___
4 Professor Ivănescu thinks Arjun has extremely unusual powers. ___
5 Tony (the presenter) doesn't think he'd ever be able to lift the car. ___
6 Arjun used hysterical strength. ___
7 Whenever our muscles hurt, it means we're damaging them. ___
8 The cyclist suffered permanent injuries. ___

**C** LISTEN FOR CAUSATION Listen again. Which pairs of events are examples of correlation (a)? Which are examples of causation (b)? Use the information in the box to help you.

> **Identifying causation**
>
> It's important to distinguish between **correlation** (= two or more things happen at about the same time) and **causation** (= one thing causes another thing to happen). Common ways of signalling causation include:
> - linking expressions (e.g. *as a result of*, *due to*, *thanks to*, *that's why*).
> - conditionals (e.g. *If X hadn't happened, Y might not have happened*).
> - past perfect in time clauses (e.g. *After I'd done X, Y happened*) rather than past simple (e.g. *After I did X, Y happened*).

1 Arjun wasn't paying attention to the other vehicles. The car ran over a bicycle. a / b
2 The driver freed the cyclist. Arjun put the car down. a / b
3 They used a mobile phone. A spark caused the car to explode. a / b
4 Arjun was brave. The cyclist wasn't seriously injured. a / b
5 Arjun's back hurts now. He lifted the car. a / b
6 Tony was unable to lift the car. His muscles hurt. a / b
7 The adrenaline wore off. Arjun felt extreme pain. a / b
8 Athletes feel stressed. They can break world records. a / b
9 The cyclist survived. She spent a few weeks in hospital. a / b

**D** SPEAK Work in groups. Discuss the questions.
1 How do you think you would react in an extreme situation like the one Arjun described?
2 Have you heard of any examples of people doing amazing things in extreme situations? What happened?

76 EXTREMES

## PRONUNCIATION
Intonation in question tags

**A** Complete the extracts from *The Breakfast Show* with the correct question tag. Then listen to check.

1 So the car could have exploded at any second, _____?
2 I mean, you're a big guy, _____?
3 It's weird, _____?
4 I mean, a car weighs, what, a tonne and a half, _____?
5 So that's what helped Arjun, then, _____?
6 We can't harness this strength in everyday life, _____?
7 I'm just a normal guy, _____?
8 Anyway, let's have a break now, _____?

**B** Listen again. Try to copy the intonation.

**C** SPEAK Work in small groups and discuss the extreme human abilities shown in pictures 1–5. Use question tags to ask questions, make suggestions, check assumptions and invite agreement.

*Let's start with this one, shall we? It's bungee jumping, is it?*

## SPEAKING HUB

**A** PLAN You are going to conduct a daytime TV interview about examples of extreme achievements. Work in groups of three. Use pictures 1–5 to help you.

**Student A:** You are the **interviewee**. You can talk about a real experience from your life, or you can invent the details.

**Student B:** You are an **expert** (e.g. a university professor). You have been invited to explain Student A's abilities/achievements. You can use your real knowledge or invent details.

**Student C:** You are the **interviewer**. It's your job to make the interviewee and the expert feel comfortable, and to make the TV show entertaining for the audience at home.

**B** PRACTISE Practise your interview. Try to use the vocabulary, grammar and pronunciation from this lesson in your interviews.

**C** PRESENT Act out your interview for the class.

**D** REFLECT Which of the interviews was the most believable? Which was the most entertaining?

- Describe reactions to extreme experiences
- Describe extreme situations and achievements

# 7.2 Extreme jobs

- Discuss extreme jobs
- Deal with difficult interview questions

- **G** – *what* clefting and *all* clefting
- **P** – *any* and *quite*
- **V** – polysemy; intensifiers
- **S** – understanding reference within texts

## READING

**A SPEAK** Work in pairs. Look at the pictures. Why do people choose to work in such extreme places?

**B READ FOR MAIN IDEA** Read *Risky business*. Match the statements (1–6) with the workplaces (a–c).

1 It's dangerous if you go up too fast. ____
2 The weather may prevent you from working. ____
3 You'll need to work at least half a year. ____
4 You'll earn a lot of money. ____
5 It's hard to get a job there. ____
6 It takes over a week to get home. ____

a  The Antarctic
b  At extreme heights
c  Under the ocean

**C READ FOR REFERENCES** What do the reference devices (1–10) in the article refer to? Use the information in the box to help you.

1 _____    6 _____
2 _____    7 _____
3 _____    8 _____
4 _____    9 _____
5 _____   10 _____

### Understanding reference within texts

Reference devices (e.g. pronouns, articles, contrast linkers, comparatives) link different parts of a text.

**Anaphoric reference:** refers back to something mentioned earlier in the text.

**Cataphoric reference:** refers forward to something mentioned later in the text.

**Exophoric reference:** refers to things outside the text, e.g. *you* (the reader), *they* (people in general).

**D SPEAK** Work in pairs and discuss the questions. Do any of the jobs in the article appeal to you? Which would you hate?

# RISKY BUSINESS

¹They say over half of us are doing jobs that we don't care about, and a further 16% actively hate our jobs. If you're **sick** of the nine-to-five, here are some of the more extreme places where you can actually make a living.

## ANTARCTICA

Unfortunately, it's not exactly easy – or cheap – to visit Antarctica as a tourist. So if you really want to go, what you should do is get a long-term job, not a holiday job: no employer is going to pay your airfare if you're planning to stay for less than six months.
There are scientific jobs for biologists, glaciologists, geologists, meteorologists, oceanologists, and so on. Trouble is, there's plenty of **competition** for them, with hundreds of applicants for each vacancy. Your best chance of **landing** ²one is to be a well-qualified specialist already, ideally with a doctorate or two.
There are also a few support jobs for engineers, technicians, divers, radio operators, etc. Just be warned: you'll spend most of your time on the base, where you'll quickly get bored with the same faces every day. Due to the extreme weather, it's usually too dangerous (or too expensive) to venture out into the wilderness for some sightseeing.

## AT EXTREME HEIGHTS

For ³those of us who get dizzy at the thought of standing on a chair, the prospect of climbing up a radio mast, wind turbine or skyscraper is the stuff of our worst nightmares. But for ⁴the lucky few who have no fear of heights, there are plenty of career opportunities.
⁵It's not especially glamorous, but the easiest way to make a career at heights is as a window cleaner. You can literally start at the bottom – all you'll need is a ladder and a bucket – and gradually work your way up to office blocks and skyscrapers.
A rather ⁶more lucrative career for real-life 'high-climbers' is as a tower climber. These brave people spend their time 100 to 150 metres above the ground, inspecting cellular phone towers for damage, changing light bulbs, replacing cables, etc. One of the biggest challenges is that they need to work in all **conditions**, including the cold, the wind and the rain, all of which add to the level of danger. The ⁷one exception is thunderstorms, which tower climbers steer well clear of.

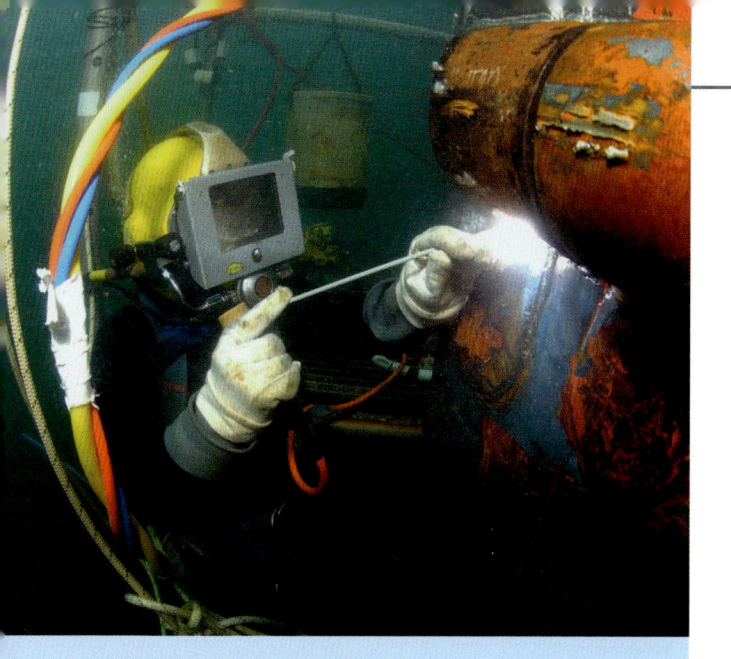

## ON THE OCEAN FLOOR

[8]It's one of the most bizarre careers imaginable. [9]These people do construction, maintenance and demolition work 300 metres or more beneath the ocean's surface. To survive the extreme **pressure** at such depths, they spend weeks or months at a time living in tiny pressurised containers, either deep underwater or inside pressure tanks on board ships. Welcome to the world of the saturation diver.

Breathing pressurised air causes inert gases to dissolve in your blood and body tissues. If you were to release the pressure suddenly, by coming to the surface, the bubbles formed would quickly kill you. To avoid this, saturation divers spend several hours building up to the necessary pressure, saturating their bodies with inert gases. At the end of their work, they spend as much as eleven days de-pressurising, before finally returning to normal life.

Saturation divers carry out essential work for some of the world's richest businesses, so [10]it's no surprise to find that they're extremely well-paid. However, before sending off your **application**, you need to consider how you'd feel about spending months in a tiny metal container with your co-workers, constantly aware that the failure of a single pressure valve would mean certain death.

### Glossary
**lucrative (adj)** bringing a lot of money
**venture (v)** to go somewhere unpleasant, dangerous or exciting

## 7.2

## VOCABULARY
Polysemy

**A** Choose the correct definition of the words in bold from *Risky business*. Use the context in the article and the information in the box to help you.

> **Polysemy**
> Polysemy is where a word has two or more related meanings. Sometimes different meanings have different grammatical properties (e.g. countable/uncountable).

| 1 | sick | a | feel unwell |
| | | b | bored or tired of something |
| 2 | competition | a | rivalry |
| | | b | a contest |
| 3 | to land | a | bring a plane down |
| | | b | get something you want |
| 4 | condition(s) | a | weather |
| | | b | an important part of a contract |
| 5 | pressure | a | a feeling of too much work |
| | | b | a 'pushing' force |
| 6 | application | a | a way of using something |
| | | b | a document stating why you want a job |

**B** In which pair of meanings from Exercise A is one meaning countable and the other uncountable? In which pair is one meaning always plural?

**C** Go to the Vocabulary Hub on page 146.

## GRAMMAR
*what* clefting and *all* clefting

**A** Complete the rules with examples from the article.

> ***what* clefting and *all* clefting**
>
> Form: *what/all* + FIRST FOCUS + *is/was* + SECOND FOCUS
> Example: *What you need to succeed is mental strength.*
>
> We can use *what* clefting to focus attention on two different parts of a sentence by keeping them separate.
>
> 1 You should get a long-term job. → _____
>   *All* clefting has the extra meaning of *only*.
>
> 2 You'll <u>only</u> need a ladder and bucket. → _____

**B** Go to the Grammar Hub on page 134.

## SPEAKING

**DISCUSS** Work in pairs. Think about the advantages and disadvantages of the jobs in the article. Your partner is planning to apply for one of the jobs. Give your partner advice using *what* clefting and *all* clefting.

EXTREMES 79

## 7.2

### LISTENING

**A SPEAK** Work in pairs. Have you ever had a stressful job interview? What happened?

**B** Read *Extreme job interviews*. Rank the questions in order from hardest to easiest (1–7).

**C LISTEN FOR DETAIL** Listen to a recruitment specialist giving advice about the questions below. For each question, make notes on the dos and don'ts for job interviewees.
7.3

**D LISTEN FOR GIST** Now listen to some extracts from an interview for a job as a marketing designer. Does Oscar (the interviewee) follow the recruitment specialist's advice for each question?
7.4

**E LISTEN FOR DETAIL** Listen again. Choose the correct options (a, b or c) to answer the questions.
7.4

1. How would Oscar feel on a desert island?
   a  lonely	b  inspired	c  upset
2. What would be Oscar's priority as a dinosaur?
   a  pleasure	b  beauty	c  safety
3. How does Oscar feel at the end of each day?
   a  relieved	b  disappointed	c  exhausted
4. Which one of the following is NOT mentioned as a use for a stapler?
   a  tissue-holder	b  child's toy	c  doorstop
5. How many pizzas does Oscar think a typical American eats each year?
   a  12	b  144	c  300
6. How does Oscar feel about looking after his brothers and sisters?
   a  grateful	b  frustrated	c  proud
7. How does Oscar feel about people who don't like him?
   a  grumpy	b  indifferent	c  superior

**F SPEAK** Work in pairs. Ask and answer the questions from *Extreme job interviews*.

# EXTREME job interviews

These days, recruiters are going to extremes to sort the best from the rest. The following questions, all taken from real job interviews, have no correct answer. But they are designed to show how you cope with stress and how creative you are. They might also reveal the real 'you' behind the business suit and the polished CV.

- What would you take with you to a desert island and why?
- If you could be any dinosaur, which dinosaur would you be?
- What's your biggest weakness?
- Name four uses for a stapler, without the staples.
- How many square metres of pizza are eaten in the US each year?
- What's the most interesting thing about you that we wouldn't learn from your CV?
- How would your worst enemy describe you?

## VOCABULARY
### Intensifiers

**A** Complete the sentences from the interview with intensifiers in the box. Sometimes more than one answer is possible.

| altogether | immensely | noticeably | outright | practically |
| radically | relatively | remarkably | somewhat | utterly |

1 I find writing poetry _____ calming.
2 I'd be _____ devastated if I couldn't record my ideas on paper.
3 Compared to the ground, the sky would be a _____ good place.
4 I tend to be _____ disorganised.
5 I learnt some _____ simple techniques, and I've improved _____ since then.
6 I'm not _____ sure how typical I am.
7 I'm not _____ different from the average American …
8 It was often _____ impossible to study.
9 I'm not the sort of person who has _____ enemies.

**B** Work in pairs. Complete the sentences with an intensifier from Exercise A.

1 _____ means 'to a huge extent'.
2 _____ is mainly used before negative adjectives and adverbs.
3 _____ means 'compared to other things'.
4 _____ means 'a little'.
5 _____ means 'so much that it's obvious or easy to see'.
6 _____ is often used in negative sentences, especially with 'sure'.
7 _____ is often used before nouns with a negative meaning.
8 _____ means 'not quite 100%, but as good as 100%'.
9 _____ is often used before 'different'.

**C** Go to the **Vocabulary Hub** on **page 146**.

**D SPEAK** Work in small groups. Offer advice for preparing for and coping with extreme job interviews. Use intensifiers in your advice.

## PRONUNCIATION
### *any* and *quite*

**A** Listen to the extracts from the recruitment specialist's advice. Underline *any* and *quite* when they are stressed. (7.5)

1 Almost any other answer is much better …
2 So don't just say any old number that pops into your head.
3 … on a desert island, without any other people …
4 … the sense of freedom would be quite exhilarating.
5 It takes quite a lot of self-discipline …
6 It's been quite challenging …

**B** Listen and underline the sentence (a or b) in which *quite* or *any* is stressed. (7.6)

1 a The interview was quite difficult.
  b The interview was quite impossible.
2 a Don't say anything!
  b Don't say anything!
3 a Her house was quite dirty.
  b Her house was quite filthy.
4 a Any questions can be answered.
  b Any questions can be answered.

## SPEAKING HUB

**A PLAN** Work in groups of three. You are going to interview several candidates for a job. First, decide what the job is, what exactly it involves and what sort of candidate you are looking for. Then plan four or five extreme questions for your interview. Use the ideas below or your own ideas.

- If you could be any …, what would you be?
- Name four uses for a …
- How many … could you fit inside this room?
- How would … describe you?

**B PREPARE** Discuss what would be a 'good' or 'bad' answer for each of your questions, bearing in mind the type of candidate you are looking for.

**C INTERVIEW** Interview two candidates from other groups. At the end of each interview, provide feedback on what the candidate did well/badly and give advice on how to improve.

**D DISCUSS** Work in your original groups to choose the best candidate for your job. Make sure you justify your choice. Share your decision and reasoning with the class.

- Discuss extreme jobs
- Deal with difficult interview questions

# Café Hub

## 7.3 Push your limits

A — fronting    S — changing and recycling topics

## ▶ Driving on the edge

**A** Work in pairs. Look at the picture and discuss the questions.
1. Where do you think this is?
2. What do you think it would be like to be a bus driver in these mountains?

**B** ▶ Watch the video. Check your answers to Exercise A.

### Glossary
**abrasive (adj)** having a rough surface
**canyon (n)** a long deep valley with steep sides made of rock
**maze (n)** a set of small streets, roads, paths, etc that it is easy to get lost in
**slope (n)** a surface or piece of land that has one end higher than the other end

**C** ▶ Watch the video again. Complete the sentences with between one and three words.
1. The mountains of Northern Peru consist of a network of _____, basic roads and deep canyons.
2. Glorioso is considered a _____ amongst some of the villagers in Huancabamba.
3. The truck tyres need to be changed after ten weeks as the roads here are so _____.
4. Annually, over a _____ people die on the mountain roads of Peru.
5. The passengers on the bus are not _____.
6. The secret to a long _____ as a Peruvian bus driver is to take your time.

## AUTHENTIC ENGLISH

**A** Work in pairs. Read the information in the box. Complete the sentence from the video.

*And that's _____ to a long career as a Peruvian bus driver – taking the mountains at their own pace.*

### Fronting
Fronting involves moving information to the front of a sentence, often to give it emphasis. It is often used in informal spoken English, for example, *Really good it was – best film I've seen for ages.*

Whole clauses can be fronted, for example, *Why they decided to buy that house, I couldn't tell you.*

**B** Work in pairs. Rewrite the sentences to create emphasis. Begin each sentence with the underlined word.
1. I'll never know <u>why</u> Maria married Tony.
   _____
2. He didn't know <u>whether</u> he'd got the job or not.
   _____
3. I'll be there <u>in</u> about twenty minutes.
   _____
4. It cost me <u>three</u> hundred pounds.
   _____
5. I just don't know <u>how</u> you put up with your boss.
   _____
6. It started to snow <u>all</u> of a sudden.
   _____
7. It must have cost <u>an</u> absolute fortune.
   _____
8. An old woman sat quietly <u>in</u> the corner.
   _____

**C** Compare your sentences in Exercise B with another pair.

# Hello from the Andes

SAM   MALCOLM   AMANDA   HARRY   EMILY

**A** Work in pairs. Discuss the questions.

1 Do you prefer travelling with other people or on your own? Why?
2 Do you know anybody that has visited many countries? What motivates them to travel?

**B** ▶ Watch the video. Who calls Sam and where are they?

**C** ▶ Watch the video again. Answer the questions.

1 Who did Fred meet by chance?
2 What does Fred's meeting make Sam think of?
3 What does Fred say about the condition of the bus?
4 What could Fred see when he looked out of the window?
5 What did Fred find comforting?
6 What does Sam suggest doing when Fred returns?

## SPEAKING SKILL

**A** What is the purpose of the phrases in bold in each of the examples from the video?

1 Sorry, not very good signal out here. **So where was I?** Oh yes …
2 **I tell you what** when you're back from the Andes, let's go for dinner.

**B** Work in pairs. Underline the words and phrases which are used to change or recycle topics in the extracts below.

1 I had just arrived in Lima and guess who I ran into?
2 Well, funny you should ask. I had a bit of an adventure getting to my adventure.
3 That reminds me of the time when I was in Spain and bumped into my next door neighbour.
4 Well, yeah … made worse by the fact it was quite an old bus.
5 For sure … which brings me back to what I was saying … Daniel suggested I come with him on a trek.

### Changing and recycling topics

We use many different set phrases to try to steer conversations towards the topics we wish to talk about.

We can use them to recycle a topic we were speaking about, for example, *as I was saying*. We can also use them to change topic, for example, *that's like the time when*.

## SPEAKING HUB

**A PREPARE** Student A: you are going to describe your exciting journey to your partner. However, your partner is going to try to distract you and talk about himself/herself.

Student B: you are going to listen to your partner describing a journey. However, you are not very interested in what your partner has to say and you want to talk about yourself and your experiences.

**B PRESENT** Perform your conversation. Change roles.

A: *Why I'd decided to drive through the wilderness alone, I couldn't tell you.*
B: *Speaking of which, I'm going camping in the wilderness next month.*

**C REFLECT** Work in small groups. Perform and listen to each other's conversations again. Give feedback using the points below.

- use of language
- pronunciation
- fluency
- interaction

○─ Tell a story about an exciting journey

➤ Turn to page 162 to learn how to write a cover letter for a dream job.

# Unit 7 Review

## VOCABULARY

**A** Match numbers (1–10) to letters (a–j) to form full sentences.

1. I'm frustrated because I
2. I thought she was so courageous
3. I became hysterical
4. I always get grumpy
5. I'm quite resilient
6. They were disgusted by
7. As a child, I was indifferent
8. I try to be humble
9. I felt devastated about
10. He acted superior

a. when I'm tired.
b. to my classmates' bad behaviour.
c. about my success when I meet strangers.
d. when she chased away the burglars.
e. can't do anything to help.
f. losing all that work.
g. around the others, as if he were the best player.
h. and couldn't calm down for ages.
i. the condition he left the flat in.
j. so I'm sure I'll get over this setback.

**B** Complete the sentences with the correct form of the words in the box. Use each word twice.

sick   competition   condition   application

1. Unfortunately your _____ for the job hasn't been successful.
2. We can't go out in these _____! We'll get wet!
3. I'm _____ of his excuses. He's just lazy!
4. The product can be used in a number of ways – it has many _____.
5. I enter a lot of _____ but I never win.
6. There's a lot of _____ for each place on the course.
7. I find an early night helps if you are feeling _____.
8. You can go out on _____ that you're home by 10 pm.

**C** Put the lines (a–h) in order so that they form a paragraph.

a. long periods – the world-record free-diver, Herbert Nitsch, can go an utterly
b. dangerous changes of pressure. Nitsch's record of 253 metres was spoiled
c. different to normal deep-sea diving, because the divers have practically
d. easy compared to the challenge of coping with immensely
e. somewhat by the medical problems he suffered as a result.
f. Free diving is radically
g. incredible nine minutes without breathing. But holding your breath is relatively
h. no equipment. It involves holding your breath for remarkably

## GRAMMAR

**A** Complete the sentences with words from the box. Each word can be used more than once.

is   was   until   that   not   because   who   it

1. It was _____ I was scared _____ I decided not to climb the cliff.
2. It's _____ adrenaline that I'm looking for; it _____ a sense of flow.
3. It wasn't _____ I reached the top _____ I realised how high the cliff was.
4. When I said 'Stop being stupid', it was _____ you I was talking to; _____ was James I was talking to.
5. It _____ at that moment _____ I realised I was no longer afraid.
6. It _____ to impress my friends _____ I tried to lift the car.
7. It's you _____ is causing most of the delays, _____ us!

**B** Find and correct the mistakes in five of the sentences.

1. All what I'm trying to say is you should be careful.
2. What you should avoid to do is to pretend you don't have any weaknesses.
3. What I did was stretched my arms to calm my nerves.
4. All I remember is staring out into the abyss and feeling sick.
5. What happened next was that some people call an ambulance.
6. All they did was watch TV.

# 8 WELL-BEING

*The part can never be well, unless the whole is well.*
Plato

Sunset swimming washes away the day's cares.

## OBJECTIVES

- discuss wellness treatments
- talk about health and technology
- talk about sports psychology
- discuss nutrition and fitness
- explain and give instructions about a process
- write a summary

**Work with a partner. Discuss the questions.**

1 Look at the picture. Do you often swim in lakes, rivers or the sea? How is it different from swimming in a pool?
2 Read the quote. What does Plato mean? Do you agree?
3 Do you think it's easy for people to stay healthy these days? Why/Why not?

# 8.1 Health and wellness

- Discuss wellness treatments
- Talk about health and technology

- G – relative clauses with complex relative pronouns
- P – building suspense
- V – health problems
- S – identifying writers' opinions

## VOCABULARY
### Health problems

**A** Work in pairs. Discuss the questions. Try to write down five words for each question.

1 Name five parts of the body connected to the five senses.
2 Name five joints.
3 Name five parts of the body that people have more than two of.
4 Name five parts of the body that can be used as verbs.

**B** Work in pairs. Match the words in bold in 1–9 with the definitions (a–i).

1 **fracture** a rib/your leg
2 **dislocate** your shoulder/thumb
3 a **sore** throat/back
4 **pull** a muscle
5 **sprain** your ankle/your wrist
6 **inflamed** joint/skin
7 skin **rash**
8 fast/slow **heart rate**
9 high/low **blood pressure**

a the force at which the blood flows through the body
b twist (a joint)
c the speed that your heart beats
d break or crack (a bone)
e painful
f force a joint out of its socket
g red and swollen
h red spots on the skin
i overstretch or tear

**C** Go to the Vocabulary Hub on page 147.

**D** SPEAK Work in pairs. What can people do to avoid having the health problems in Exercise B? What can people do if they have these problems?

## READING

**A** SPEAK Work in pairs. Have you ever tried any wellness treatments (e.g. a massage, a sauna, a spa)? Did you enjoy them? Did they have any lasting benefits?

**B** READ FOR MAIN IDEA Read *From forest bathing to halotherapy*.

Which treatments are good for …

1 your lungs?
2 your heart?
3 reducing stress?
4 your skin?
5 insomnia?

**C** READ TO IDENTIFY OPINIONS Work in pairs. Read the article again and discuss the questions. Use the information in the box to help you.

1 What is the writer's attitude to the things she is writing about? Find examples of three types of language which show her attitude.
2 What is the purpose of this article? Is it mainly written to inform, entertain or persuade?

### Identifying writers' opinions

Writers can choose particular words and phrases to show their opinion of a topic.

- Adverbs can show a positive attitude (*interestingly, surprisingly, intriguingly*), a negative attitude (*disappointingly, infuriatingly, predictably*) or a sceptical or cautious attitude (*supposedly, allegedly, presumably*).
- Different structures can be used to show writers believe something is true (*it is good for the heart*), they have a neutral stance about reported information (*it is said/thought to be good for the heart*) or they are uncertain or even sceptical (*it is supposed/meant/claimed to be good for the heart*).
- Writers can also use colloquial asides, including tag questions and rhetorical questions (*sounds fascinating, doesn't it?*) to comment on information. They can use humour, sarcasm and irony to show a sceptical attitude.

**D** SPEAK Work in pairs. Do you agree with the writer's attitude to the treatments? Why/Why not?

## SPEAKING

**DISCUSS** Work in groups. Discuss the questions.

1 Why do some people prefer alternative treatments to conventional medicine?
2 Should doctors be allowed to recommend wellness treatments and alternative medicine?
3 Should companies be allowed to offer scientifically unproven wellness treatments?

WELL-BEING

# FROM **FOREST BATHING** TO **HALOTHERAPY:** THE **FIVE LATEST WELLNESS TRENDS**

Know your 'sound lounger' from your carbon dioxide bath with our guide to the latest and not-so-greatest spa innovations.

'Wellness' is all the rage these days, but we've noticed that some therapies doing the rounds at hotel spas right now sound suspiciously basic. Surely oxygen therapy is just breathing, right? Decide for yourself, as we explore a few of the more interesting treatments we've spotted on spa menus around the world.

### Forest bathing or 'going for a walk'

Forest bathing is based on the Japanese practice of *Shinrin-yoku*. That may sound like some sort of elaborately mystical ritual, but in fact involves simply 'being in the forest'. You might call it walking, or even sitting, in, you know, a forest. The practice is supposed to exercise the mind as well as reduce stress by bringing you back to nature. Perhaps eager to jazz up the concept, The Mayflower Grace Hotel in Connecticut has put together a forest-bathing package that involves 90 minutes of skin-cleansing treatments, using plant-derived lactic acid and exfoliators made with peat enzymes and berries. Finally, a 'plant hydrosol ionising mist' supposedly boosts your lymphatic system with a 'stimulating breeze'.

### Carbon dioxide dry bath or 'sitting in a bag'

Does lying fully clothed on a bed while wrapped in a bag of carbon dioxide sound fun? Didn't think so, but in the Czech Republic it's all the rage. In the west of the country – an area known for its natural gas – you can have a large bag wrapped around you all the way from your toes to under your arms and watch it slowly inflate with $CO_2$. The treatment is meant to slow your heart rate, reduce your blood pressure and improve circulation, but this happens by the gas seeping into your clothes and skin – that thought would put most people's blood pressure up, not down.

### So Sound lounger or 'napping and listening to music'

Yes, Tibetan singing bowl therapy has been around for centuries, but it's now been upgraded for the digital age. The So Sound lounger is meant to help you relax by, well, sitting in a lounger and listening to music. Revolutionary stuff. You're supposed to be able to take a 'therapeutic nap' while the lounger sends musical vibrations through your body … A bit like an airport massage chair, perhaps?

### Halotherapy or 'a salty room'

Halotherapy is actually a fancy name for salt therapy. In a natural setting, this treatment would mean sitting in a salt cave and breathing in the dry, salty air, which is supposed to be good for respiratory and skin conditions. Now hotels are replicating salt caves; the Windsor Arms Hotel in Toronto has created a room filled with salt and negative ions that has darkened ambient lighting to replicate natural salt caves found in Europe. Supposedly this also helps strengthen the immune system, among other health benefits.

### Oxygen therapy or 'breathing'

Oxygen therapy is supposed to help with headaches, depression and sleep deprivation by – that's right – breathing oxygen. It involves being hooked up to a machine, sticking some tubes up your nose and, well, breathing.

## Glossary

**circulation (n)** the continuous movement of blood around your body
**lymphatic (adj)** relating to the body's liquid lymph, or involved in moving lymph around your body
**mystical (adj)** relating to or involving mysterious religious or spiritual powers
**nap (v)** to sleep for a short period of time, usually during the day
**ritual (n)** a formal ceremony

## 8.1

### LISTENING

**A SPEAK** Work in pairs. Discuss the questions.
1 Do you own any gadgets that monitor your health? If so, how often do you use them?
2 What are some of the benefits and drawbacks of these devices?

**B LISTEN FOR GIST** Listen to a conversation between friends discussing technology to help you stay healthy and answer the questions.
1 What kinds of health data can be provided by the devices they talk about?

2 What four devices do they talk about?

**C LISTEN FOR DETAIL** Listen again and answer the questions.
1 Why are they talking about wellness technology?

2 Why do Cheryl and Luke think that wellness technology is a good idea?

3 Why is Jake uncertain?

**D DISCUSS** Work in pairs. Discuss the questions.
1 Would you use any of the devices the speakers discussed? Why/Why not?
2 Do you think it's useful for people to collect data about their health?

### GRAMMAR
Relative clauses with complex relative pronouns

**A** Read the extracts from the conversation. Underline the relative clauses and circle the relative pronouns.
1 Wellness technology is technology with which we can improve our health and well-being.
2 I've just read several news stories about people whose lives may have been saved because their smart watch alerted them to a problem.
3 I'm meeting the person [who is] writing the article with me for lunch today.
4 It's basically a thermometer which a smartphone can be attached to.
5 This device has an automated diagnosis feature whereby it checks the symptoms of the person to whom it's attached against a database.

88   WELL-BEING

**B** Complete the rules (1–6) with the words in the box and the example sentences from Exercise A. You may use the words in the box more than once.

> informal   formal   whereby   whom   whose

### Relative clauses with complex relative pronouns

**Advanced relative pronouns**

1 Use _____ to add information about someone's possessions.
2 Use _____ to add information about a method (mainly used in formal English).
3 Use _____ to add information about a person where they are the object of the clause (mainly used in formal English).

**Prepositions and relative pronouns**

4 In _____ English, prepositions usually come at the end of the relative clause.
Example: _____
5 In _____ English, prepositions come before the relative pronoun.
Examples: _____
and _____

**Reduced relative clauses**

6 In _____ English, we can often omit *who*, *that* or *which* in relative clauses – and in relative clauses that use *be*, we can leave out the pronoun + the part of *be*.
Example: _____

**C** Complete the sentences with the correct relative pronoun. Add a preposition if needed.

1 The device _____ I'm most interested is something that helps me eat healthily.
2 Wellness devices are the technology _____ people will be able to extend their lives.
3 Companies need to develop security systems _____ it's impossible for hackers to gain access to users' private health data.
4 I don't understand people _____ first thought when they are sick is to look up their symptoms online rather than go to the doctor.
5 The people _____ wellness technology will make the biggest difference are older people.

**D** **SPEAK** Work in pairs. Do you agree with the sentences in Exercise C?

**E** Go to the Grammar Hub on page 136.

## PRONUNCIATION
### Building suspense

**A** Listen to the example sentences from the conversation. Underline the word where the speaker changes pitch.

1 So check out my brand new smart watch!
2 You'll never guess what … I've just been commissioned to write an article about wellness technology.
3 For example, on this smart watch take this handy heart rate tracker.
4 And if you forget, it starts flashing red.

**B** Complete the sentences so they are true for you.

1 The app I use most on my phone is …
2 The person I send most messages to is …
3 In one of the messages I received recently, someone said …

**C** Work in pairs. Present the information in Exercise B to your partner. Use pitch and pauses to build suspense.

## SPEAKING HUB

**A** **PLAN** Work in groups. Imagine that you work for a technology start up. Your group needs to think of a health and wellness product idea and pitch it to potential investors. Discuss your ideas and think about the following questions.

- Will your idea help prevent health problems, encourage healthy behaviour or help people who are already sick?
- What problem do people have that your idea could help to solve?
- Is your idea for a device, an app or a service?
- Who is the target market for your idea?
- How will you make it easy for users to use your product or service?
- What are the benefits for users of your product or service?

**B** **PREPARE** Prepare a presentation about your idea. Think of ways to sell the idea to your classmates.

**C** **PRESENT** Present your idea to the class. Then as a class, vote on the best idea.

○─ Discuss wellness treatments
○─ Talk about health and technology

## 8.2 Sport and wellness

- Talk about sports psychology
- Discuss nutrition and fitness

**G** – pronouns and determiners
**V** – idioms; describing taste
**P** – pronunciation of idioms
**S** – understanding speech with background noise

### LISTENING

**A SPEAK** Work in pairs. Discuss the questions.
1. Do you know any players or teams that use a sports psychologist?
2. How do sports psychologists help athletes?

**B LISTEN FOR GIST** 🔊 8.3 Listen to the first part of a podcast about sports psychology. What are the two training techniques the sports psychologist mentions?

**C LISTEN FOR DETAIL** 🔊 8.3 Listen again and answer the questions.
1. What example situation does Professor Kumar give for using therapy?
2. How do Professor Kumar's positive thinking techniques help athletes?

**D LISTEN WITH NOISE** 🔊 8.4 Listen to the second part of the podcast. Some parts are quite hard to hear because of background noise. Which two main sports psychology techniques does the interviewee use in her training sessions? Use the strategies in the box to help you.

1 _____
2 _____

> **Understanding speech with background noise**
>
> If there's a lot of background noise and you can't ask the speaker to repeat what they said:
> - use the context of the situation to help you. Remember that you don't need to understand every word that is spoken to get the gist of what somebody is saying. Use your knowledge of the topic to help fill in the gaps.
> - remember that speakers stress the most important words, so these words should be easier to hear. Use this information plus the context to help make intelligent guesses about what the people are saying.

**E LISTEN FOR DETAIL** 🔊 8.4 Listen to the second part of the podcast again and answer the questions.
1. What problem had the football team been facing?
2. What kind of coaching style does she say many players won't accept?
3. What kind of coaching style does Bill prefer?

**F SPEAK** Work in pairs and discuss the questions.
1. Do you think sports psychologists are important?
2. Which techniques do you think would be most helpful for you when playing sport?
3. How difficult did you find it to understand what the speaker was saying when there was background noise?

### VOCABULARY
#### Idioms

**A** Look at the three groups of idioms (1–12). Complete the headings for each group with the words in the box.

> body   sport   food

_____ idioms

1. My <u>gut feeling</u> is we'll lose the match.
2. Their striker <u>was head and shoulders above</u> the rest of us.
3. <u>Keep an eye out for</u> John – we're supposed to meet him at the stadium.
4. _____

_____ idioms

5. It wasn't a big problem, but he was really <u>making a meal of it</u>.
6. He says he knows Ronaldo, but you have to <u>take what he says with a pinch of salt</u>.
7. What she said about coaching <u>gave me food for thought</u>.
8. _____

_____ idioms

9. The other athletes are really good. I think she's <u>out of her depth</u>.
10. I can't win, so I think it's time to <u>throw in the towel</u>.
11. I thought I'd finished my part of the work, but then they suddenly <u>moved the goal posts</u>.
12. _____

**B** Put the underlined idioms below into the correct group in Exercise A.

- They have times when they doubt their abilities or <u>get cold feet</u> because they're anxious about competing.
- It's all about staying calm and focused, so they can <u>give it their best shot</u>.
- I need someone to nag me and tell me to up my game, but I know that's <u>not everyone's cup of tea</u>.

**C** Match the underlined idioms (1–12) in Exercise A with the meanings (a–l).

a something to think about carefully
b change the rules or aims
c watch for
d feel nervous
e make something seem more important or serious than it really is
f be the most likely to win something
g lack the required ability or knowledge
h much better than
i be sceptical about something as it may not be accurate or true
j to have an instinctive feeling about
k try your hardest
l not something that everyone likes

**D SPEAK** Work in pairs and discuss the questions.

1 Do you usually have a gut feeling about who will win a sports game?
2 Have you ever felt out of your depth playing a game or sport?
3 Do you keep an eye out for new trends in fitness and nutrition?
4 What kinds of sport are not your cup of tea?
5 Do you know anyone who is head and shoulders above the rest at a sport?

## PRONUNCIATION
Pronunciation of idioms

**A** Listen to the sentences. Circle the prominent words in the underlined idioms.
8.5
1 I had a gut feeling.
2 It's time to throw in the towel.
3 He was really making a meal of it.
4 Keep an eye out for the others.
5 You have to take what she says with a pinch of salt.

**B** Complete the advice for sports players with your own ideas.

1 If you feel out of your depth, …
2 If you have cold feet, …
3 You should always keep an eye out for …
4 If you want to give something your best shot, …
5 If your opponent is making a meal of something, …
6 Take it with a pinch of salt if …

**C** Work in pairs. Read the sentences you wrote in Exercise B to your partner. Do you agree with your partner's advice?

## SPEAKING

**A** Work in groups. Rank the following in order of how important they are for success in sports.

- coaching
- diet and nutrition
- insights from technology
- natural ability
- physical fitness
- sports psychology
- training facilities

**B DISCUSS** Work in groups and discuss the questions.

1 Could students benefit from using sports psychology techniques? How?
2 Could people at work benefit from using sports psychology techniques? How?

**C** Share your ideas with another group.

## 8.2

### READING

**A SPEAK** Work in pairs. What kind of diet should an athlete have?

**B SKIM** Read *Should athletes go gluten-free?* about someone trying out a diet. Which foods did the writer eat? Which did the writer have to avoid?

**C READ FOR DETAIL** Read the article again and answer the questions.
1. Why did he decide to try this diet?
2. What problems did he experience?
3. What was his conclusion about the effectiveness of the diet?

**D** Work in pairs and discuss the questions.
1. Have you tried a gluten-free diet?
2. Would you like to try a gluten-free diet? Why/Why not?
3. Would might be the advantages and disadvantages?

## Should athletes go *gluten-free*?

For those who are gluten intolerant, a diet that is gluten-free is a necessity rather than a choice. But there are some who may be motivated to try this diet for other reasons. When tennis player Novak Djokovic became world number one, he credited going gluten-free as the reason for his success. Some athletes have followed suit and switched to a gluten-free diet and some are already swearing by its effects. So, I'm going gluten-free for two weeks to see if it makes me a better football player.

**DAY 1** Going gluten-free means no bread and no cereal, so I had nice **tangy** grapefruit for breakfast. Then for lunch, I had a big salad full of nice **crisp** lettuce and **crunchy** carrots. I was briefly impressed by how healthy I was being. But then I worked out in the afternoon, and was suddenly ravenous.

**DAY 2** I was overjoyed when I saw the gluten-free section of my local supermarket stuffed full of packets of bread, pasta, cakes, and biscuits – all long lost friends! ¹I put several in my basket. Then I added some more packets just in case. At home, I made myself my first sandwich for two days. Disappointingly, the bread was incredibly dry and incredibly **bland**.

**DAY 3** ²I'd been planning to have grapefruit some days and melon some days, but I was so hungry today that I had both. However, the grapefruit tasted **sour**, so I decided to try one of my gluten-free cupcakes instead. It didn't look that **appetising** but it was actually pretty good – **moist**, unlike the bread, and with very sweet, **sticky** icing. Relieved that I had found some comfort food, I had two more before lunch.

**DAY 4** A revelation! Perhaps the gluten-free bread would be passable as toast? I spread a generous amount of honey on top. Maybe too much as it was a bit **soggy** – but it actually tasted OK. A relief, because I didn't fancy grapefruit or melon for breakfast again.

**DAY 5** For variety, I decided to try some probiotic food – food rich in healthy bacteria that are said to be good for gut health. I'd been told kefir, a fermented milk drink, is a good way to kick things off. It looked like milk, but it smelled interesting – slightly **cheesy** but also vinegary. Tentatively, I poured some into a glass. It had a **creamy** texture, but it was also a little **gritty**. And it tasted like a slightly **acidic**, **fizzy** glass of milk. I'd found something else I could have for breakfast!

**DAY 6** A Japanese friend had warned me that natto – another probiotic food made from fermented soya beans – is a bit of an acquired taste. I could see what she meant right away. It looked **slimy** and had a very **pungent** aroma – almost like burnt tyres. I think the beans actually had a pretty **mild** taste, but the smell was so strong that it was hard to tell. ³I couldn't eat much, so I reached for some gluten-free cakes instead, which I ate with some kombucha, a sweetened tea that looked a little **murky**. Despite the **cloudy** appearance it was nice, although it didn't exactly taste like tea.

**DAY 7** I met some friends for a game of football. The jury was still out as to whether the diet had had any effect. Unfortunately, there wasn't much to see. I hadn't morphed into an overnight football sensation. So, is going gluten-free better for sports performance? It seems highly unlikely. And if you do need to go gluten-free, you should work with a sports nutritionist to create a diet to suit your training needs.

### Glossary

**appetising (adj)** appetising food smells or looks very good
**morph (v)** to change from one thing into another by small and interconnected steps
**overjoyed (adj)** extremely pleased
**the jury is still out (phr)** used for saying that people have not yet decided what they think about someone or something

WELL-BEING

## GRAMMAR
### Pronouns and determiners

**A** Look at the sentence from the article *Should athletes go gluten-free?* Which of the underlined words in the sentence is followed by a noun? What does the word not followed by a noun refer to?

<u>Some</u> athletes have followed suit and switched to a gluten-free diet and <u>some</u> are already swearing by its effects.

**B** Choose the best words to complete the rules.

> **Pronouns and determiners**
>
> Words such as *this*, *these*, *many*, *several* and *some* can be used as both pronouns and determiners. To understand whether the word is being used as a pronoun or determiner, we need to look at the context.
>
> 1 Pronouns *are / are not* followed by a noun. They are used in place of a noun. We need to use the context to understand what the pronoun refers to.
>
> 2 Determiners *are / are not* followed by a noun. They are used to say which thing or how many things are being talked about.

**C** Look at the underlined sentences (1–3) in the article in *Should athletes go gluten-free?* For each sentence, decide which words are pronouns and which are determiners. Then decide which nouns the pronouns refer to.

**D** Go to the Grammar Hub on page 136.

## VOCABULARY
### Describing taste

**A** Complete the table with the words in bold from *Should athletes go gluten-free?* Some words can go into more than one category.

| Look | Smell | Taste | Texture |
|------|-------|-------|---------|
|      |       |       |         |

**B** Go to the Vocabulary Hub on page 147.

**C** SPEAK Work in pairs. Discuss the questions.

1 Describe a food you have eaten because you wanted to be healthy. Did it have any effect?
2 Describe a food you have eaten from another country. Did you like it?
3 Describe the most unusual thing you have ever eaten. Would you recommend it to other people?

## SPEAKING HUB

**A** PREPARE Work in small groups. Imagine you are a fitness instructor or personal trainer. You are pitching your services to a famous athlete. To win the pitch, you need to create the best plan to help him or her prepare for an important competition. First decide what kind of athlete you are pitching to.

**B** PLAN Create a plan to help the athlete. Use the questions to help you.

- What are the best mental techniques to help him or her prepare for the competition?
- What should he or she do to prepare physically?
- What is the best diet for him or her to follow?

**C** PRESENT Present your plan to the class.

**D** DISCUSS Discuss the plans with the class. Which plan was the best?

○ Talk about sports psychology
○ Discuss nutrition and fitness

# Café Hub

## 8.3 Health hacks
**A** – reformulating  **S** – repairing misunderstandings

## ▶ Is it good for you?

**A** Work in pairs. Look at the picture and discuss the questions.
1. Are these foods healthy? Why?
2. Would you eat the food shown in the picture? Why/Why not?

**B** ▶ Read the terms below. Now watch a video about food packaging. Tick (✓) the terms you see or hear.

- [ ] source of fibre
- [ ] high in iron
- [ ] high in vitamins
- [ ] low in salt
- [ ] high in vitamin D
- [ ] source of calcium
- [ ] gluten free
- [ ] good
- [ ] low in calories
- [ ] 100% natural
- [ ] OK for veggies
- [ ] high fibre
- [ ] nature is power
- [ ] high in Omega 3
- [ ] organic
- [ ] no refined sugars
- [ ] no added nonsense
- [ ] veggie-friendly
- [ ] low sugar
- [ ] no added salt

### Glossary
**back up (phrasal verb)** to show that an explanation or belief is probably true
**bend the rules (phrase)** to allow something that is not normally allowed
**dupe (v)** to trick someone into believing something that is not true or something that is stupid or illegal
**manipulate (v)** to influence someone or to control something in a clever or dishonest way
**tricks of the trade (phrase)** quick and effective methods used by experienced people in a particular profession

**C** ▶ Watch the video again. Complete the summary.

A normal supermarket has thousands of products with ¹_____ information. Food producers cannot make health ²_____ about products unless they can support them with ³_____. However, they often manipulate the ⁴_____ to make their foods appear healthier. People generally only notice certain ⁵_____ when food shopping. Some terms such as 'good' and 'natural' are ⁶_____ and can be used without any evidence of health ⁷_____.

## AUTHENTIC ENGLISH

**A** Work in pairs. Read the sentences from the video and the information in the box. Which of Babita's words has Richard reformulated?

**Babita:** *So, we're being duped, we're being fooled, are we?*
**Richard:** *Well, we're being manipulated.*

### Reformulating
We reformulate when we want to express that we don't necessarily agree with what another person has said or with their point of view. We often reformulate by using *well* and then the same structure the other person has used.

**B** Match the sentences (1–6) with the replies (a–f).
1. New York's the greatest city in the world.
2. They're definitely lying to us, aren't they?
3. What they're doing is illegal.
4. All health claims on food have to be backed up with scientific evidence.
5. You hated the film then?
6. So, Maria doesn't want to come to the party then?

a. Well, they're not being completely honest.
b. Well, they're definitely bending the rules.
c. Well, some have to be backed up with evidence.
d. Well, it's certainly the most exciting.
e. Well, she wants to come but she's working really late.
f. Well, I didn't like it very much.

**C** Work in pairs. Write responses to the sentences.
1. I bet the film was amazing, wasn't it?
2. What they're doing is immoral.
3. The apartment's filthy.

**D** Work in pairs. Practise the exchanges you wrote in Exercise C.

94 WELL-BEING

## ▶ Healthy display

SAM  MALCOLM  AMANDA  HARRY  EMILY

**A** Work in pairs. Discuss the questions.
1. Where do you get recipes from?
2. Are you good at following recipes or do you prefer to improvise?

**B** ▶ Watch the video. Complete the recipe.

### Amanda's HEALTHY BROWNIE RECIPE

**INGREDIENTS**
One ¹_____ of coconut oil
Two egg whites
² _____ yoghurt
small amount of sugar
³ _____ cocoa powder
⁴ _____ flour
⁵ _____ of dark chocolate

**METHOD**
Step one: ⁶_____ the oven.
Step two: ⁷_____ egg whites from yolks.
Step three: ⁸_____ egg whites, coconut oil, yoghurt and sugar.
Step four: Add cocoa powder and wholewheat flour to wet ⁹_____.
Step five: ¹⁰_____ mixture until incorporated.
Step six: Add chips of chocolate.
Step seven: Spread the ¹¹_____ in a pan.
Step eight: Put the pan in the oven for ¹²_____ minutes at 260 degrees Fahrenheit.

**C** Where does Harry think he went wrong with the recipe?

## SPEAKING SKILL

**A** Work in pairs. Complete the example in the video. Why does Sam use a question tag here?

> **Sam:** Now you did separate the egg whites from the yolks, _____?

**B** Read the information in the box. Which strategy (a–c) has been used in the sentences from the video (1–4)?

### Repairing misunderstandings
When we don't understand another person or another person doesn't understand us there are a number of things we can do to repair the misunderstanding.
a Tag questions to check that we have understood correctly or that the other person has understood correctly.
b Clarifying instructions to signal that we are going to go over instructions again.
c Restating to clarify what we mean. We can also say what we don't mean.

1. OK … maybe let's go over them again. ___
2. Not whisk … mix. ___
3. Remember to add chips … not chunks … chips of dark chocolate. ___
4. Hold on, Fahrenheit? You mean Celsius, don't you? ___
5. OK, let's go through it one more time. ___

**C** Work in pairs. Take it in turns to read aloud the sentences (1–5) in Exercise B. Try to copy the intonation of Sam and Harry in the video.

## ○ SPEAKING HUB

**A** PLAN You are going to give instructions on a process you know well. Choose one of the ideas below or use your own idea.
- recipe
- how to repair something
- sport or exercise tips
- professional or academic process

**B** PREPARE Make notes on how you are going to explain the process to your partner.

**C** PRESENT Work in pairs. Explain your process to your partner. Ask your partner to retell you the process. Clarify any misunderstandings. Change roles.

*Well, no … that's not quite right. You should make sure you stretch first.*

○— Explain and give instructions about a process

➤ Turn to page 163 to learn how to write a summary of a text about stress.

# Unit 8 Review

## VOCABULARY

**A** Choose the correct word to complete the sentences.

1. I went to see the doctor when I had a *rash / sprain* on my chest.
2. I'm really stressed at the moment, so my blood *pressure / rate* is a little high.
3. I'm on crutches because I've *fractured / pulled* a bone in my foot.
4. Do you have any eye drops? I've been looking at a screen all day and my eyes are really *inflamed / sore*.
5. I *pulled / sprained* my wrist when the ball hit my hand.
6. I think I *fractured / pulled* a muscle at the gym, so I'd better put some ice on it.
7. Do you ever track your heart *rate / pressure* while you're exercising?

**B** Match the questions (1–12) with the answers (a–l).

1. Do you ever get cold feet before speaking in public?
2. Do you always give it your best shot when you play sports?
3. Do you always keep an eye out for good places to eat?
4. Which sports are not your cup of tea?
5. Have you heard something that you've had to take with a pinch of salt?
6. Did you feel like throwing in the towel when it got tough?
7. When was the last time you felt out of your depth?
8. Who is a sports player who is head and shoulders above his peers?
9. Do you offer to help out when you see someone making a meal of something?
10. What was the last thing you read that gave you food for thought?
11. Are your gut feelings usually right?
12. Has anyone ever moved the goal posts while you were working on something?

a. Yes, because I'm incredibly competitive.
b. Messi is clearly one the best players in history.
c. At times in the race I wanted to give up, but you have to keep going.
d. No, I don't usually get nervous.
e. A teacher once changed the title of an essay.
f. I'm not a big fan of rugby or cricket.
g. There was a great article in the paper about innovation the other day.
h. Yes, a friend told me a story. But he always exaggerates.
i. Not usually, I find it a bit embarrassing.
j. Not really. I search for things online.
k. I once took an exam that was much too difficult for me.
l. Rarely. I'm not good at predicting things.

**C** Choose the correct word to complete the sentences.

1. I don't like soft biscuits. They need to be *crunchy / sharp / soggy*.
2. I don't often eat seaweed. It's a bit too *crisp / murky / slimy* for me.
3. Pasta can often be too *bland / pungent / sour*, so I always add lots of parmesan cheese.
4. I tend to order a *mild / gritty / sticky* curry when I have Indian food.
5. I like lemon dressing on my salad to give it a *creamy / soggy / tangy* flavour.
6. I never buy *mild / pungent / fizzy* drinks in case they've been shaken up.
7. I love eating *cheesy / gritty / sticky* things like toffee apples and candy floss.

## GRAMMAR

**A** Correct the mistakes in the sentences.

1. My smartwatch has a feature that you can share your exercise data with friends.
2. There's an app which in you can record your fitness data.
3. This is the device that being used to monitor people's blood sugar levels.
4. The inventor is someone which people like to read about.
5. I don't know who's smartwatch this is.
6. This is the diet tracking service which I subscribe.

**B** Complete the text with the words or phrases in the box.

> a large number of   both   either
> most people   one   others   some people

### The raw food diet

These days, there are ¹_____ diets that claim to be the best way to stay healthy. ²_____ is the raw food diet. According to this diet, ³_____ cooked and processed foods are unhealthy, so people should not eat ⁴_____. ⁵_____ follow a raw vegan diet, whereas ⁶_____ eat animal products, too. The diet includes fruits, vegetables, nuts, seeds and, for the non-vegans, meat. ⁷_____ who follow the diet, whether vegan or not, also eat fermented foods, such as sauerkraut and kimchi.

# 9 BEHAVIOUR

> Behaviour is the mirror in which everyone shows their image.
>
> Johann Wolfgang von Goethe

Caught red … and blue … and green handed.

## OBJECTIVES

- talk about group behaviour
- discuss factors that affect behaviour
- discuss animal behaviour
- talk about behavioural experiments
- give and justify your opinion on social engagement
- write a conclusion to an academic report

Work with a partner. Discuss the questions.

1 Look at the picture. How do children learn to behave? What influences our behaviour as we grow?

2 Read the quote. What aspects of our image/character might we deliberately try to show through our behaviour? What might we reveal accidentally?

3 What would a stranger guess about your character from your behaviour? What might they assume incorrectly?

# 9.1 Language and behaviour

- Talk about group behaviour
- Discuss factors that affect behaviour

**G** – noun phrases   **V** – slang   **P** – pronouncing vague expressions   **S** – understanding rapid colloquial speech

## VOCABULARY
### Slang

**A  SPEAK**  Read the dictionary definition. Work in groups and discuss the questions.

1. Can you think of any examples of slang (in English or your language)?
2. What problems can slang cause for language learners?

---

**slang** – definition and synonyms
NOUN  Pronunciation  /slæŋ/

Words or expressions that are very informal and are not considered suitable for more formal situations. Some slang is used only by a particular group of people.

---

**B**  Read and listen to some examples of informal English. In pairs, try to work out the meaning of the underlined slang expressions.

1. I could do with some new wheels but they'd set me back at least ten grand … and I'm completely skint.

2. Hey, can you lend me ten bucks? Ah, sweet. That's awesome, dude.

3. I don't mean to whinge, but the office do last night was a total shambles. I was so gutted!

4. This bloke offered me a brand new telly for fifty quid, so I'm like 'Sounds dodgy to me – it's probably nicked or something.'

5. I wanted to hang out with my buddies tonight but I'm totally beat, so I guess I'll just chill out and crash instead.

6. I'm well chuffed cos I got myself a new flat. So I'm sorted now.

**C**  Now listen to a more neutral version of the same sentences to check your ideas.

**D  DISCUSS**  Work in small groups. Discuss the questions. Use words in Exercise B.

1. When was the last time you whinged about something?
3. What events have you been to that were a complete shambles? What happened?
4. When was the last time you felt well chuffed or gutted? Why?

## LISTENING

**A SPEAK** Work in pairs. Do you speak or behave differently depending on who you are with?

**B LISTEN FOR GIST** Listen to a group of people taking part in a psychology experiment. Then answer the questions.

1. How many participants are in the group?
2. Where are the experimenters?
3. What's the purpose of the experiment?
4. What five tasks does the experiment include?

**C LISTEN FOR DETAIL** Listen again. Are the statements true (T) or false (F)? Correct the false sentences.

1. Lisa volunteered to take part for free. T / F
2. Lisa's group was due to start at 11:30. T / F
3. All four members of the group agree to eat the doughnuts. T / F
4. Lisa knew for certain that her answer about the lines was wrong. T / F
5. Sometimes PTU affects everyone in a group. T / F
6. The participants think 'yummy' is a cool word. T / F
7. Groupthink is mainly associated with teenagers. T / F
8. The experimenters were surprised by Lisa's behaviour. T / F

**D LISTEN TO RAPID SPEECH** Listen to some extracts from the conversation. Cross out the words and sounds that the speakers leave out. Put brackets [ ] round the phrases they link together. The first two have been done for you. Use the information in the box to help you.

### Understanding rapid colloquial speech

Rapid colloquial English is especially difficult to understand because:
- speakers use a lot of slang and idioms.
- sounds, syllables or even whole words are often left out.
- common phrases like *what do you* and *going to* are linked together.

1. G~~ood~~ morning. How ~~are~~ [you doing?]
2. [Don't know] what they're testing.
3. Are we supposed to wait?
4. We've got to go and teach.
5. Shall we get cracking?
6. It's obvious.
7. Do you think they're for us?
8. What about you, Jake?
9. Shall we have some more?
10. What are you on about?

**E SPEAK** Work in groups and discuss the questions.

1. Do you think you would respond to the tasks in the same way as Lisa?
2. Have you ever experienced PTU? Think about your experiences as a language learner.
3. Have you ever encountered groupthink or something similar? What happened?

## PRONUNCIATION
### Pronouncing vague expressions

**A** Underline the vague expressions in the extracts from the conversation. Use the information in the box to help you.

### Pronouncing vague expressions

Vague expressions are a way of showing that we're not being too precise. They are especially common in informal English.

Vague expressions are usually pronounced very quickly, with no stressed syllables. The word *of* is often reduced to *a* (e.g. *kinda, sorta*). The word *and* becomes *n*.

1. Something about perception skills and stuff like that.
2. There were two blokes here earlier, psychology professors or whatever.
3. How groups influence our behaviour, and so on.
4. I thought my eyes were playing tricks on me in some way!
5. Sometimes it's easier to follow the crowd, in a sense, than to trust your own eyes!
6. Everyone else is nodding their heads, or something like that.
7. I felt kind of stupid.
8. You must think I'm some sort of sheep!

**B** Listen to check your answers. Then practise saying the sentences.

## SPEAKING

**DISCUSS** Work in small groups and discuss the question. Use the vague expressions in the list and slang from this lesson in your discussions.

> **How can we avoid the problems of group behaviour? Think of at least five practical steps.**

- and so on
- and stuff like that
- in a/some sense/way
- kind/sort of (+ adjective/verb)
- more or less
- or something (like that)
- or whatever
- some kind/sort of (+ noun)

BEHAVIOUR

## 9.1

### READING

**A SPEAK** Work in pairs. Do you think the language you speak could affect any of the areas below? Why/Why not?

- how rich you are
- how you play
- your health

**B SKIM** Read *Does your language affect your behaviour?* Were any of your ideas from Exercise A mentioned?

**C READ FOR MAIN IDEA** Read the article again. Answer the questions.

1. How did Chen try to show that language (not other factors) affects our behaviour?
2. Why does our language affect our behaviour, according to Chen?
3. How could Chen's ideas make the world a better place?
4. What other behaviours are connected with our language, according to Chen?
5. What other factor (apart from grammatical structures) might affect how speakers of certain languages behave?
6. What claim is the main focus of the article?
7. What's the problem with the classification of English?
8. Which language feature did Chen use to categorise languages?

**D SPEAK** Work in groups and discuss the questions.

1. Do you agree with Chen's claims?
2. How else could we explain his correlations?
3. Do you often make long-term plans for the future (e.g. saving for retirement)?
4. Do you consider yourself an impulsive person or someone who likes to plan?

# DOES YOUR LANGUAGE AFFECT YOUR BEHAVIOUR?

In 2013, Keith Chen, a behavioural economist at Yale University, made headlines around the world with the extraordinary claim that the language we speak can have a significant impact on [1]our propensity to save, plan and prepare for the future.

Chen divided the languages of the world into two categories: strong FTR (future tense reference) languages, which need markers like 'will' to signal the future, and weak FTR languages, which don't. In English (a strong FTR language), you can't say 'it snows tomorrow'; you usually have to add 'will' or 'going to'. In weak FTR languages like Mandarin, it's normal to say, 'it snows now' and 'it snows tomorrow', using the same verb form in [2]both these cases.

Chen's remarkable finding was that speakers of weak FTR languages save 25% more money for the future than speakers of strong FTR languages. Chen's interpretation of this correlation is that for speakers of weak FTR languages, the future feels like part of the present, while speakers of strong FTR languages save much less because the future feels more remote to them.

Remarkably, Chen's correlations held not only for savings rates, but also for overeating, smoking, drinking, debt and lack of physical exercise. In each case, speakers of weak FTR languages were significantly healthier and took fewer risks, presumably because they felt [3]a strong connection with their future selves.

While Chen's study provoked considerable interest and enthusiasm from the general public, the backlash from linguists and other academics has been just as striking. One criticism involves the possible confusion of correlation with causation. The link between languages and behaviour may in fact be due to other factors, such as age, education or income levels. Chen took great care to control for all these factors, by comparing families where the only difference was [4]the language spoken at home. However, many academics still feel deeply uncomfortable with the idea of a causal relationship behind the apparent correlation.

One alternative possibility is that it's the connotations of a language that affect our behaviour, rather than any grammatical properties of the language itself. For example, languages such as English might encourage a live-for-today attitude as a result of people's associations of that attitude with English-speaking countries.

In a 2010 study, Dirk Akkermans and colleagues set out to find out more by asking bilingual speakers of English and Dutch to play a game. [5]Those who had lived in English-speaking countries were found to be considerably more competitive when playing in English rather than Dutch. However, those who had experienced only limited exposure to the culture of English-speaking countries were found to be no more competitive when playing in English or Dutch, strongly suggesting that it's the culture of English-speaking countries, not the language itself, that is making the difference.

A second major concern with Chen's study is that his division of the world's languages into two categories, strong and weak FTR, seems overly simplistic. For example, while English does require a future tense marker in predictions like 'it'll rain tomorrow', future markers are optional in other future constructions (e.g. 'I'm leaving tomorrow') and virtually outlawed in conditional clauses (e.g. 'If it rains …'). The future in English is complex, as [6]pretty much every learner can attest, so its classification as strong FTR feels debatable at best. Similar objections could be raised for many other languages.

Overall, despite [7]the many legitimate concerns, Chen's analysis of the correlation can't be dismissed out of hand. Further research is needed, ideally with a more sophisticated classification of languages. However, if [8]Chen's conclusions that grammar influences behaviour prove correct, the implications will be profound. Wouldn't it be great if we could solve [9]all our financial and health problems simply by outlawing words like 'will'!

"Chen, M Keith. 2013. "The Effect of Language on Economic Behavior: Evidence from Savings Rates, Health Behaviors, and Retirement Assets." American Economic Review, 103 (2): 690-731."

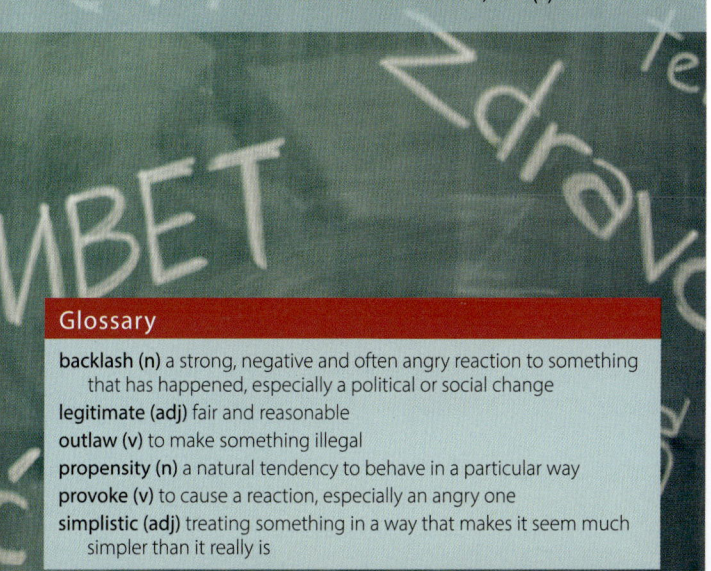

### Glossary
**backlash (n)** a strong, negative and often angry reaction to something that has happened, especially a political or social change
**legitimate (adj)** fair and reasonable
**outlaw (v)** to make something illegal
**propensity (n)** a natural tendency to behave in a particular way
**provoke (v)** to cause a reaction, especially an angry one
**simplistic (adj)** treating something in a way that makes it seem much simpler than it really is

## GRAMMAR
### Noun phrases

**A** Complete the rules with the examples (1–9) from the text.

#### Noun phrases
Long noun phrases (NPs) are especially useful in formal and academic writing because they can contain as much information as a full sentence.

Most NPs start with a number, a quantifier (e.g. *some*, *all*) and/or another determiner (e.g. *the*, *my*, *these*).

**a** *all* and *both* can be used before a determiner without *of*: ___ / ___

**b** *many*, *few*, *little* and numbers can be used after a determiner: ___

**c** Some quantifiers can be modified with phrases like *almost* or *not quite*: ___

Common structures at the end of an NP include:

**d** relative clauses: ___

**e** reduced relative clauses: ___

**f** preposition phrases: ___

**g** *that*-clauses ___

**h** *to* + infinitive ___

**B** Go to the **Grammar Hub** on **page 138**.

**C** SPEAK Work in small groups. Build 'monster noun phrases' around the nouns in the box, as in the example.

> behaviour   experiments   language

A: *My friends' behaviour is strange.*
B: *A lot of my best friends' behaviour is strange.*
C: *Quite a lot of my best friends' behaviour when they're tired is strange.*

## SPEAKING HUB

**A** DISCUSS Work in small groups. Go to the **Communication Hub** on **page 152**.

**B** PLAN Choose one of the ideas in Exercise A. Create a list of at least five pieces of evidence to support or challenge the idea.

**C** PREPARE Work in pairs. Explain your pieces of evidence to your partner. Listen to your partner's evidence. Give feedback and ask questions.

**D** PRACTISE Practise presenting your evidence. Use your partner's feedback to improve your presentation.

**E** PRESENT Report your evidence to the class. Be prepared to answer questions.

**F** REFLECT Decide which evidence you found most convincing and why.

○ Talk about group behaviour
○ Discuss factors that affect behaviour

BEHAVIOUR

## 9.2 Animal behaviour

- Discuss animal behaviour
- Talk about behavioural experiments

**G** – participle clauses and verbless clauses
**P** – intrusive stops
**V** – verb + object + infinitive; gestures and body language
**S** – identifying outcomes of scientific research

### READING

**A SPEAK** Work in pairs and discuss the questions.

chimpanzees   dolphins   crows and jays   dogs

1 Which of the animals listed in the box are intelligent?
2 How do we know?
3 How could we find out?

**B SKIM** Read *Understanding animal behaviour* quickly. What does the writer say about the questions in Exercise A?

# Understanding animal behaviour
*By Peter Aldhous*

We gaze into the eyes of a chimp and see a reflection of ourselves. We glance at a crow and see an alien being. Such biases skew our understanding of what non-human intelligence looks like.

The best known experiment designed to probe animal minds is the 'mirror test'. Having been given time to interact with a mirror, chimps are marked with a dye and anaesthetised. After coming round, they look into the mirror while touching the marked area. From this behaviour, researchers have concluded that the chimps know they are looking at themselves – one of the hallmarks of an advanced mind. Other animals that have passed the test include manta rays and dolphins.

My issue with the mirror test isn't the meaning of success, but rather how to interpret failure. Do most animals fail because they lack a concept of self, or is the test irrelevant to species that don't use vision for social communication? How would you design a similar test using smells for a dog or ultrasound for a dolphin? When a dolphin **hears its own echoes coming** back in altered form, it might well be thinking: 'Yes, that's me' – but how would we know?

In New Caledonian forests, Gavin Hunt of Massey University **watched crows fashion** twigs into hooks to capture insects from holes. Seeming to understand cause and effect, crows are capable of astounding feats of meta-tool use: using one tool to manipulate another in order to achieve an ultimate goal.

In fact, they seem better than chimps at translating their skill in solving one problem to another conceptually similar one. In the trap-tube test, an animal must use a stick to obtain food from a tube. Pushing it in one direction **helps them get** the reward; pushing it in the other **makes the food fall** into a trap. Crows that have already solved this problem can apply their skills when presented with the trap-table test, which looks different but has the same rule: Don't **let the food drop** down the hole. For chimps, prior experience with the trap tube gives no advantage on the trap table.

Understanding the wider scope of corvid cognition meant entering the birds' world to devise experiments to probe their mental processes. Nicky Clayton did this while at the University of California in the late 1990s. After being told confidently by a psychologist colleague that animals lack 'episodic' memory – an ability to remember the 'what, where and when' of past events – Clayton decided to check for herself. While studying western scrub jays, she realised that the birds' habit of burying food provided a prime opportunity to test their memories.

Clayton first **had the jays bury** insect larvae and peanuts in sand-filled trays. Having learnt that the larvae tasted bad after a few days, if just four hours had elapsed, the jays sought out the places where they had hidden them. But if several days had passed, they went for the hidden peanuts. This was an impressive demonstration of 'episodic-like' memory. Clayton has also found that jays will selectively bury certain types of food when aware that it is likely to be scarce in future. So now we apparently have jays planning ahead, in addition to acting on specific memories of the past.

When I visited Clayton and her scrub jays, it was a while before I **saw one of the birds** bury an item of food – apparently my presence had interrupted them. 'They're checking you out,' Clayton told me. I stared back, struck by the gulf between us. Despite having read the scientific papers and knowing how cognitively sophisticated scrub jays are, I experienced no emotional connection.

### Glossary

**elapse** (v) if time elapses, it passes
**feat** (n) something impressive and often dangerous that someone does
**gulf** (n) a large and important difference between people or groups
**hallmark** (n) typical feature

**C READ FOR OUTCOMES** Complete the notes about the research. Use the information in the box to help you.

> **Identifying outcomes of scientific research**
>
> When you read about scientific research, it's important to distinguish between:
> - results (what happened?)
> - conclusions (what did we learn?).
>
> You can then decide if you agree with the conclusions.

**Mirror test**
1 **Results:** Chimps look in mirror and _____.
2 **Conclusions:** Chimps know _____.

**Trap-tube/-table test**
3 **Results:** Crows _____ from one test to another; for chimps _____.
4 **Conclusions:** _____ at translating skills to conceptually similar problems

**Insect larvae vs peanuts**
5 **Results:** Jays went to larvae locations after _____, but to peanut locations after _____.
6 **Conclusions:** Jays possess _____.

**D SPEAK** Work in pairs and discuss the question. How might research like this change the way we treat animals?

## VOCABULARY
Verb + object + infinitive

**A** Look again at the examples in bold in *Understanding animal behaviour*. Then complete the rules with verbs from the text.

> **Verb + object + infinitive**
>
> A very small number of verbs are followed by an object and an infinitive without *to*.
> 1 Sense verbs: _____, _____, _____ and *feel* are followed by an infinitive to describe a complete event, or an *-ing* form to describe a process or series of events.
> 2 Causative verbs: _____, _____ and _____. After help, both an infinitive and *to* + infinitive are possible.

**B** Go to the Vocabulary Hub on page 147.

## GRAMMAR
Participle clauses and verbless clauses

**A** Complete the sentences from the article with one word.

1 _____ been given time to interact with a mirror, chimps are marked with a dye.
2 After coming round, they look into the mirror while _____ the marked area.
3 Nicky Clayton did this _____ at the University of California in the late 1990s.
4 After _____ told confidently by a psychologist colleague that animals lack 'episodic' memory … Clayton decided to check for herself.
5 Having _____ that the larvae tasted bad after a few days … the jays sought out the places where they had hidden them.
6 Clayton has also found that jays will selectively bury certain types of food when _____ that it is likely to be scarce in future.
7 I stared back, _____ by the gulf between us.

**B** Match the sentences (1–7) in Exercise A with the rules (a–c).

> **Participle clauses and verbless clauses**
>
> Participle clauses use participles (e.g. *doing, done, being done, having done, having been done*) instead of a subject + verb.
> a When a clause starts with a participle, the meaning is often *when/after* ___, ___ or *because* ___.
> b Many participle clauses start with prepositions (e.g. *before, after, despite*) ___.
> c After some conjunctions (*if, when, while, although*), we can leave out the subject and *be*. Usually this leaves a participle ___.
> When *be* was the only verb, we are left with a 'verbless clause' ___, ___.

**C** Go to the Grammar Hub on page 138.

## SPEAKING

**SPEAK** Work in groups. Discuss your experiences and opinions of animal intelligence. Then use participle clauses to report back to the class.

## 9.2

## LISTENING

**A SPEAK** Work in groups. Discuss the questions.

1 Do you have any lucky charms that you use before exams or other stressful situations? Do you know anybody who uses these lucky charms?
2 Do you have any lucky rituals or routines that you follow, e.g. before watching your favourite sports team? Do you know anybody who follows these lucky rituals?

**B LISTEN FOR MAIN IDEA** Listen to a radio show about behavioural psychology and answer the questions.

1 How did the pigeons get food?

2 What's the connection between the experiment with pigeons and the one with people?

3 How do the three people at the end try to influence events?

**C LISTEN FOR DETAIL** Listen again. Choose the correct endings.

1 In the famous pigeon experiment, the mechanism always delivered food …
   a after the same amount of time had passed.
   b at random times.
   c when the pigeons performed a particular action.
2 As the food continued to be delivered, the pigeons …
   a changed their actions.
   b became more sure they could affect the delivery.
   c became more desperate.
3 The experiment with people …
   a showed humans weren't so easily convinced.
   b showed very similar results.
   c used food as well to trick the participants.
4 The person who seems most convinced of their power to control events is …
   a the football fan.
   b the exam-taker.
   c the lottery player.

**D SPEAK** Work in groups and discuss the questions.

1 Do the behaviours and rituals described in the radio show prove that pigeons and people are stupid/irrational? Or is there a benefit in believing we can influence things beyond our control?
2 What other examples can you think of, where people (or animals) try to control things that are beyond their control?
3 What are some dangers of this type of behaviour?

## PRONUNCIATION
Intrusive stops

**A** Listen carefully to some extracts from the radio show. Which sound (/p/, /t/ or /k/) can you hear in each of the underlined words?

1 A kind of bizarre pigeon <u>dance</u>. /p/ /t/ /k/
2 Such actions can <u>influence something</u> beyond our control. /p/ /t/ /k/
3 After completely random <u>lengths</u> of time. /p/ /t/ /k/
4 I was a <u>youngster</u>, and my aunt gave me a lucky <u>hamster</u> mascot. /p/ /t/ /k/

**B** Work in pairs. Practise saying the sentences in Exercise A.

**C** Which six words in the box can have intrusive stops? Listen to check. What's different about the other three words?

> becomes   influence   intense   once
> prince   strength   things   warmth   wins

**D** Work in pairs. Write a sentence using at least three of the words in Exercise C. Then give it to another pair for them to attempt to say correctly.

*The more influence the prince has, the more intense he becomes.*

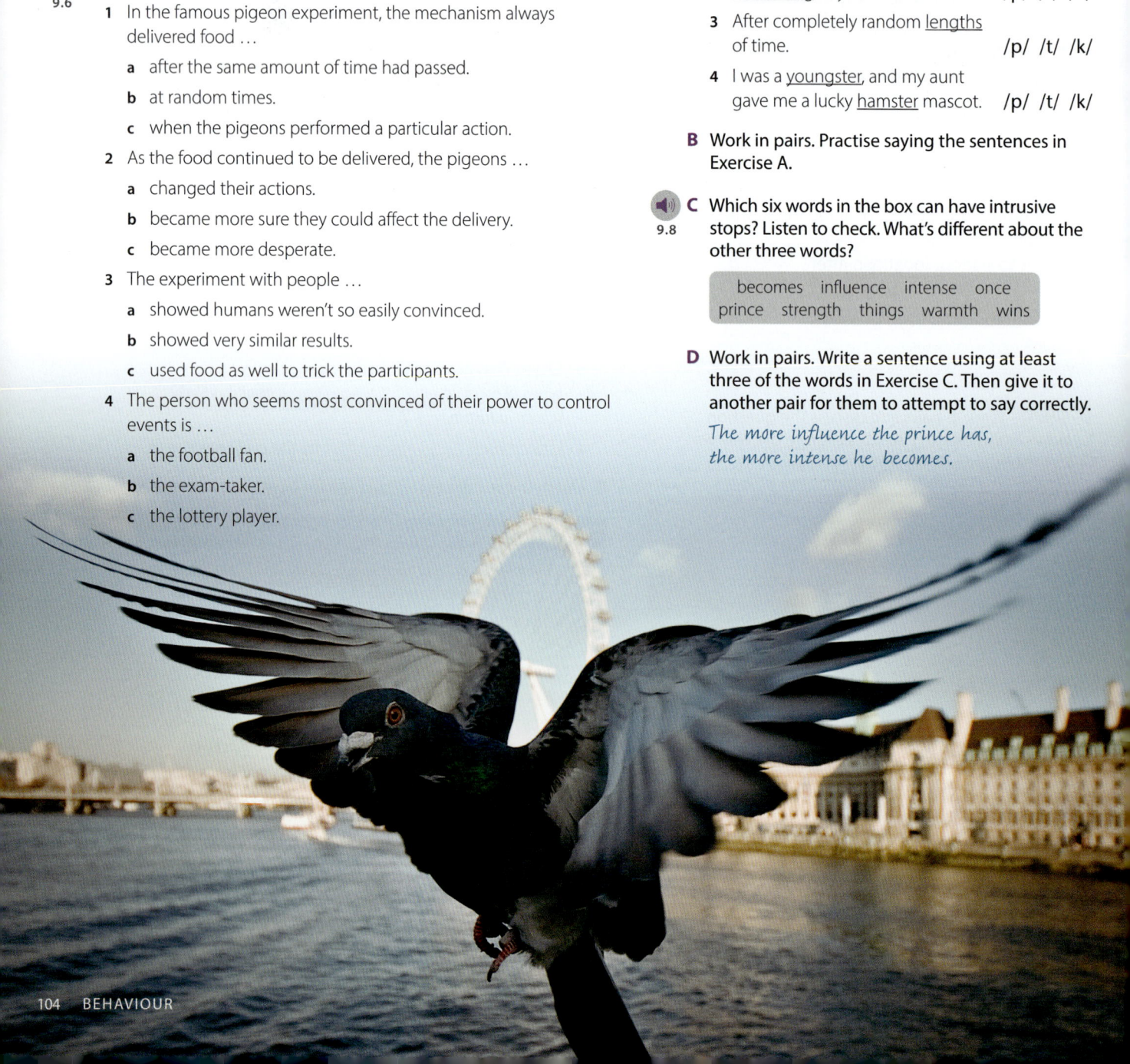

104 BEHAVIOUR

## VOCABULARY
### Gestures and body language

**A** Match the gestures (1–7) with the body parts (a–g). Choose each body part once. When would you use each gesture?

1 blink / wink
2 shrug
3 point / bend / wiggle
4 nod / shake
5 fold / cross
6 cross / bend
7 raise

a your finger(s)
b your eyebrows
c your head
d your legs
e your eyes
f your shoulders
g your arm(s)

**B** Complete the sentences with the correct form of a verb in the box. Which body part does each verb involve?

> beckon   fidget   gaze   glare   grin   lean   smirk   stare

1 Stop _____ at those people's clothes! It's really rude! They're looking back now!
2 You look so happy in that photo! You're _____ from ear to ear!
3 I love _____ out to sea and dreaming of what's on the other side.
4 Stop _____ with your keys and pay attention!
5 During the test, the teacher _____ for me to come to the front of the class.
6 Don't _____ against that cupboard! It's not very stable.
7 When he beat me at tennis, Harry just _____ and said, 'I guess I'm better than you.'
8 I could tell you were angry by the way you _____ at me.

**C** Go to the Vocabulary Hub on page 147.

**D** SPEAK Work in groups and discuss the questions.

1 Which gestures can you use to show that you're happy/interested/bored?
2 How might you show that you don't like someone?
3 How could you communicate with a stranger who doesn't speak your language?

**E** Work in groups to play a game. One of you is the facilitator; the others are players. Facilitator – go to the Communication Hub on page 153. Players – go to the Communication Hub on page 150.

## SPEAKING HUB

**A** PREPARE Work in groups. You are going to design and conduct a behavioural experiment to test an assumption. You can use one of the ideas below or your own ideas.

**Assumption 1:** Our body language communicates more information than the words we use.

**Assumption 2:** We can't help nodding or shaking our heads when we say *yes* or *no*, or shrugging our shoulders when we say *I don't know*, even if the movements are extremely tiny.

**Assumption 3:** We can't help mirroring other people's gestures and body language. We copy them subconsciously.

**B** PLAN Work out how you could test the assumption on other members of the class.

- How will you set up the experiment?
- What will you tell the participant(s)?
- What will you be looking out for?
- How might your observations confirm or undermine the initial assumption?

**C** CONDUCT Take turns to conduct your experiments with other members of the class.

If you're participating in another group's experiment, try to act naturally. Don't try to guess what the experimenters are testing – and don't try to influence their results.

If you're an observer, watch both the experimenters and the participants carefully. Try to work out what the experiment is testing.

**D** DISCUSS Report back to the class on what you learnt from your experiment. Ask other observers for their conclusions. How could you refine your experiment to learn more?

- Discuss animal behaviour
- Talk about behavioural experiments

# Café Hub

## 9.3 Model behaviour
A – end up    S – backtracking and reformulating

## ▶ All together now

**A** Work in pairs. Look at the picture and discuss the questions.
1. What is happening in the picture?
2. Which other animals behave in this way? Why?

**B** ▶ 00.00–01.51 Work in pairs. Watch the first part of a video. Check your answers to Exercise A.

### Glossary
**evacuation (n)** the process of removing people from a building or an area that is not safe
**scenario (n)** a situation that could possibly happen
**simulate (v)** to produce the features of something in a way that seems real but is not
**swarm (v)** to go somewhere as part of a large crowd

**C** ▶ 00.00–01.51 Watch the first part of the video again. Complete the sentences with the best option (a, b or c).

1. Doctor Ed Codling is a …
   a   mathematician.
   b   biologist.
   c   mathematical biologist.
2. The experiment replicates how people on their own react in …
   a   a fire.
   b   an earthquake.
   c   a plane accident.
3. Doctor Codling wants to observe participants that …
   a   look confident and assume they can find the exit.
   b   remain calm and find the exit.
   c   panic and follow another person.
4. When Doctor Codling blows his whistle he wants them to leave out of …
   a   the north exit.
   b   the south exit.
   c   either the north or south exit.

**D** Work in pairs. Discuss the questions.
1. What do you think the result of the experiment will be?
2. How many people do you think will go the right or the wrong way?
3. Why did people behave in the way they did?

**E** ▶ 01.51–02.35 Watch the second part of the video. Check your answers to Exercise D.

## AUTHENTIC ENGLISH

**A** Work in pairs. Read the sentence from the video. Choose the correct options in the box.

*I mean, I've done it before, you just **end up** following someone who looks the most confident in the room.*

### end up
We use *end up* to describe being in a particular place or state after doing something or because of doing it. It is used when the subject *did / didn't* intend or expect this.

**B** Work in pairs. Respond to the sentences using *ended up*.
1. You missed your plane.
   *I ended up sleeping at the airport.*
2. The film you wanted to see was sold out.
   _____
3. After travelling around the world for years, Marta unexpectedly settled down in Ireland.
   _____
4. I thought I'd passed the exam but I failed.
   _____
5. Alan kept on arriving late for work.
   _____
6. We had booked a holiday but had to cancel it because my boyfriend was ill.
   _____

**C** Compare your answers with another pair.

## ▶ Follow the herd

**SAM  MALCOLM  AMANDA  HARRY  EMILY**

**A** Work in pairs. What do you think the phrase *follow the herd* means?

**B** ▶ Watch the video. Answer the following questions.
1. What is Amanda writing an article about?
2. What motivated people to use the Social Stairs?
3. What doesn't Harry understand?
4. Why does Sam want Amanda to tell him what she finds out?

## SPEAKING SKILL

**A** Work in pairs. Complete the examples from the video.

1. Oh, _____ like that piano staircase in Stockholm?
2. _____, the piano staircase had an escalator next to it.
3. You _____ about that other example – the Social Stairs or something like that?
4. Oh, yeah. The Social Stairs. _____.
5. Or _____, they liked hanging out together.

**B** ▶ Watch the video again to check your answers to Exercise A.

**C** Choose the correct options to complete the information.

### Backtracking and reformulating
When we correct something that has been previously said we ¹**backtrack** / **reformulate**. When we say something previously said in a different way we ²**backtrack** / **reformulate**.

**D** Work in pairs. Decide which of the examples in Exercise A are backtracking (b) and which are reformulating (r).

1. ___   2. ___   3. ___   4. ___   5. ___

## ○ SPEAKING HUB

**A PREPARE** You are going to discuss the following question.

Do you think a sense of community is declining in modern society. Why/Why not?

Make notes on what you are going to say and how to justify your opinion. Be prepared to reformulate your arguments.

**B DISCUSS** Work in small groups. Present your opinion to the rest of the group. Respond to what the other members in your group say.

*We've ended up being very isolated ... or to put it another way ... lonely.*

**C REFLECT** Give feedback to the other members of your group. Consider the following points.
- reformulation
- fluency
- pronunciation
- interaction

○— **Give and justify your opinion on social engagement**

➤ Turn to page 164 to learn how to write a conclusion to an academic report.

# Unit 9 Review

## VOCABULARY

**A** Complete the conversation with the words in the box.

> awesome   bloke   chill out   chuffed   dodgy
> dude   gutted   quid   shambles   was like

**A:** Hey, ¹_____. You look happy. What's up?

**B:** I'm well ²_____! I just got ten ³_____ for taking part in an experiment.

**A:** ⁴_____! What did you do?

**B:** I had to use sticks to push food out of a tube, but it kept dropping into a hole. Total ⁵_____! I was well ⁶_____, but the ⁷_____ who was in charge ⁸_____, ⁹'_____, man! Don't worry!'

**A:** Sounds a bit ¹⁰_____ to me. What were they testing?

**B:** Whether people are smarter than crows! Crazy, huh!

**B** Find and correct the mistake in three of the sentences.

1. The researchers watched one chimp hide the food.
   _____
2. We weren't let to watch the experiment.
   _____
3. I'll have my assistant to contact you next week.
   _____
4. I felt a mosquito bite me last night.
   _____
5. I can't help you to pass the exam, but I can help you avoid mistakes.
   _____
6. A crow was seen use one tool to make another.
   _____

**C** Choose the correct words to complete the blog post.

### How to listen – and show you care

- ¹*Lean / Glare / Raise* towards the other person slightly.
- Don't ²*fold / gaze / wink* your arms or ³*fidget / shake / wiggle* with pens, keys, etc.
- Keep neutral facial expressions – a smile might look like a ⁴*gaze / raise / smirk*.
- Don't speak. Instead, ⁵*bend / nod / wink* your head slowly to show understanding, ⁶*cross / point / raise* your eyebrows to show interest, or ⁷*bend / shrug / wiggle* your shoulders to show you don't know.
- Keep eye contact but don't ⁸*cross / grin / stare*. You're allowed to ⁹*beckon / blink / glare*!

## GRAMMAR

**A** Reorder the sentences to make noun phrases.

1. You usually have to use / forms / available / future / the / two / that / of / one / are /
   _____
2. The research focused on / for / are making / the / that / worrying / of / preparation / the future / lack / extremely / most people /
   _____
3. all / behaviour / Practically / into / research / my / animal / shows they're smarter than we think
   _____
4. The accident occurred because of / the event / for / failure by / such / the organisers / almost / to plan / the / large crowds / complete / to attend /
   _____
5. problem / the / ways / these / approaching / Both / of / are flawed
   _____
6. We are aware of / that / be expressed / the / only / animal intelligence / of / many / a / can / few / ways /
   _____

**B** Complete the sentences with participle clauses. Use the verbs in brackets.

1. _____ a big breakfast earlier, I skipped lunch. (*eat*)
2. The octopus uses a coconut shell as a shelter if _____. (*attack*)
3. _____ to understand the rules, the pigeon solved the puzzle quickly. (*seem*)
4. _____ to be at the airport at 4 am, we weren't happy about the 10-hour delay. (*tell*)
5. When _____ your bags, remember to leave space for souvenirs. (*pack*)
6. Despite not _____ at university, she has produced some excellent research. (*study*)

BEHAVIOUR

# 10 SOCIETY

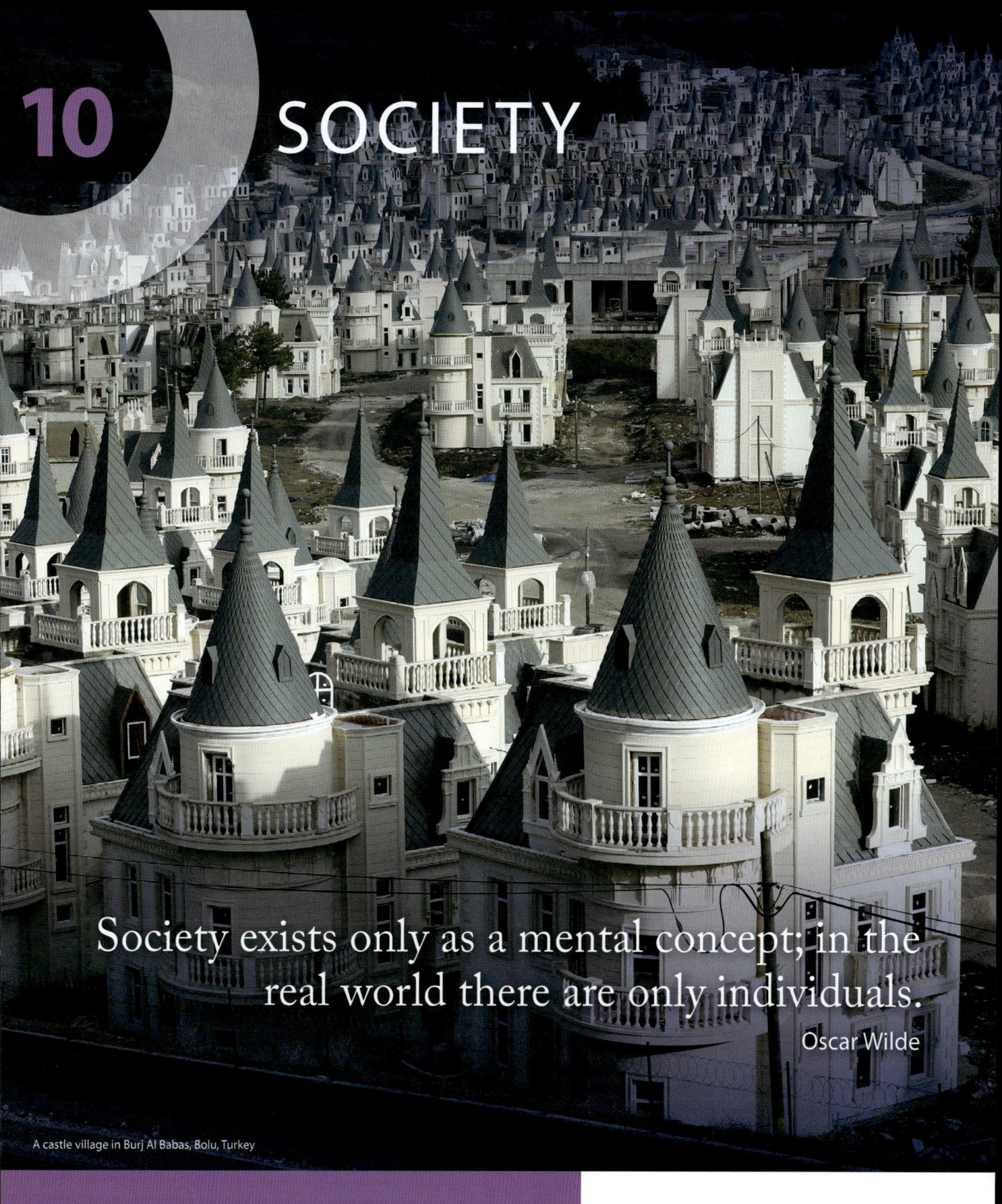

> Society exists only as a mental concept; in the real world there are only individuals.
>
> Oscar Wilde

A castle village in Burj Al Babas, Bolu, Turkey

## OBJECTIVES

- discuss issues related to tourism
- present solutions to urban problems
- talk about political activism
- discuss how to make a difference
- debate for and against a motion
- write a persuasive essay

Work with a partner. Discuss the questions.

1. Look at the picture. What type of person might live in a place like this?
2. Read the quote. What do you think Wilde means? Do you agree?
3. What would be the advantages and disadvantages of living in an unusual place like the one in the picture?

SOCIETY 109

# 10.1 Urban problems

- Discuss issues related to tourism
- Present solutions to urban problems

**G** discourse markers
**P** introducing new information
**V** culture and heritage; nouns with *to*
**S** integrating information from different texts

## READING

**A SPEAK** Work in pairs. What are some advantages and disadvantages of increased tourism for a city?

**B SCAN** Read the three newspaper articles. What problem of tourism are they discussing?

### Has tourism reached its limit?

Being **designated** as a UNESCO World **Heritage** site helps **preserve** a site and **refurbish** its facilities – as well as boosting tourism. Yet, it can end up **endangering** the site. A famous example is Machu Picchu, the **ruins** of an Inca **settlement** in Peru, which is being destabilised owing to tourists littering, climbing on the ruins or even taking pieces of it home.

In response to similar problems, Venice has capped the number of tourists allowed to enter its most famous areas. Niagara Falls requires visitors to buy tickets which say when they can enter the site, whereas the Taj Mahal has increased entrance fees for tourists to actually try to put people off visiting.

#### Glossary

**booming (adj)** if an activity is booming, it is becoming very popular
**destabilise (v)** to cause problems for a country, government, or person in authority so that they become less effective
**elitist (adj)** supporting or based on a system in which a small group of people have a lot of advantages and keep the most power and influence

**C SYNTHESISE INFORMATION** Imagine that you are writing an essay about tackling the problem you identified in Exercise B. Complete the notes using information from all three articles. Use the information in the box to help you.

> **Integrating information from different texts**
>
> Sometimes you need to get information from multiple sources to understand a topic.
> - Be clear about your purpose for reading. What questions are you trying to answer?
> - Underline the main ideas in the texts and look for arguments connected to your topic.
> - Use headings to organise the information you are looking for. Make notes under these headings as you read more texts.

**Notes**

Issues caused by the problem
_____

Ideas for dealing with the problem
_____

Criticism of these ideas
_____

**D DISCUSS** Work in pairs. Look at your notes in Exercise C and discuss the best methods for solving the problem.

### Is tourism tax fair?

The New Zealand government recently announced that it will start charging tourists a tax of approximately NZ$35 (£18). The government claims this **fund** will be spent on infrastructure and the natural **habitat** of New Zealand's wildlife.

Is this reasonable? Tourists already contribute to the economy by paying for hotels, food and souvenirs. It's not as elitist as charging higher entrance fees to attractions, but it is still enough to put some tourists off.

Some might question if the fee is masking a failure to manage tourism properly. Should governments be responsible for not only attracting tourists, but better ensuring they are able to handle the influx of visitors?

SOCIETY

## VOCABULARY
### Culture and heritage

A Match the words in bold in the articles with the meanings (1–10).

1 _____ = the type of place where an animal lives or a plant grows
2 _____ = the parts of a building that remain after it has been damaged
3 _____ = a large amount of money
4 _____ = to take care of something and prevent it being damaged
5 _____ = a place where people live
6 _____ = relating to the style or design of a building
7 _____ = to formally choose someone or something for a role or special status
8 _____ = objects, traditions and beliefs important to a society's history or culture
9 _____ = to put something at risk of being destroyed or becoming extinct
10 _____ = to repair or improve a building

B Go to the Vocabulary Hub on page 148.

C SPEAK Work in pairs and discuss the questions.

1 Are there any habitats where endangered species live in your country?
2 Should your country's government provide a larger fund to preserve cultural sites?
3 How important is architectural style to your country's heritage?

## Tackling tourism with tech

Tourism in Amsterdam is booming, with over 14 million visitors a year to enjoy the canals and the mix of **architectural** styles. The Amsterdam tourism board felt limiting tourist numbers was too extreme, so they turned to technology to deal with potential overcrowding.

Many tourists visit the Van Gogh Museum in the morning and take a cruise on the canal in the afternoon. So the tourism board has launched an app providing information on how busy the attractions are and suggesting alternative destinations.

## GRAMMAR
### Discourse markers

A Choose the correct discourse markers to complete the sentences.

1 A top tourist attraction is the Grand Bazaar in Istanbul *owing to / despite* its spectacular architecture and wide range of shops.
2 The Zócalo in Mexico, another very popular attraction, hosts a large number of events throughout the year. *Yet / Moreover*, it is home to the Metropolitan Cathedral and the National Palace.
3 Some of the most popular tourist attractions are in the US – *as a matter of fact / namely* Times Square, Central Park and Union Station.
4 Theme parks are also among the most popular tourist destinations. Disneyland in Florida, *in any case / for instance*, is a very popular destination.
5 *Conversely / Whereas* several of the world's most popular tourist attractions are in the US, one of the most popular destinations in Europe is Paris.

B Complete the rules with words and phrases in Exercise A.

> **Discourse markers**
>
> 1 Use *despite*, _____ and _____ to join two clauses. They can come at the beginning of the sentence (followed by a comma) or in between the two clauses.
> 2 Use *as a matter of fact, conversely, in any case,* _____ and _____ to connect ideas in two sentences.

C Go to the Grammar Hub on page 140.

D Work in pairs. Make sentences using the prompts below plus a discourse marker.

1 there are some great tourist sites in my city
2 people who live near tourist sites often get angry with tourists
3 tourists have a reputation for bad behaviour
4 many cities around the world are keen to attract tourists

## SPEAKING

A SPEAK Work in pairs and discuss the questions.

1 How important is tourism to your country?
2 Do you believe tourism is mainly good or bad for a city? Why?

B DISCUSS Work in groups. Try to gain a consensus on question 2 in Exercise A. Use the steps below to help you.

- Get everyone's view.
- Allow speakers time to justify their views.
- Establish agreement: think about ways of doing this fairly.

C PRESENT Present and justify your position to the class.

## 10.1

### LISTENING

**A SPEAK** Work in pairs and discuss the questions.

1 What kind of place do you like to work or study in? Why do you like this place?
2 What are your favourite buildings in your city? Why do you like them?

**B LISTEN FOR GIST** Listen to the first part of a radio report about building design. Generally speaking, how can the design of a building affect people?

**C LISTEN FOR DETAIL** Listen to the next part of the radio report and note down how these specific features can affect people.

1 Light: _____
2 Shapes and lines: _____
3 Colours: _____
4 Shop facades: _____
5 Spaces between buildings: _____

**D SPEAK** Work in pairs and discuss the questions.

1 What do you think of the different ideas? Do you think they make a difference?
2 Why do you think many buildings don't follow the recommendations discussed in the programme?

### VOCABULARY
Nouns with *to*

**A** Circle the nouns followed by *to* in the extracts from the radio programme. Use the information in the box to help you.

> **Nouns with *to***
>
> Several nouns are often followed by *to* + the infinitive. You can remember which ones they are by thinking about the adjective or verb forms of these words – because they are also normally followed by *to* + infinitive, e.g. *Architects normally start with the wish to design innovative buildings.*

1 And if people feel better about their environment, they have a higher inclination to interact positively with the people around them.
2 People have a tendency to be less productive if their desk is more than 7.5 metres away from a window.
3 … whereas plain, monotonous facades make people anxious and give them the urge to hurry past.
4 The project's failings were a reminder for architects to think not just about the look of buildings, but also about how people would interact within the spaces they create.

**B** Match the underlined nouns (1–10) with their meanings (a–j).

1 Most architects have a <u>desire to</u> create beautiful rather than functional buildings. ____
2 Most people in big cities show a <u>reluctance to</u> talk to strangers. ____
3 Governments have an <u>obligation to</u> limit the population of their cities. ____
4 Cities need to be doing a lot more in <u>readiness to</u> deal with swelling populations. ____
5 The <u>refusal</u> of many cities <u>to</u> provide seating in public places is a mistake. ____
6 A <u>failure to</u> learn from environmental psychology will lead to higher crime rates. ____
7 People need frequent <u>reminders to</u> behave considerately in cities. ____
8 Companies have a <u>responsibility to</u> make sure building design has a positive effect on their staff. ____
9 People in cities have a <u>tendency to</u> feel isolated because they are too busy to socialise. ____
10 There should be a greater <u>urge to</u> limit noise and sound pollution in cities. ____

a something that helps you remember something
b an unwillingness
c preparation
d not doing something that you were expected to do
e a wish
f saying that you will not do something
g a strong feeling of wanting or needing to do something
h responsibility
i a habit of behaving in a particular way
j a duty

**C** Work in pairs. Do you agree with the sentences in Exercise B?

**D** Work in pairs. Complete the sentences with your own ideas.

1 Architects have a tendency to …
2 In my city, most people show a reluctance to …
3 Most people have no desire to …
4 Local planners have a responsibility to …

Google Global HQ

## PRONUNCIATION
Introducing new information

**A** Listen to the extracts from the radio programme. Does the pitch of the speaker's voice go up or down on the underlined words?

10.3

1 As the city evolves, its population has swelled to over 21 million, making Beijing one of the most populated cities in the world. <u>And</u> the more people there are, the more challenging it becomes to provide comfortable environments for people to live and work in.

2 They found that people strongly preferred daylight to electric light – and, <u>as a matter of fact</u>, other research has shown that people have a tendency to be less productive if their desk is more than 7.5 metres away from a window.

3 Apparently, people feel more comfortable in places with round shapes and curved lines. <u>On the other hand,</u> straight lines and sharp edges have been shown to create feelings of fear.

4 One interesting study showed that people are more relaxed when they see lively and interesting shop facades, <u>whereas</u> plain, monotonous facades make people anxious and give them the urge to hurry past.

**B** Work in pairs. Practise saying the sentences. Listen carefully. Did your partner use a higher pitch on the correct word?

1 Although most people think that living in a city is exciting, it's actually quite boring for many people.

2 Rather than developing urban areas, we should be developing rural areas.

3 Companies are now embracing ideas from environmental psychology rather than ignoring them.

4 The offices of large companies are being designed to encourage positive feelings in staff. People's homes, however, are much less likely to receive the same attention.

## SPEAKING HUB

**A PLAN** Work in small groups. Imagine that your city is holding an election for a new mayor. Make a list of some of the biggest problems about living in your city and brainstorm some solutions to these problems.

**B PREPARE** You support a candidate in the election. Prepare a short speech to try to persuade people to vote for your candidate. You should:

- decide which three problems your candidate will solve
- be ready to explain the problems
- be ready to explain how your candidate will fix them
- make sure that each member of your group has something to say.

**C PRESENT** Give your speeches and listen to the other groups' speeches.

**D DISCUSS** As a class, decide which candidate you want to be mayor.

*For me, the best speaker by far was …*
*While I liked all the candidates, the one that really stood out was …*

○- Discuss issues related to tourism
○- Present solutions to urban problems

SOCIETY 113

# 10.2 How to change the world

- Talk about political activism
- Discuss how to make a difference

**G** – ellipsis and substitution  **V** – word building  **P** – managing conversations  **S** – recognising shifts in register

## READING

**A SPEAK** Work in pairs and discuss the questions.

1 If you were concerned about a local issue, would you contact your local politician about it?
2 Do you think that political activism (e.g. demonstrations or petitions) can make a difference?

**B READ FOR MAIN IDEA** Read the article *Political activism* and choose the best summary.

1 The younger generation are becoming very active in politics and many are choosing to become politicians so they can make the world a better place.
2 The younger generation are more interested in campaigning for specific causes than getting behind a particular political party.
3 The younger generation are completely uninterested in politics and prefer to focus on their friendships, hobbies and interests.

**C READ FOR DETAIL** Read the article again and answer the questions.

1 Is the writer part of the younger or older generation?
2 Why is the younger generation disillusioned with the political system?
3 What three issues has the Harry Potter Alliance taken an interest in?
4 What does the writer mean when he says that 'we're moving from a vision of civics that is party-based and partisan to one that's personal and pointillist'?

**D SPEAK** Work in pairs. Discuss the question. Some people label the kind of political activism described in the article as 'slacktivism'. Do you think this is a fair criticism?

# Political activism is as strong as ever, but now it's digital – and passionate

**The new generation of digital natives are not apathetic about politics, but they see online campaigns as more effective than lobbying a politician or joining a party.**

Like most Americans of my generation – born in 1973 – I learnt about civics from television. On Saturday mornings, our childhood diet of cartoons was regularly interrupted for *Schoolhouse Rock*, three-minute animated musical lessons on science, grammar and the workings of government. Today it's hard to teach civics in three-minute snippets because the way we participate in civic life is changing shape – and changing very quickly. The vision of participatory citizenship that I grew up with – read a newspaper, vote in elections and if you're really incensed, write to your congressional representative – is utterly unpersuasive and unappealing to the students I teach. Digital natives, born and raised in an atmosphere of interactivity, are acutely aware of how insensitive most governments are to participation and how little meaningful interaction they can expect from their elected representatives and other government officials.

This distaste for participation in dysfunctional political systems is easily misread as apathy, leading legislators and educators to declare 'a crisis in civics' as young people participate in elections at a much lower rate than their parents. But that misses a key shift: digital natives are participating in civic life in ways where they feel they can have an impact and these points of impact are often outside government.

Take the Harry Potter Alliance, a group of teen and twenty-something fans of JK Rowling's books and movies, who are organising online and searching for ways to live out the values of Harry Potter and Dumbledore's Army here in the Muggle world. Their past campaigns have purchased thousands of books for underfunded public libraries and sent planeloads of health supplies for Haitian crisis response. Now they're working to persuade Warner Bros to buy Fairtrade chocolate for the sweets sold as tie-ins to the movies, bombarding the company with 'howlers', open, digital letters that demand it consider the ethical concerns of Harry Potter's fans.

## VOCABULARY
### Word building

**A** Complete the Example column with words from the article. Use the information in the box to help you.

> **Word building**
>
> We use suffixes to change the form of words. For example, we can add *-ness* to the end of an adjective to turn it into a noun (*ready* becomes *readiness*). Being aware of different suffixes can help you to understand what kind of word is being used.

| Suffix | Add to … | to make… | Example |
|---|---|---|---|
| -al | a noun | an adjective | *ethical* |
| -ate | a noun | an adjective | |
| -ic | a noun | an adjective | |
| -ical | a noun | an adjective | |
| -ive | a verb | an adjective | |
| -hood | a noun | a noun | |
| -ity | an adjective | a noun | |
| -ship | a noun | a noun | |

**B** Go to the **Vocabulary Hub** on **page 148**.

## SPEAKING

**DISCUSS** Work in small groups. Discuss the questions.

1 What do you think are some of the biggest problems in the world today? Make a list and rank the problems.
2 What could people do to raise awareness of the top three issues on your list? How could people try to get companies, individuals or governments to change their behaviour?
3 If a friend of yours wanted to become involved in political activism, would you encourage him or her or dissuade him or her from doing so? Why?

---

Not every digital native is an engaged, active citizen (and not every young person is a digital native) and not every online campaign has an impact. But it's too easy to dismiss digitally-rooted activism as naive 'slacktivism'. Online activism is having an impact, but it often focuses in areas outside formal political participation. Civic participation of the young uses a broad suite of tools to affect a wide range of targets.

Coders write open-source security software in the hope of frustrating NSA surveillance, while community organisers fund neighbourhood gardens through Kickstarter. This emergent civics targets governments, corporations, communities and the media. It harnesses social media, crowdfunding, social entrepreneurship and open-source software as well as law and politics, to bring about change.

No wonder it's hard to get our heads around it. We're moving from a vision of civics that's party-based and partisan to one that's personal and pointillist. Parties offer a way to have an opinion (often an ill-informed one) on every issue, while participatory civics centres on issues that people are passionate about. While my generation tends to see the world in terms of issues important to Republicans or Democrats, my students often see the world in terms of the issues their friends care about, a political identity built on the passions of people important to them. This isn't civics in crisis – it's civics in flux, civics that's changing with the people who practise it.

> **Glossary**
> **dysfunctional** (adj) not working normally
> **howler** (n) a silly and embarrassing mistake
> **incensed** (adj) extremely angry
> **lobby** (v) try to influence politicians or people in authority on a particular subject
> **snippet** (n) a small piece of something, especially information or news

SOCIETY

## 10.2

### LISTENING

**A SPEAK** Work in pairs. Discuss the questions.
1. What job did you want to do when you were younger?
2. Do you still want to do that job? Why/Why not?

**B LISTEN FOR MAIN IDEA** 10.4 Listen to a conversation about finding a job after university. Answer the questions below.
1. What kind of job was Robin interested in before?
   _____
2. What kinds of jobs is Robin thinking about doing now?
   _____

**C LISTEN FOR DETAIL** 10.4 Listen again and answer the questions.
1. What made Robin think about pursuing a different career?
   _____
2. What does Joanna think about the jobs Robin is thinking of doing?
   _____
3. What advice does Mr Evans give Robin about finding the job he wants to do?
   _____
4. How did the philosophy graduate decide to help people?
   _____
5. Does Joanna agree with Mr Evans' advice?
   _____

**D LISTEN TO REGISTER** 10.5 Listen to extracts from the conversation. For each, decide if Robin is using formal or informal register. Use the information in the box to help you.

> **Recognising shifts in register**
>
> People speak differently in formal and informal/casual situations.
>
> In formal situations, speakers:
> - use longer, more complete sentences
> - use careful pronunciation
> - are less direct
> - use formal words and phrases.
>
> In informal/casual situations, speakers use:
> - short sentences, contracted forms and often omit words
> - less careful pronunciation
> - more informal words and phrases (phrasal verbs, vague language and slang).

1. informal / formal          4. informal / formal
2. informal / formal          5. informal / formal
3. informal / formal          6. informal / formal

**E SPEAK** Work in pairs and discuss the questions.
1. What kind of job do you think Robin should do? Why?
2. What do you think about the idea of working in finance to help charities?
3. If you want to donate to charity, what's the best way to choose the charity?

## GRAMMAR
### Ellipsis and substitution

**A** Look at the extracts from the conversation. The speakers omitted some words. Complete the sentences with the omitted words.

1 I've just been trying to sort out my CV and _____ looking for some interesting stuff to apply to.
2 _____ any idea what you're going to do?
3 You could train to be a teacher or _____ just volunteer in your spare time.

**B** Look at the underlined words in the sentences. What words do they replace?

1 **A:** So … you going to work at your dad's company then?
   **B:** Hmm … hope <u>not</u>.
2 If you haven't read it, you should <u>do</u>.
3 **A:** I was thinking about some kind of voluntary work.
   **B:** You should definitely <u>do it</u>.

**C** Complete the rules using examples in Exercises A and B.

> **Ellipsis and substitution**
>
> *Ellipsis* means omitting unnecessary words. We can omit:
> 1 the subject + modal: _____
> 2 the subject + auxiliary verb: _____
> 3 a verb phrase
> 4 an adjective: _____.
>
> In spoken English, it's also common to leave out words if our meaning is obvious from the context. We can omit:
> 5 the subject
> 6 the subject + auxiliary verb.
>
> *Substitution* means avoiding repeating something by using words like:
> 7 *do*: _____
> 8 *not*: _____
> 9 *do so / do it / do that*: _____.

**D** Go to the Grammar Hub on page 140.

**E** SPEAK Work in pairs. Cross out the words that can be omitted in these sentences. Then discuss whether you agree or disagree with them.

1 Charity workers should not receive high salaries and they should not get bonuses.
2 Some charity workers are very persistent and I wish they weren't so persistent.
3 Animal charities often receive the most money, but they shouldn't receive the most money.

**F** Work in pairs. Replace parts of the questions with *do so*, *not* or *so*. Then ask your partner the questions.

1 Would you ever go overseas to do voluntary work? If you went overseas to do voluntary work, where would you go?
2 Do you think having voluntary work on your CV makes a big difference to recruiters or does it not make a big difference to recruiters?
3 If your company or university allowed you to take a week off to do voluntary work, would you take a week off to do voluntary work?

## PRONUNCIATION
### Managing conversations

**A** Listen to extracts from the conversation. For each extract, decide if the intonation on the second speaker's words rises (↗) falls (↘) or rises then falls (↗↘).

1 ___   2 ___   3 ___   4 ___   5 ___

10.6

**B** SPEAK Work in pairs. Think of an anecdote for one of these topics. Listen to your partner and use appropriate reactions to keep the conversation going.

- some good advice a teacher gave me
- a time I made a difference

## SPEAKING HUB

**A** PREPARE Work in two groups. You are going to roleplay an event where charities look for funding. Group A – you are fundraisers for a charity. Decide what type of charity you work for. Group B – you are funding organisations. Decide what types of charities you want to give money to and why.

**B** PLAN Group A – plan how you will persuade people to support your charity. Group B – think of questions you will ask charities that want your funding.

**C** PRESENT Talk to students from the other group. Try to persuade them to support your charity or ask them questions about their work.

**D** REFLECT Who was able to convince the most people to support their charity? Why were they successful?

○ Talk about political activism
○ Discuss how to make a difference

# Café Hub

## 10.3 Changing cities
A – describing a scene in real-time
S – using vague language

### ▶ Mexicable

**A** Work in pairs. Look at the pictures and discuss the questions.
1. What are some of the different uses of cable cars?
2. Are there cable cars in your city or country? How are they used?

**B** ▶ Watch the video. Tick (✓) which of the following you see.
1. A man admiring spectacular views from a cable car. ☐
2. A man in a wheelchair going up a ramp. ☐
3. A man in a wheelchair entering a cable car. ☐
4. Tourists taking photos from a cable car. ☐
5. Mechanics repairing an engine. ☐
6. A man wheeling himself along a pavement. ☐

**C** ▶ Watch the video again. Complete the sentences with between one and three words.
1. Abe likes the cable car station because there's a wheelchair entrance and _____.
2. Victors says the advantages of cable cars are that they avoid stoplights and _____.
3. The cable cars from Stations 1 to 4 are moved by _____.
4. *Mexicable* connects some of the poorest and _____ areas of the city.

### Glossary
**feat (n)** something difficult needing a lot of skill, strength, bravery, etc to achieve it
**haphazard (adj)** done in a way that does not seem to be carefully planned or organised
**loop (n)** a round shape or curve made by a line curling back towards itself
**mural (n)** a large painting on the wall of a room or building

**D** Work in pairs. Try to remember what you heard. What do these numbers and dates refer to?
1. 22 million _____
2. 2016 _____
3. 6 _____
4. 26 _____
5. 30,000 _____
6. 4 _____
7. 7 _____
8. 3 _____

## AUTHENTIC ENGLISH

**A** Work in pairs. Read the sentence from the video and the information in the box. Underline the descriptive words. What do they mean?

*The views from the Mexicable – you've got this sprawling city and these murals and the amazing colours on the houses, it's just breathtaking!*

### Describing a scene in real-time
When we describe a scene in real-time we often use visually descriptive language to bring the scene to life and paint a mental picture in the listener's mind.

**B** Read the sentences. What is being described in each sentence?
1. There's this sea of golden shifting sand, spectacular dunes and a fierce, burning sun.
2. Just look at the gorgeous lush green meadows and peaceful grazing sheep.
3. I've never seen such deep valleys and magnificent snow-capped peaks.
4. Everywhere you look there are towering skyscrapers, bustling streets and stunning street art.
5. You've got these picturesque narrow streets, an enchanting medieval square and beautiful, cosy cottages.

**C** Work in pairs. Describe a scene to each other using descriptive language. Student A – go to the **Communication Hub** on **page 152**. Student B – go to the **Communication Hub** on **page 155**.

118  SOCIETY

# ▶ Everything's changing

SAM   MALCOLM   AMANDA   HARRY   EMILY

**A** Work in pairs. Discuss the questions.

1. What developments are happening where you live?
2. Are the developments positive or negative? Why?

**B** ▶ Watch the video. Does everybody have a similar opinion about the new cable car?

**C** ▶ Watch the video again. Answer the following questions.

1. Why is parking and traffic worse according to Emily?
2. What is being built over the river?
3. What does Malcolm say will happen to the area soon?
4. How much would it cost Emily to rent a bigger business space?
5. Why is Harry looking forward to the cable car?
6. What improvements have there been to the area according to Amanda?
7. How was Sam able to set up his café according to Harry?

## SPEAKING SKILL

**A** Work in pairs. Look at the extracts from the video. Why have the speakers used the underlined phrases?

> **Amanda:** Also, the area was quite run down with high unemployment and <u>all the rest of it</u>.
>
> **Malcolm:** I had to park all the way over on <u>whatsitsname</u> and walk here.

**B** Read the information in the box. Underline the vague language in the sentences from the video.

### Using vague language

We often use vague words when we can't find the exact expression we need.

a List completers – when someone is unable to complete everything on a list.
b Placeholders – a speaker cannot remember something.
c Evasion – not wanting to say something exactly.
d Quantities – when we're not sure of the exact figure.

1. It doesn't help either that they're building that thingy over the river.
2. I hardly recognise the neighbourhood any more with all the new shops, the road system and stuff like that.
3. It was two thousand odd pounds for the month.
4. Well, yeah, sort of … it is convenient … but if I can't afford to stay in the area they won't be much good to me.
5. It will also encourage tourism and who knows what else.
6. Crime in the area is down about 20% in the past four years.

**C** Work in pairs. Match the examples (1–8) from the video with the functions (a–d) in the box.

## ○ SPEAKING HUB

**A PREPARE** You are going to debate the following motion. Decide who in the class will be *for* and *against* the motion.

All vehicles should be banned from city centres.

**B PLAN** In your groups, make notes for your side of the argument. Think about:

- environment
- convenience
- public transport
- cost

**C PRESENT** Join together with the other group and hold a debate.

*Without cars you could have more public spaces, street cafés and all the rest of it.*

**D REFLECT** Hold a vote on whether you agree or disagree with the motion.

○– Debate for and against a motion

➤ Turn to **page 165** to learn how to write a persuasive essay about living in the city or countryside.

SOCIETY

# Unit 10 Review

## VOCABULARY

**A Complete the article with the words in the box.**

architectural   designated   endangered   fund   habitat
heritage   preserve   refurbish   ruins   settlement

### UNESCO
### World Heritage Sites

The aim of the World [1]_____ list is to help countries [2]_____ sites of 'outstanding universal value'. To be [3]_____ as a World Heritage site, a place must meet one of ten criteria, such as being an [4]_____ masterpiece, a human [5]_____ or the [6]_____ of one representative of a particular culture, a place of exceptional natural beauty, or a place that is the natural [7]_____ of an [8]_____ species.

Once a site is selected for the list, the World Heritage [9]_____ can provide money to protect or [10]_____ the site – and being on the list usually provides a significant boost to the number of tourists visiting the site.

**B Choose the correct words to complete the sentences.**

1 Architects have *an urge* / *a responsibility* to provide people with enough daylight.
2 People have a *reluctance* / *tendency* to be less productive if there is background noise.
3 The government needs frequent *desires* / *reminders* to tackle the problem of air pollution.
4 The government's *readiness* / *refusal* to invest in rural areas has led to overcrowding in cities.
5 Architects have *a failure* / *an obligation* to talk to the people who will use a building before they design it.

**C Choose the correct words to complete the sentences.**

1 Young people don't like politics because it is too *formal* / *formality*.
2 People often vote for the person with the strongest *personal* / *personality* rather than the best plans.
3 The *public* / *publicity* should have a vote on major political decisions.
4 Social media enables much easier *interactive* / *interactivity* with politicians.
5 Politicians' *personal* / *personality* lives should remain private.
6 People who don't vote have let down their *communal* / *community*.

## GRAMMAR

**A Complete the article with the words or phrases in the box. There are five you do not need to use.**

as a matter of fact   conversely   despite
for instance   in any case   moreover
namely   owing to   whereas   yet

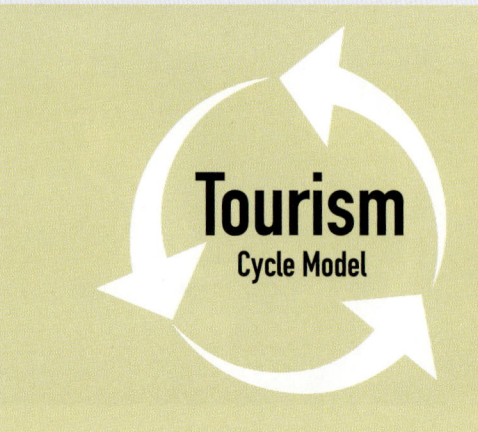

### Tourism Cycle Model

Tourist sites go through similar stages as they grow. First of all, adventurous tourists start coming to a place. [1]_____ this interest, local people set up businesses to cater for tourists. They open hotels and restaurants, [2]_____. After that, larger companies start to invest in the area – [3]_____, by building large hotels and catering to large groups. The tourism industry begins to dominate the area, while, [4]_____, other industries begin to shrink. As the number of visitors increases, the area becomes less attractive and visitors begin to go elsewhere. [5]_____, the facilities begin to become dated and damaged. If there is no further investment, the area will go into decline.

**B Match numbers (1–6) to letters (a–f) to form full sentences.**

1 It's better to give money to a charity than
2 You should donate clothes or
3 Some charities are really wasteful with their donations
4 If a friend asks you to donate to a charity,
5 Some people are really good at volunteer work,
6 It's a good idea to choose one or two charities to support

a volunteer your time rather than give money.
b and when you do, you can give bigger donations.
c you should do so.
d to an individual.
e and I wish they weren't.
f but I'm not.

120 SOCIETY

# Irregular Verbs

| Infinitive | Past simple | Past participle |
|---|---|---|
| be | was/were | been |
| become | became | become |
| begin | began | begun |
| break | broke | broken |
| bring | brought | brought |
| build | built | built |
| buy | bought | bought |
| can | could | (been able to) |
| catch | caught | caught |
| choose | chose | chosen |
| come | came | come |
| cost | cost | cost |
| cut | cut | cut |
| drink | drank | drunk |
| eat | ate | eaten |
| fall | fell | fallen |
| feel | felt | felt |
| find | found | found |
| forget | forgot | forgotten |
| get | got | got |
| give | gave | given |
| go | went | gone/been |
| grow | grew | grown |
| have | had | had |
| hear | heard | heard |
| hit | hit | hit |
| hold | held | held |
| hurt | hurt | hurt |
| keep | kept | kept |
| know | knew | known |
| leave | left | left |
| lend | lent | lent |
| let | let | let |
| lose | lost | lost |
| make | made | made |
| mean | meant | meant |
| meet | met | met |
| must | had to | (had to) |
| pay | paid | paid |
| put | put | put |
| read | read /red/ | read /red/ |
| ride | rode | ridden |
| run | ran | run |
| say | said | said |
| see | saw | seen |
| sell | sold | sold |
| send | sent | sent |
| set | set | set |
| shut | shut | shut |
| sing | sang | sung |
| sit | sat | sat |
| sleep | slept | slept |
| speak | spoke | spoken |
| spell | spelt/spelled | spelt/spelled |
| spend | spent | spent |
| stand | stood | stood |
| steal | stole | stolen |
| take | took | taken |
| teach | taught | taught |
| tell | told | told |
| think | thought | thought |
| throw | threw | thrown |
| understand | understood | understood |
| wear | wore | worn |
| win | won | won |
| write | wrote | written |

## PHONETIC SYMBOLS

### Single vowels

| | | |
|---|---|---|
| /ɪ/ | fish | /fɪʃ/ |
| /iː/ | bean | /biːn/ |
| /ʊ/ | foot | /fʊt/ |
| /uː/ | shoe | /ʃuː/ |
| /e/ | egg | /eg/ |
| /ə/ | mother | /ˈmʌðə/ |
| /ɜː/ | word | /wɜːd/ |
| /ɔː/ | talk | /tɔːk/ |
| /æ/ | back | /bæk/ |
| /ʌ/ | bus | /bʌs/ |
| /ɑː/ | arm | /ɑːm/ |
| /ɒ/ | top | /tɒp/ |

### Diphthongs

| | | |
|---|---|---|
| /ɪə/ | ear | /ɪə/ |
| /eɪ/ | face | /feɪs/ |
| /ʊə/ | tourist | /ˈtʊərɪst/ |
| /ɔɪ/ | boy | /bɔɪ/ |
| /əʊ/ | nose | /nəʊz/ |
| /eə/ | hair | /heə/ |
| /aɪ/ | eye | /aɪ/ |
| /aʊ/ | mouth | /maʊθ/ |

### Consonants

| | | | | | |
|---|---|---|---|---|---|
| /p/ | pen | /pen/ | /s/ | snake | /sneɪk/ |
| /b/ | bag | /bæg/ | /z/ | zoo | /zuː/ |
| /t/ | tea | /tiː/ | /ʃ/ | shop | /ʃɒp/ |
| /d/ | dog | /dɒg/ | /ʒ/ | television | /ˈtelɪvɪʒən/ |
| /tʃ/ | chip | /tʃɪp/ | /m/ | map | /mæp/ |
| /dʒ/ | jazz | /dʒæz/ | /n/ | name | /neɪm/ |
| /k/ | cake | /keɪk/ | /ŋ/ | ring | /rɪŋ/ |
| /g/ | girl | /gɜːl/ | /h/ | house | /haʊs/ |
| /f/ | film | /fɪlm/ | /l/ | leg | /leg/ |
| /v/ | verb | /vɜːb/ | /r/ | road | /rəʊd/ |
| /θ/ | thing | /θɪŋ/ | /w/ | want | /wɒnt/ |
| /ð/ | these | /ðiːz/ | /j/ | yes | /jes/ |

# Grammar Hub

## 1.1 Nominal clauses

- Nominal clauses function like nouns. They can be used as the subject or object of a sentence, after a preposition, an adjective or the verb *to be*.
- Nominal *-ing* clause (also known as a 'participle clause'):

    *Wearing a uniform* can help people feel part of the team. (as subject)
    I don't enjoy *wearing formal clothes*. (as object)
    I'm excited about *buying some new outfits*. (after a preposition)

- Nominal *that* clause:

    *That she won again this year* is not surprising. (as subject: this use is rare)
    I explained *that she would have to buy a new outfit*. (as object)
    I'm worried *that I won't fit in*. (after an adjective)

- Nominal question clause:

    *What you wear* is entirely up to you. (as subject)
    My appearance certainly affects *how I feel*. (as object)
    Fiona felt embarrassed because of *how she looked*. (after a preposition)

- Nominal *to* + infinitive:

    *To spend so much money on clothes* is totally unnecessary. (as subject: this use is rare)
    It's a good idea *to wear smart clothes for an interview*. (as object)
    I was surprised *to learn about the dress code*. (after an adjective)

- We often use phrases like *The fact/idea that …* or *The experience/problem of …* to introduce a nominal clause.

    *The fact that you got a high grade* shows how hard you worked.
    *The experience of travelling on the Orient Express* was one she would never forget.

> **Be careful!**
> - Because *that* clauses and *to* + infinitive clauses can sometimes sound unnatural as subjects, we often use *it* as an empty subject.
>
>     *It doesn't surprise me that you hate shopping.*
>     NOT *That you hate shopping doesn't surprise me.*

## 1.2 Comparatives and superlatives

- We only use *than* after comparative adjectives and adverbs when it is followed by the thing we are comparing it with.

    *CDs are more expensive than they used to be.*

> **Be careful!**
> *CDs are only fractionally more expensive today.* NOT *CDs are only fractionally more expensive than today.*

- We don't put *the* before a superlative when we use a determiner.

    *Here's our cheapest smartphone.*
    NOT *Here's our the cheapest smartphone.*

- To compare things that are the same, we can use *as* + adjective/adverb + *as* …

    *Dance music is as popular as it ever was.*

- We leave out the second + *as* when the adjective/adverb isn't followed by the thing we're comparing it with.

    *None of our audiences have been as large!*
    NOT *None of our audiences have been as large as!*

- We can use *the … the* with comparatives to show that two changes are closely connected. As one thing changes, it makes the other thing change.

    *The cheaper the technology, the worse quality it is.*
    *The bigger, the better!*

- We can use the structure *more than* with a small number of verbs (*compensate for, double, fulfil, make up for, meet*)

    *His enthusiasm and intelligence more than compensated for his lack of experience.*

- To show that there is a big difference between two things we can use one of these modifiers before the comparative adjective: *a good/great deal, a lot, considerably, dramatically, far, significantly, much*.

    *The new building is considerably bigger than the old one.*

- To show that there is a small difference, we use these words and phrases before the comparative adjective: *a bit/little, a fraction, fractionally, marginally, rather, slightly, somewhat*.

    *The first film was fractionally longer than the sequel.*

- We can modify superlative adjectives using: *by far, far and away, easily, the very*.

    *Tom is by far the cleverest boy in the class.*
    *Tom is the cleverest boy by far.*

- We can also make a superlative stronger by inserting *possible* after the superlative and before the noun.

    *The shopping centre was built in the best possible location.*

- We can also use modifiers before the structure *as … as*: *almost, at least, easily, every bit, half, just, twice*.

    *My old phone was every bit as good as this new one.*

# Grammar Hub

## 1.1 Nominal clauses

**A** Correct the mistakes in each sentence.
1 It's an unwritten rule what employees must stick to the dress code.
2 The fact of you wear a uniform sends a certain message about your status.
3 You'll regret not to wear smarter clothes to yesterday's interview.
4 David insisted on that he pay for all the designer clothes I'd chosen!
5 The reason for Sarah's absence that she never received her invitation.
6 That I had forgotten was that the restaurant only lets in smartly dressed customers.
7 The clothing company more than double its annual profits.
8 Sandra always wants to buy clothes at the possible lowest price.

**B** Choose the correct options to complete the conversation.

Joey: I'm really keen ¹*to start / about starting* my new job next week.
Phoebe: I'm sure ²*you to / that you will* fit in really well.
Joey: They explained ³*that they have / having* a dress code there. So … ⁴*that I buy / buying* a smart suit is my first priority! Will you come and help me choose one?
Phoebe: Of course. I think you should be prepared ⁵*to spend / that you spend* quite a bit of money.
Joey: What do you mean?
Phoebe: You must know ⁶*that / the fact* an expensive suit will last longer than a cheap one?
Joey: Oh, I see ⁷*what / that* you mean. OK. But ⁸*I'm needing to know / what I really need to know* is what colour to choose!

**C** Complete the second sentence so that it has a similar meaning to the first sentence, using the word given. Write between two and five words.

1 That designer clothes are hugely expensive is well-known.
FACT

_____
designer clothes are hugely expensive is well-known.

2 It's none of my business what he does in his free time.
SPENDS

_____
his free time is none of my business.

3 The purchase of expensive school uniforms is a problem which many parents face.
OF

Many parents face _____
_____ expensive school uniforms.

▶ Go back to page 3.

## 1.2 Comparatives and superlatives

**A** Choose the correct options to complete the sentences.
1 Thank goodness I have tech-savvy friends like you – you're _____.
   a the best     b the best friend
2 I think we need to replace our company logo with something _____.
   a funkier than     b funkier
3 Winning the Young Tech Designer of the Year was _____ moment!
   a the my proudest     b my proudest
4 Your handwriting is _____ Carol. Well done!
   a the neatest handwriting     b the neatest
5 We've redesigned our website so that it's _____.
   a more user-friendly     b user-friendlier
6 CDs weren't around for very long, and CD burners disappeared almost _____.
   a as quickly     b as quickly as

**B** Write one word in each gap to complete the sentences.
1 My sister is a great _____ more concerned about appearances than I am.
2 A tailored jacket is _____ and away the most important item of clothing in your wardrobe.
3 I dress _____ fraction more informally on Fridays, but I don't feel comfortable in casual clothes.
4 In my opinion, having the right image is every _____ as important as saying the right thing.
5 Chelsea only ever buys the _____ best in terms of clothing and accessories.

**C** Complete the sentences using a word from the box and your own ideas.

| considerably   half   marginally   twice |

1 The green dress costs €25. The blue dress costs €27.
   The blue dress costs _____.
2 My sister is a fashion vlogger and earns ten times more than I do!
   My sister earns _____.
3 We were expecting 100 people at the fashion show, but only 50 came.
   Only _____ we expected came to the fashion show.
4 I believe that you have to do double the work of others to be sure of success.
   I believe that you have to work _____.

▶ Go back to page 7.

# Grammar Hub

## 2.1 Narrative tenses

| | Active | Passive |
|---|---|---|
| Past simple | **I realised** it was a great idea. | **We were given** a month to finish the job. |
| Past continuous | **We were hoping** for a better result. | **The plans were being drawn up** at the time. |
| Past perfect simple | **They had already bought** the site. | **The architects had been chosen.** |
| Past perfect continuous | **We had been walking** for hours. | |

- We use the past simple in a story or narrative to explain the main events.

  *We **met** on Saturday, outside Victoria train station.*

- We use the past continuous to describe the background to a story, actions in progress at a particular point or, together with the past simple, to describe actions or situations that were interrupted by shorter events.

  *The sun **was shining** when Amy **left** the house.*

- We use the past perfect simple to show that one event happened before the other.

  *He **had waited** for over an hour by the time she finally arrived.*

- We use the past perfect continuous, often together with the past simple, for actions that were in progress before another action in the past.

  *I **had been working** all day so I **decided** not to go out that night.*

- We can use the past simple with *did* + infinitive for emphasis.

  *He **did** look very anxious when he left.*

> **Be careful!**
> - We don't often use the passive form of past perfect continuous.
>
>   *Someone had been watching us.* NOT *We had been being watched.*

## 2.2 Future in the past

| | Future in the past |
|---|---|
| Past continuous | We **were travelling** to Australia the next day. |
| *was/were going to* | Sam **was going to start** looking for another job. |
| *would* + infinitive | I thought it **would be** nice to take a gift. |
| *was/were to* + infinitive | Jody **was to contact** me as soon as her plane landed. |
| *was/were to* + perfect infinitive | Jody **was to have contacted** me as soon as her plane landed. |
| *was/were about to* + infinitive | We **were about to leave** the house when the phone rang. |

- When we are talking about the past, we sometimes need to talk about things that had not yet happened. We can use the past continuous or *was/were going to* for this.

  *When I saw her, she **was leaving** the next day.*
  *Jim **was going to** meet Mary that evening.*

- We can use the past form of *will* (*would*).

  *That discovery **would turn** out to be important later on.*

- We can also use past forms of the verb *be* with the infinitive or the perfect infinitive. The infinitive can be used for events that came true or didn't come true.

  *He **was to deliver** the report on Tuesday. (And he did.)*
  *He **was to deliver** the report on Tuesday. (But he failed.)*

  The perfect infinitive is usually only used for events that didn't come true.

  *He **was to have delivered** the report on Tuesday. (But he failed.)*

- We can also use past forms of *be* + *supposed to* + infinitive or perfect infinitive. These are often, but not always, used for events that didn't come true.

  *He **was supposed to have delivered** the report on Tuesday. (But he failed.)*
  *He **wasn't supposed to look** at the files. (But he did anyway.)*

- To describe something that was going to happen soon, we use the past form of the verb *be* with the word *about*. Sometimes we add the word *just*.

  *She had her coat on because she **was** (just) **about to take** the dog for a walk.*

> **Be careful!**
> - You may need to make other changes to pronouns, times, places, etc, in the same way as you do in reported speech.
>
>   *Anna was leaving for Canada the following day.*
>   NOT *Anna was leaving for Canada tomorrow.*

# Grammar Hub

## 2.1 Narrative tenses

**A** Choose the option in each sentence that is NOT correct.

1 I ___ what he meant.
   a had finally been understanding
   b finally understood
   c had finally understood

2 ___ to wait in the reception area.
   a They told me
   b I was telling
   c I was told

3 Jim had been swimming earlier and his hair ___ wet.
   a was
   b had got
   c was getting

4 Angie was shocked by what she ___ at the film festival.
   a had seen
   b saw
   c has seen

5 He had got the job but he ___ the starting date.
   a hadn't been being told
   b wasn't told
   c hadn't been told

6 It was a terrible day and it ___ heavily.
   a was raining
   b had been raining
   c had been rained

**B** Correct the underlined mistakes. Sometimes more than one answer is possible.

1 I realised I <u>left</u> my money at home.
2 When I looked out of the window, I saw that it <u>rained</u>.
3 I <u>did to realise</u> that I had forgotten my keys before I left.
4 Janine changed her mind about the theatre but it was too late as I <u>already bought</u> the tickets.
5 We arrived a little early and we <u>told</u> to wait until the manager was free.
6 Greg went to see the doctor because he <u>wasn't being feeling</u> well.
7 As soon as we had finished the discussion, we <u>had left</u>.

**C** Complete each sentence with the correct form of the verb in brackets, active or passive. Sometimes more than one answer is possible.

1 I was angry because _____ (I / keep) waiting for an hour.
2 The sun was shining and the birds _____ (sing) in the trees.
3 The reason I was tired was that I _____ (have to / walk) all the way home.
4 We _____ (only / work) on the project for a week when it was cancelled.
5 Pete _____ (not / tell) about the change of plans so he knew nothing.
6 We couldn't use the living room because it _____ (decorate).

➤ Go back to page 17.

## 2.2 Future in the past

**A** Choose the correct options to complete the sentences.

1 I couldn't go to the party because I *would take / was taking* a test the next day.
2 When we were at school together, he was *becoming / going to become* a doctor.
3 They thought it *will / would* be fun to play a trick on us.
4 Our new TV was to have been *delivered / delivering* yesterday but it didn't come.
5 I *was about / about to* ask him where he got the money when he made an excuse and left.
6 When the film was released, few people thought it *would be / was being* a success.
7 The fingerprints found at the scene of the crime *were being / were to be* vital in solving it.
8 Thinking there was no way he *was going / would* to get into university, he didn't even apply.

**B** Write one word in each gap to complete the sentences.

1 Sonja _____ about to get on the train when she realised she'd left her ticket at home.
2 Philippe couldn't believe he was actually _____ to graduate in three weeks' time.
3 We all knew it _____ be fun to enter the competition.
4 Both girls truly believed they _____ going to be famous one day.
5 At that point it dawned on me that London _____ to be my new home.
6 Marie was _____ about to give in her report when she spotted the mistake.

➤ Go back to page 21.

# Grammar Hub

## 3.1 Future structures

- We can use a variety of grammatical forms to express the future, such as future forms with *will*, the present simple, the present continuous and *be going to*.

  *They'll plant some more trees over the next few weeks.*
  *When does the presentation begin?*
  *I'm going to install solar panels on my roof.*

- We use the future continuous (*will be* + *-ing*) to describe a situation that will be in progress at a particular point in the future.

  *Scientists will be making an important announcement at 3 pm.*

- We use the future perfect simple (*will have* + past participle) to describe changes that will be completed before a particular point in the future.

  *He will have fixed the air-conditioning by the end of the day.*

- We can use the future perfect simple with adverbs in the middle position after *will*.

  *Pollution in our city will **surely** have impacted quality of life by the end of the next decade.*

- We use the future perfect continuous (*will have been* + *-ing*) to focus on the future results of an earlier future process, and/or to measure the length of time of that process.

  *The crew will have been tearing down the old factory for twelve weeks by the end of June.*

### Be careful!

- We usually don't use *will* after words which signal conditional sentences such as *if*, *unless*, *when*, *while*. So we use present continuous instead of future continuous, and present perfect instead of future perfect.

  *She'll be hanging up flyers while I'm meeting with the council.* NOT *She'll be hanging up flyers while I'll be meeting with the council.*

- We can use a modal verb such as *may*, *might* or *could* instead of *will* in these future structures to express possibility.

  *They'll be switching to renewable energy soon.* (= definitely)
  *They could be switching to renewable energy soon.* (= it's possible)

- We also use phrases such as *be on the verge of* + *-ing*, *be on the brink of* + *-ing*, *be due to* + infinitive, *be set to* + infinitive, and *be about to* + infinitive to refer to the future.

  *Danielle **was on the verge of achieving** her goal.*

## 3.2 Negative inversion

- We use negative inversion when we want to emphasise a negative element of a sentence. We place the negative element at the beginning and we invert (= swap over) the subject and auxiliary verb.

  *I have never seen such waste in my life.* = ***Never have I seen** such waste in my life.*
  *I'm not saying we need to leave now.* = ***By no means am I saying** we need to leave now.*
  ***No way could I ever drive** a petrol-powered car again.*

- We add *do*, *does* or *did* in inverted clauses when there is no auxiliary verb.

  *She never received an apology.* = *Never **did** she receive an apology.*

- We use *than* after the phrase *no sooner*.

  *No sooner had she written the document **than** her computer crashed.*

- Inversion is often used with the structure *not only … but also*.

  *Not only did I meet the chancellor, but I also met the environment minister.*

- Some words and phrases change in inversions, and negative verbs become positive.

  ***Nobody** told me about that once.* → *Not once did **anybody** tell me about that.*
  *You **mustn't** say that under **any** circumstances.* → *Under **no** circumstances **must** you say that.*
  *That's **not** the only solution by **any** means.* → *By **no** means **is that** the only solution.*

- There are also some inversions which do not contain negative words and phrases. These include sentences which start with *only* for time expressions, such as *Only after*, *Only when*, *Only once*, *Only if*, *Only by*, *Only rarely*, and *Rarely*, *Hardly* and *Barely*.

  *Only by reading the instructions three times did I understand what to do.*

### Be careful!

- With some inversions, such as *No sooner … than*, *Not only*, *Hardly*, etc, it's the first verb and the subject which inverts.

  *Not only **was he late**, he was also unprepared.*
  *Hardly **had we sat down** when the fire alarm went off.*

- With other inversions, such as *Only after*, *Not until*, etc, it's the verb in the main clause which inverts.

  *Only after I'd arrived **did I realise** I'd got the day wrong.*
  *Not until he'd spent hours online **did he find** a suitable photo.*

- We don't use inversion when the negative word or phrase is the subject.

  *None of my colleagues take public transport.*
  NOT *None of my colleagues do take public transport.*

- The verb and subject invert after *neither* and *nor*.

  *None of their staff knew the answer, and **neither did we**.*
  *I haven't told anyone, and **nor has Jake**.*

## Grammar Hub

### 3.1 Future structures

**A** Match the statements (1–7) with their purposes (a–g).

1 We're going to build a zero-emissions home. ___
2 I'll call the manager, if you like. ___
3 I think you'll be famous someday! ___
4 When are they going to close down that factory? ___
5 The talk begins at 10 am. ___
6 I think I'll just take the bus instead. ___
7 With all these clouds, it's going to rain very soon! ___

a making a prediction from strong evidence
b explaining plans
c talking about a fixed scheduled event
d making a prediction based on opinion more than evidence
e making an offer
f asking about plans
g making a decision while speaking

**B** Choose the correct options to complete the sentences.

1 We'll *be testing* / *have tested* the new equipment for a few hours tomorrow.
2 They'll have *been laying* / *laid* the foundation by the end of next week.
3 I'll *be meeting* / *have met* Jim later today, if you'd like to join us.
4 Will you have *be working* / *been working* with the company for very long when you retire?
5 The company will have *built* / *been* building two new hotels by the end of the year.
6 They won't *have taken* / *be taking* questions from the audience after the talk.
7 By the time she finishes the marathon, Kayla will *have jogged* / *been jogging* for six hours.
8 He'll probably still be working unless he *decides* / *will decide* to leave it for next week.

**C** Complete the second sentence so that it has a similar meaning as the first sentence. Use between two and five words, including the word in bold.

1 Thirty minutes from now, the meeting will conclude. **DUE**
   The meeting _____ conclude in half an hour.
2 The scientists will make the discovery any day now. **VERGE**
   The scientists are _____ the discovery.
3 In less than a minute, the rocket will launch. **ABOUT**
   The rocket _____ launched.
4 The two companies are close to sealing the deal. **BRINK**
   The two companies _____ sealing the deal.
5 By the end of the year, the agreement will have expired. **SET**
   The agreement is _____ by year's end.
6 I'll be collecting samples and she'll be recording them. **WHILE**
   She'll be recording samples _____ them.

➤ Go back to page 26.

---

### 3.2 Negative inversion

**A** Rewrite the sentences (1–6) using inversion and the words given.

1 Nobody asked me if I passed my driving test.
   Not once _____.
2 I'd just arrived home when they called me back to the office.
   No sooner _____.
3 We seldom see players with such natural ability.
   Rarely _____.
4 He is really clever and incredibly funny.
   Not only _____.
5 Tina realised her purse had been stolen when she went to pay her bill.
   Only when _____.
6 You must not open that door.
   Under no circumstances _____.

**B** Write one word in each gap.

Anna was in charge of organising her company's annual conference. She had met the manager a week before to settle the plans, and no ¹_____ had they sat down to talk than the manager was called away. She waited forty-five minutes, and ²_____ until she got up to leave did the manager re-appear. On the day of the conference, ³_____ no means did everything go according to plan. Not ⁴_____ was the turnout low, but she ⁵_____ had trouble with the conference venue. ⁶_____ in a million years would she have thought things could go so wrong.

➤ Go back to page 31.

# Grammar Hub

## 4.1 Conditionals without *if*

We can use inversions to replace the word *if* in some conditional sentences.

- In first conditional sentences, we can use *should* to replace *if*.

    *Should you have any questions, please don't hesitate to call.* (= If you have … OR If you should have … )

- In second conditional sentences, we can use *were* to replace *if*.

    *Were it banned, there would be an outcry.* (= If it were banned… )
    *Were I to do the quiz, I'm sure I would win!* (= If I were to do … )

- In third conditional sentences, we can use *had* to replace *if*. This use of inversion is more common in formal language.

    *Had he used a brain training game, he would have remembered more.* (= If he had used … )

- We can also sometimes use verbs, *-ing*, past participles and the imperative in place of *if*.

| Imagine / Suppose (that) | **Suppose** (that) I had a chip in my brain, would I be smarter? |
| Assuming / Supposing / Presuming / Providing (that) | **Assuming** (that) you complete the experiment, will you have all the data? |
| | **Providing** (that) we didn't make any mistakes, the results should be correct. |
| Provided (that) | **Provided** (that) you believe in yourself, you will definitely succeed. |
| Imperative … , and | **Read** more books, **and** you will improve your memory. |

### Be careful!

- With the imperative and *Imagine/Suppose (that)*, you cannot swap the clauses round.

    *Imagine you were offered a brain implant, would you want it?*
    NOT *Would you want a brain implant imagine you were offered it?*

## 4.2 Wishes and regrets

| | | |
|---|---|---|
| wish / if only + past simple/continuous | to wish that the present was different | **I wish / If only I didn't blush** so easily. |
| wish / if only + could/would | | **I wish / If only I could stop** stammering. |
| | | **I wish / If only you would speak** more clearly. |
| wish / if only + past perfect simple/continuous | to wish that the past was different | **I wish / If only I had participated** in the study. |
| wish / if only + could have + past participle | | **I wish / If only I could have participated** in the study. |
| ought (not) to / should (not) have + past participle | | |
| ought (not) to / should (not) have been + -ing | | **I shouldn't have gazed** at the floor all the time! |

- *If only* often sounds more dramatic or emphatic than *wish*. It can be used about other people, but usually suggests the speaker's opinion.

    *If only David had known the answer!* (= I wish David had known the answer!)

- To be more formal, we use *were* instead of *was* after *I/he/she/it*.

    *If only I were more confident.*
    *He wishes he were more confident.*

- When you want to talk about your own wishes, use *could* instead of *would*.

    *I wish I could speak Chinese.* NOT *I wish I would speak Chinese.*

- We can also use *ought to have* + past participle to talk about things that were ideal or desired in the past.

    *They ought to have managed the meeting better.*

- We can use *would love to have* + past participle to talk about regrets.

    *I would love to have had enough time to explain my views.* (= I didn't have enough time and that's a shame.)

- We can also use *if* + past perfect simple + modal verbs (subordinate clause) and modal verb + *have* + past participle to talk about imagined situations in the past with regret.

    *I could have learned more, if I had prepared for the classes.*

# Grammar Hub

## 4.1 Conditionals without *if*

**A** Complete each second sentence so it means the same as the one before it.

1. If I had dropped my coffee on her carpet, I would have felt embarrassed!
   Had _____, I would have felt embarrassed!
2. If brain implants were available to everyone, I would definitely get one!
   Should _____, I would definitely get one!
3. If you practised Sudoku puzzles more, you would get better at them.
   Were _____, you would get better at them.
4. If you become dizzy after taking the medication, please contact your doctor.
   Should _____, please contact your doctor.

**B** Choose the correct options to complete the sentences.

1. *Imagine / Imagining* that you met Elon Musk, what would you say to him?
2. *Suppose / Providing* that we didn't make any errors during the experiment, the data should be correct.
3. *Look / Suppose* we look at the problem from a different angle, we might be able to find a solution.
4. *Imagine / Assuming* that she told us the truth, I think we can conclude that she's innocent.
5. *Supposing / Provided* all the participants had been men, would that have made a difference to the results?
6. *Conducting / Conduct* more research, and you will have a clearer picture.

**C** Complete the sentences with the correct form of the verbs in brackets.

1. _____ (act) confidently, and you will never again feel embarrassed.
2. Suppose you _____ (arrive) late for an exam, what would you do?
3. Provided that you think before you speak, you _____ (not say) anything silly.
4. Were I _____ (say) the wrong thing, I would apologise.
5. Assuming you _____ (prove) he was cheating, would you tell the examiner?
6. Should AI become a reality, we _____ (need) to improve human intelligence.
7. _____ (I know) that the research was unethical, I would never have taken part in it.
8. Unless the government _____ (increase) funding for the programme, the researchers will never be able to complete their study.

▶ Go back to page 41.

---

## 4.2 Wishes and regrets

**A** Choose the correct options to complete the sentences.

1. I wish I had made a better first impression. = I *made / didn't make* a good impression.
2. I wish I could understand what the lecturer was saying. = I *understand / don't understand*.
3. You shouldn't have been so clumsy! = You *were / weren't* clumsy.
4. Helena wishes her new boss was more friendly. = Her new boss *is / isn't* friendly.
5. I would love to have taken part in the experiment. = I *took / didn't take* part.
6. You ought not to have worn that eccentric outfit. = You *wore / didn't wear* an eccentric outfit.
7. If only I didn't feel so socially awkward. = I *feel / don't feel* socially awkward.
8. If only he could express himself more clearly. = He *is / isn't* able to express himself clearly.

**B** Complete the sentences with the correct form of the verbs in brackets.

1. I wish I _____ (prepare) more thoroughly for my interview yesterday.
2. If only I _____ (know) whether or not I've got the job!
3. I wish I _____ (can / get) her autograph but I wasn't brave enough.
4. If only I _____ (not / say) that I'm disorganised!
5. I wish I _____ (can / think) clearly under pressure but I get so stressed.
6. I wish I _____ (not / have to) go through job interviews!

**C** Correct the mistakes in each sentence.

1. You shouldn't have copy your essay from the internet.
2. The girls wish they was on holiday.
3. You could had told me the truth – I would have believed you!
4. I would love to had taken part in the research.
5. The scientists ought to have make their findings public.
6. Gemma doesn't wish she was so shy.
7. If only I hadn't get embarrassed with new people.
8. I could have done better, if I haven't been so nervous.

▶ Go back to page 43.

# Grammar Hub

## 5.1 The passive

| | Passive |
|---|---|
| *make* sb do sth | We **were made to wait** for over an hour. |
| Passive with *-ing* | I hate **being kept** waiting. |
| Passive with infinitive | He would like **to be given** the chance to retake the test. |
| *get* passive (informal) | They **got thrown** off the course. |
| Causative *have* and *get* | I need to **have** my phone **serviced**. |

- Remember that we use the passive when we don't say who or what causes the action (usually because the person or thing is not known, not important or not obvious).

  *We were made to sit the exam again. NOT We were made by the examination board to sit the exam again.*

- We use *by* when we know who does/did an action and we want to mention it.

  *I don't mind being told by my boss to work late but I don't like it when I have to cover for other people.*

- We can use an infinitive or *-ing* passive form, depending on the verb or construction that comes before it. Some verbs can be followed by an infinitive or *-ing* with no or little change in meaning. Prepositions are always followed by *-ing*.

  *We arranged to be paid in cash.*
  *I appreciated being told about the delay.*
  *The child loved to be / being thrown up in the air.*
  *Johnny never talks about being thrown out of college.*

- We use the causative (in any tense) when someone does something for us, or when we are victims of a crime or accident. The causative with *have* is more formal than the causative with *get*.

  *I got my hair cut. OR I had my wallet stolen on the train.*

- We can use *get* + object + past participle when we talk about causing something to happen or be done by somebody else.

  *She is popular because she gets things done.*
  *They are angry because they are not getting their parcels delivered on time.*

- We can also use *get* + object + *-ing* to talk about causing someone or something to do something.

  *The book on game theory got Susan thinking.*

> **Be careful!**
> - In both the *get* passive and the causative, *get* is usually less formal than *have*. Don't use it in formal situations.
>
>   *The letter asked us when we had had the house built. NOT The letter asked us when we had got the house built.*

## 5.2 Passive reporting structures

- Some verbs, such as *allege, assume, believe, expect, know, say, report, rumour, suppose, understand*, are often used in the passive as reporting verbs. The verb *rumour* can only be used in this way.

- We often use the impersonal *it* with these verbs.

  *It is rumoured that the Prime Minister will announce her resignation today.* (= There is a rumour that …)

- With an impersonal *it* passive, we can follow the reporting verb with either an infinitive or *that*.

  *It is understood to be a complicated situation.*
  *It is understood that the situation is complicated.*

- With a personal reporting structure, beginning with *I/you/he/she/it/we/they*, we use the past participle of the reporting verb, followed by *to* + infinitive.

| *to* + infinitive | He **is known to be** a thief. |
|---|---|
| *to* + continuous infinitive | She **is thought to be planning** a comeback. |
| *to* + perfect infinitive | They **are rumoured to have started** a secret mission. |
| *to* + perfect continuous infinitive | They **are believed to have been watching** us. |

- We can sometimes use modal verbs before the reporting verb.

  *It can be assumed that the business is still profitable.*

- In both personal and impersonal constructions, we can use the reporting verb in the past if we are referring to something people *expected/knew/thought*, etc. However, if the action was done in the past, and we are reporting it now, the verbs must reflect this.

  *He was known to be hiding.*
  *It was thought that they had failed.*
  *He is understood to have made contact.*
  *It is believed that he discovered America.*

> **Be careful!**
> - Do not use *that* in a personal passive (one that begins with *I/You/He/She*, etc).
>
>   *He is rumoured to be planning to make cuts. NOT He is rumoured that he is planning to make cuts.*

# Grammar Hub

## 5.1 The passive

**A** Find the mistakes and correct them. Some sentences are correct.
1 I was made to fill in pages of details on the form.
2 I dislike to be spoken to as if I don't understand anything.
3 He looks forward to be spoiled when he visits his family.
4 In my school, we used to get told off for the slightest things.
5 You look different – have you had your hair done?
6 Do you know what we were made do in the intelligence test?

**B** Complete the sentences with the correct -ing or infinitive passive form of the verb in brackets.
1 I miss _____ spend summer holidays on the beach. (*be able to*)
2 Justine begged _____ for the things she'd said in anger. (*forgive*)
3 The taller kids tended _____ for basketball, regardless of their ability. (*choose*)
4 The manager wouldn't tolerate _____ with. (*disagree*)
5 Paul didn't mention _____ by the police – do you think he's hiding something? (*stop*)
6 He couldn't remember _____ onto an elephant, although he had the photo to prove it had happened. (*lift*)

**C** Complete the sentences in the passive or causative.
1 Active: They made him sign the document.
   Passive: He _____.
2 Active: If you're not careful, they'll throw you out.
   Passive: If you're not careful, you'll _____.
3 Active: I'd like to know how much it costs for you to clean my car professionally.
   Causative: I'd like to know how much it costs to _____.
4 Active: How on earth are we going to find someone to repair that window on a Sunday?
   Causative: How on earth are we going to get _____?
5 Active: I'm sure they didn't tell me to be here half an hour early.
   Passive: I don't remember _____.
6 Active: Someone will steal your car if you leave it there.
   Causative: You'll get _____.

➤ Go back to page 51.

## 5.2 Passive reporting structures

**A** Choose the correct options to complete the sentences.
1 We are supposed *to be / to be being* there at nine o'clock.
2 It is rumoured *to be / that* the company is in difficulty.
3 Two members of staff are alleged to *transfer / have transferred* money into private accounts.
4 It *is / was* originally thought that they were related.
5 They are believed to *plan / be planning* a trip abroad.
6 The police are known to *be / have been* following him for the past few months.
7 It was thought that there *was / to be* a secret tunnel, but nothing has been found.
8 On her first day, *it / she* was expected to write three reports.

**B** Complete the text with a suitable form of the verbs in the box.

announce   discuss   focus   look   make   plan

### Director disputes

Home   Articles   About us   Contact

Following tomorrow's meeting, Collins is expected ¹_____ his resignation. The company is thought ²_____ to specialise in the near future. They are expected ³_____ on only one product, and Collins is known ⁴_____ his objections to this very clear on several occasions in the past. Although Collins is understood ⁵_____ the situation with top management for several weeks, the company is now rumoured ⁶_____ for a way to force him out.

**C** Rewrite the sentences using both personal and impersonal passive structures. Use the reporting verb in bold.
1 People **believe** he is very rich.
   He _____.
   It _____.
2 Some people **report** that he was awarded over one million dollars.
   He _____.
   It _____.
3 They **say** she knows her subject inside out.
   She _____.
   It _____.
4 Critics **claim** that the game's story is too complex.
   The game _____.
   It _____.
5 Many **think** that it is a complex problem.
   The problem _____.
   It _____.
6 People **assume** she is shy but she's just quiet.
   She is _____.
   It is _____.

➤ Go back to page 55.

# Grammar Hub

## 6.1 Past modals of speculation and deduction

- We use *must* + *have* + past participle for things we believe logically happened.

  *It's a huge book, so it **must have taken** her a long time to research and write.*

- We use *could/might/may well* + *have* + past participle for things we believe likely happened.

  *They're still not sure what caused the fire but it **may well have been started** deliberately.*

- We use *could/might/may* + *have* + past participle for things we think possibly happened.

  *The plane **might have crashed** in the mountains but they never found the wreckage.*

- We use *can't/couldn't* + *have* + past participle to say something was not logically possible.

  *They **couldn't have built** this massive fort in just a week.*

### Be careful!

- Although *could/might/may have* + past participle all mean the same thing, *might/may not have* expresses possibility, whereas *couldn't have* expresses certainty.

  *It's possible that Aled didn't see the email. = Aled may/might not have seen the email. NOT Aled couldn't have seen the email.*

- We can use phrases that start with *There is* + *a/an/the* + adjective + noun + (*that*) to speculate, with adjectives such as *distinct*, *fair*, *high*, *remote*, *slim* and *slight*, and nouns such as *chance*, *likelihood* and *possibility*.

  *There is a **distinct possibility that** he picked up the illness while in the jungle.*

- We can also use phrases that start with *It is* + adverb + adjective + (*that*) to speculate, with adverbs such as *extremely*, *highly*, *reasonably*, *somewhat* and *quite*, and adjectives such as *likely* and *possible*.

  *It's **quite possible that** rival explorers sabotaged their plans.*

## 6.2 -ing and infinitive forms

- We use *-ing* after a preposition.

  *She praised the journalist **for exposing** the injustice.*
  *They're not interested **in finding** out the truth.*

- We also use *-ing* after expressions such as *It's no good…*, *It's not worth…*, *There's no point (in)…* and *…have a good time/difficulty/fun/problems…* .

  *It's **not worth publishing** the article if it will get you fired.*
  *There's **no point (in) helping** people who are ungrateful.*
  *You'll **have difficulty justifying** that answer.*

- We use *to* + infinitive after adjectives, nouns, quantifiers and the word *time*.

  *She's **eager to get** started on her work.*
  *They urged **people to take** shelter in the new facility.*
  *The report is lengthy, and there's **too much to read** in one night.*
  *Let's pick a good **time to review** the materials.*

### Be careful!

- We use *to* + infinitive after the word *time*, but after the phrase *have a good/great time…*, we use *-ing*.

  *It's time to make a decision. NOT It's time making a decision.*
  *We had a great time painting the wall. NOT We had a great time to paint the wall.*

- Some verbs can be followed by *-ing* (e.g. *appreciate*, *suggest*) and some can be followed by *to* + infinitive (e.g. *attempt*, *manage*). Some can be followed by either, usually with a change of meaning (e.g. *remember*, *stop*, *try*).

  *Why don't you **try doing** some research online?*
  *(= experiment)*
  *I **tried to get** in touch with Jan but couldn't find her anywhere.*
  *(= attempt)*

- We can use *-ing* or infinitive without *to* after the object of sense verbs like *hear*, *see*, etc. The infinitive without *to* emphasises a complete action that is seen or heard, while the *-ing* emphasises an ongoing activity.

  *I **saw her drinking** the coffee.*
  *(= The action was in progress. I didn't see her finish the coffee.)*
  *I **saw her drink** the coffee.*
  *(= The action was completed. I saw her finish the coffee.)*

# Grammar Hub

## 6.1 Past modals of speculation and deduction

**A** Find and correct mistakes in some of the sentences.

1. You may have been exhausted after such a long journey.
2. She must be lying. She might not have travelled all that distance in one day. It's impossible!
3. They could have taken a wrong turning, but it's hard to tell at this stage.
4. He must well have taken his bike with him as he loves cycling.
5. Janessa couldn't possibly have climbed Mt Kilimanjaro with a broken ankle.
6. She can't have been a globetrotter in her youth because she has souvenirs from all round the world.
7. Jonathan must not have got our message. I suppose we'll only find out when we hear from him.
8. They must have already left because their room is empty and their bags are gone.

**B** Choose the correct options to complete the sentences.

1. There is *a distinct possibility* / *extremely possible* that they checked in under a false name.
2. It is *a slim chance* / *somewhat likely* that the courier company had the wrong address.
3. There's *highly possible* / *a remote chance* that the Sphinx was carved more than 10,000 years ago.
4. There isn't *the slightest possibility* / *highly unlikely* that anyone survived that plane crash.
5. It's not *a distinct likelihood* / *completely impossible* that she made her way out of the cave alive.
6. There's *somewhat possible* / *a reasonable chance* that Geoff kept copies of all the correspondence.

**C** Complete the text with the words in the box.

| couldn't   it   might   must   there   well |

Cabeza de Vaca may ¹_____ have been one of the luckiest and unluckiest explorers ever. Of the 600 men on his 1527 expedition to the Americas, he was one of only four to survive. While they probably imagined a difficult journey, they ²_____ have known the misfortune that awaited them. They risked it because ³_____ was a possibility of finding gold. Before they even set foot on land, 100 men deserted. They ⁴_____ have been too exhausted to continue.

Shortly before reaching the coast, a hurricane killed 60 more. On land, the Apalachee people they encountered weren't very hospitable. ⁵_____ is likely they sensed the explorers' ill intentions. The Spanish tried to escape, and they ⁶_____ have been successful except for another hurricane! More men died, the natives in Texas enslaved them, and it was ten years before Cabeza de Vaca and his last three men were finally free.

➤ Go back to page 63.

---

## 6.2 -ing and infinitive forms

**A** Choose the correct options to complete the sentences.

1. It's no good ___ him for information. He doesn't give anything away.
   a to ask          b asking
2. It's time ___ our invention to the test!
   a putting         b to put
3. Despite putting his heart and soul into the project, he had a hard time ___ it.
   a to finish       b finishing
4. Even though the city has got money, they have little ___ to those in need.
   a to give         b giving
5. It's correct ___ that her life was a true rags-to-riches story.
   a saying          b to say
6. I'm not very keen on ___ a meeting on a Saturday.
   a to arrange      b arranging
7. The police didn't have enough evidence ___ the crime.
   a to solve        b solving
8. Jason found it harder ___ with his colleagues after the disagreement.
   a to work         b working

**B** Write the correct form of the verb in brackets.

1. Justin was disciplined for _____ (*express*) not finishing his assignment.
2. She brought food for the picnic, but there wasn't enough _____ (*go*) round.
3. It's not worth _____ (*do*) such hard work for so little money.
4. I'm sorry, but this is a bad time _____ (*discuss*) this topic.
5. Is she having difficulty _____ (*adjust*) to her new life?
6. They advised him on _____ (*invest*) in new business ventures.
7. There are many ideas here _____ (*help*) you get started on the project.
8. Your plan failed miserably. Have fun _____ (*explain*) that to the boss!
9. I saw them _____ (*steal*) the bike. I witnessed the whole thing from start to finish.

➤ Go back to page 67.

# Grammar Hub

## 7.1 *it* clefting

- We can use the structure *It + is/was +* 'focus' *+* defining relative clause to focus on a particular piece of information in a sentence. This focus could be:

| a person/people | It was **Tenzing Norgay and Edmund Hillary** who first reached the summit of Mount Everest. |
|---|---|
| a time | It was **1953** when Sir John Hunt successfully led the expedition to reach the summit of Mount Everest. |
| a place | It is **Mount Everest** which has always captured people's imaginations. |
| a thing or idea | It was **the challenge of the climb** which inspired generations of climbers. |
| a clause with *because* | It was **because he had almost reached the summit one year previously** that Tenzing Norgay was hired for the expedition. |
| a clause with *to +* infinitive | It was **to show his respect for the people of Nepal** that Sir Hunt asked Tenzing to make the final climb to the summit. |
| a clause with *until* | It wasn't **until years later that Tenzing revealed** which climber had first stepped onto the summit of Mount Everest. |

### Be careful!

- In sentences like this, we usually leave out the second defining relative clause to avoid repeating the same information.

  *It wasn't John Hunt who first climbed Everest – it was Edmund Hillary.*
  *NOT It wasn't John Hunt who first climbed Everest – it was Edmund Hillary who first climbed Everest.*

---

## 7.2 *what* clefting and *all* clefting

- We can use a *what* clause *+ be +* second clause in order to emphasise the information in the second clause.

  With this structure, the information in the *what* clause is usually known or understood whereas the information in the second clause is usually new and therefore the main focus of the sentence.

  *What Prianka wants is to escape the rat race.*
  *What they needed, after their walk in the snow, was a hot bath.*
  *What he decided to do was to change careers.*

- To emphasise a verb in the second clause, we can use the structure: *what* clause with *do + be +* second clause. We can use the infinitive with or without *to* after the verb *be*.

  *What he does is (to) climb cellular phone towers.*

- We can use *All* instead of *What* at the beginning of the first clause. This emphasises the idea of there being 'only one thing'.

  *All you need to do in the interview is (to) act naturally.* (= the only thing you need to do)

- It is also possible to use *Why, Where, How, When* to begin this kind of cleft sentence.

  *Why he enjoys extreme sports is a mystery to me.*

### Be careful!

- The structure *what* clause *+ be +* second clause is reversible.

  *What he enjoys about his job is living in the wilderness. OR Living in the wilderness is what he enjoys about his job.*

- The structure *what* clause with *do + be +* second clause is not reversible.

  *What they did was move to the countryside. NOT Move to the countryside was what they did.*

# Grammar Hub

## 7.1 *it* clefting

**A** Write one word in each gap to complete the responses.

1. Did you know that Jack was going to come with us?
   No, it _____ a surprise that he decided to come.
2. What time did Antonio arrive home?
   It was seven o'clock _____ I heard his key in the lock.
3. Was he worried about the cost of fixing his laptop?
   No, it was losing all his work _____ he was more worried about.
4. You've met my sister, haven't you?
   No, it was your brother _____ I met.
5. Did you recognise Stella straight away?
   No, it wasn't _____ somebody introduced us that I realised it was her!

**B** Read the questions. Use *it* clefting and the information in brackets to complete the answers.

1. What first got you interested in rock climbing? (*my friend Seb*)
   _____ first got me interested in the sport.
2. What do you think attracts people to Yosemite? (*the idea of being in the wilderness*)
   I think _____ attracts so many people to go there.
3. When did you set out to climb the Half Dome? (*early in the morning*)
   _____ we set out.
4. When did you realise how high the Half Dome is? (*only when I reached the top*)
   _____ I realised how high up it is!

**C** Complete the second sentence so that it has a similar meaning to the first sentence, using the word given. Write between two and five words.

1. Susan wasn't hysterical, Jane was.
   WAS
   It _____ hysterical, not Susan.
2. Not until after we were rescued did I realise the danger we had been in.
   UNTIL
   It _____ were rescued that I realised the danger we had been in.
3. We took part in the charity walk because we wanted to raise money.
   IT
   _____ money that we took part in the charity walk.
4. What caused her to fail the interview was her over-confidence.
   WAS
   It _____ caused her to fail the interview.
5. I believe yoga will help you to relax.
   THAT
   It _____ yoga will help you to relax.
6. Somebody else upset Mzia, not you.
   YOU
   It _____ upset Mzia.

▶ Go back to page 74.

## 7.2 *what* clefting and *all* clefting

**A** Reorder the words to make sentences.

1. about the winter / dislike / is / What / the long nights / I
   _____.
2. I / want / a normal life / All / is
   _____.
3. we're / a solution to our problems / to find / is / here / What
   _____.
4. the last train / we missed / happened / that / What / was
   _____.
5. I / to ask you / did / All / a simple question / was
   _____.
6. I / remember / All / is / really difficult / the questions / were / that
   _____.

**B** Rewrite these sentences using *what* clefting or *all* clefting.

1. I've found that working underwater isn't as bad as it sounds.
   What _____.
2. I'm only saying that you should think twice before moving to Antarctica.
   All _____.
3. I'm going to look for a job as a window cleaner.
   What _____.
4. I only asked for your opinion.
   All _____.
5. I bought a ladder and a bucket.
   What _____.

▶ Go back to page 79.

# Grammar Hub

## 8.1 Relative clauses with complex relative pronouns

- We use *whose* to add information about someone's possessions.

  *I was happy to meet Georgia, **whose** sister had helped me find a place to stay.*

- We use *whereby* to add information about a method (formal).

  *They introduced a new system in the company **whereby** everybody has a full induction on their first day.*

- We use *whom* to add information about a person where they are the object of the clause (formal).

  *The people **whom** I asked were all in favour of the plan.*

- In very formal English, we place the preposition (generally only with *whom*, *whose* and *which*) before the relative pronoun.

  *The Prime Minister, **in whose** honour the event was being held, welcomed all the guests.*
  *The person **on whom** I depend the most …*
  *The place **to which** I often return …*

- In less formal English, we put the preposition at the end of the clause.

  *Martin, **whose** house I was **staying in**, was a very tidy person.*
  *The person (who) I depend **on** the most …*
  *The place (which) I often return **to** …*

- Formal constructions can use a variety of prepositions depending on meaning.

  *The person **in whom** I have the most confidence …*
  *The person **to whom** I sent the letter …*
  *The person **for whom** the money was being raised …*

> **Be careful!**
>
> - The relative pronoun *whom* is very formal. We don't usually use it with a preposition at the end of the clause.
>
>   *The person to whom you gave the money …*
>   NOT *The person whom you gave the money to …*

## 8.2 Pronouns and determiners

- We use determiners before nouns to identify a number, an amount or a group.

  *We have **a few** tomatoes.*
  *I had **a couple of** cups of coffee while I was waiting.*
  *You need to get **some** fresh air.*

- Some common determiners include: *a/an*, *the*, *this/that/these/those*, *all*, *some (of)*, *none*, *(a) little*, *(a) few (of)*, *my/your/their/its*/etc, *any*, *much*, *more*, *both (of)*, *enough*, *a lot of*, *other*, *each/every*, *one/two/three*/etc, *either (of)*.

- We can use some common determiners like *millions of*, *loads of*, *tons of* when we want to exaggerate a point, especially in informal English.

  *I feel so guilty because I ate **loads of** chocolate last night.*

- Pronouns can be the same words as determiners but they are not followed by a noun. They replace the noun, often to avoid repeating it.

  *You look like you need water – I'll get you some.*
  NOT *You look like you need water – I'll get you some water.*

- Some common pronouns include: *I/he/they*/etc, *me/you/him/her*/etc, *this/that/these/those*, *there*, *some*, *mine/yours/his*/etc, *both*, *several*, *anyone/something*/etc, *others*, *none*, *either*.

- We can also use *one* or *one's* as pronouns to refer to people in general. These are especially used to make generalisations in formal English. *One's* indicates possession.

  *Diets make **one** realise how much food can impact **one's** life.*

> **Be careful!**
>
> - Some pronouns cannot be used as determiners.
>
>   *That glass is mine.* NOT *That is mine glass.*
>
> - Some determiners cannot be used as pronouns.
>
>   *That is my glass.* NOT *That glass is my.*

# Grammar Hub

## 8.1 Relative clauses with complex relative pronouns

**A** Choose the correct options to complete the sentences.

1. Do you know the name of the person to *who* / *whom* the letter must be addressed?
2. That's Melanie, *whose* / *who* mother is the manager of our company.
3. This is the mobile *which* / *whereby* I am most interested in.
4. His father, *to whom* / *whom* he would often go for financial help, had refused to give him more money.
5. We need to find a solution *whereby* / *which* everyone will be happy.
6. The new supermarket will benefit the villagers, *among whom* / *for whom* there are a number of families without cars.

**B** Complete each sentence with a word or phrase from the box.

| for whom   into which   into whose   whereby   whose   with which |

1. A pedometer is a mechanical or digital device _____ we count steps taken while walking.
2. The owner, _____ pocket the pedometer can be slipped, can then use it to calculate their distance travelled.
3. More recently, mobiles have started featuring fitness apps, _____ pedometers or 'step counters' have been incorporated.
4. Some experts claim that people _____ daily number of steps is lower than 10,000 should be concerned about their health and fitness.
5. Most fitness experts agree that any method _____ our steps can be counted is a useful one.
6. Pedometers make people _____ exercise is not a priority aware of their daily activity and motivate them to do more.

**C** Match the sentence beginnings (1–6) with the endings (a–f) to make sentences.

1. We reached an agreement ___
2. He was uncomfortable because it was a situation in ___
3. Paula is a person whose ___
4. This will be popular with the team, among ___
5. The explorer contracted an illness from ___
6. We still hadn't met Mr Dawson, in whose ___

a. mood never changes.
b. which he never recovered.
c. house we were all staying.
d. whereby everyone was satisfied.
e. whom any extra support is appreciated.
f. which he had never been before.

➤ Go back to page 88.

## 8.2 Pronouns and determiners

**A** Underline the determiners in each sentence. Some sentences have more than one determiner.

1. I could do with a little help starting this fitness programme.
2. The doctor said I should leave the car at home and do more walking.
3. Both of the sports centres in my area are too far to walk to.
4. There was little point in talking to him since he wouldn't listen.
5. One of the techniques is bound to suit you.
6. The canteen had two healthier options but I didn't fancy either of them.

**B** Change one determiner into a pronoun in each sentence by crossing out some words.

1. Some people have a gluten-free diet because they genuinely can't eat it without getting sick, but many people believe that avoiding gluten is just healthier.
2. I try to drink a couple of litres of water every day, but I'm pretty sure that I don't drink enough water.
3. A lot of people I know are cutting back on sugar and caffeine, but I don't want to cut back on either sugar or caffeine.
4. I've started following a vegan diet so I like to try vegan restaurants, but there are only a few vegan restaurants in my area.
5. I prefer fruit and vegetables that have been grown organically to those fruit and vegetables that haven't.
6. The government should make companies that produce food with a lot of sugar use less sugar to help people have better diets.

**C** Complete each sentence with the correct pronoun. More than one answer is sometimes possible.

1. Jack couldn't decide which of the two sandwiches to get so he just bought _____.
2. Some people enjoy running, while _____ find it really boring.
3. Now I can't tell which shoes are _____ – they look the same as yours.
4. 'Which of the two matches do you want to watch on TV?' '_____ – I really don't mind.'
5. I know we said we'd buy oranges but _____ don't look very nice.
6. We haven't got any football boots in stock but we'll be getting some new _____ in next week.

➤ Go back to page 93.

# Grammar Hub

## 9.1 Noun phrases

- We can use possessive adjectives, quantifiers, numbers and modified quantifiers before nouns to make noun phrases.

| Article/determiner | **Those** researchers are highly qualified. |
|---|---|
| Possessive adjective | **Their** study is well funded. |
| Quantifier | **Many** eager participants started immediately |
| Number | **Two of the five** speakers disagreed. |
| Modified quantifier | **Almost every single** student showed up early. |

- We can use relative clauses, prepositional phrases, *that* clauses and *to* + infinitive after nouns to make noun phrases.

| Relative clause | **The clinic where she works** just closed. |
|---|---|
| Reduced relative clause | **The woman sitting down** is my colleague. |
| Prepositional phrase | They shared **a wealth of knowledge**. |
| *that* clause | I question **the idea that humans are still evolving**. |
| *to* + infinitive | They looked for **a cheap place to eat and sleep**. |

- We can use phrases such as *the fact that*, *the idea that* and *the belief that* to turn a sentence into a noun phrase.

*A language dies every two weeks. That is regrettable.* (= *The fact that a language dies every two weeks is regrettable.*)

*People believe language strengthens social ties. This is supported by research.* (= *The belief that language strengthens social ties is supported by research.*)

## 9.2 Participle clauses and verbless clauses

- We use present and past participles as well as combinations of both to form participle clauses.

  ***Feeling** unsure of the results, Mary tested the configuration once more.*
  ***Left** to their own devices, children can solve complex problems.*
  ***Having** just finished his research, Travis went for a walk to relax.*

- We can use prepositions such as *before*, *after* and *despite* before participle clauses with present participles (but not past participles).

  ***Before arriving** at the office, Susan texted her boss.*
  *NOT Before arrived at the office, Susan texted her boss.*

- We can use conjunctions such as *if*, *when* and *while* before participle clauses with both present and past participles.

  ***While waiting** for the bus, Paula had a marvellous idea.*
  ***When pressed** to answer questions, Jonathan became very nervous.*

### Be careful!

- Participle clauses appear near the nouns they refer to. When that noun is missing, or the clause appears closer to another noun which it doesn't refer to, it becomes a 'dangling participle' and is grammatically incorrect.

  *While doing research, Frank noticed the room getting cold. NOT While doing research, the room got cold. (Incorrect: the room wasn't doing research)*

- When the participle clause involves using the verb *be*, we can omit the verb altogether and the clause becomes 'verbless'.

  *Too impatient to wait, Paul barged in and demanded the results.* (= *Being too impatient to wait, ...*)

- We can start a clause with just a participle, with words such as *when*, *after* or *because* being implied.

  *Hearing the news, Alex leapt for joy!* (= *After hearing the news, Alex leapt for joy!*)

## 9.1 Noun phrases

**A** Choose the option which is closest in meaning to the sentence.

1 Lisa questioned many of her professors, and only one gave a clear answer.
   a Many of the professors Lisa questioned only gave one clear answer.
   b Only one of the many professors Lisa questioned gave a clear answer.

2 I have two younger brothers, and they are language experts.
   a Both of my younger brothers are language experts.
   b Two of my younger brothers are language experts.

3 Very few of the participants enjoyed the study.
   a Almost all of the participants disliked the study.
   b Quite a few of the participants enjoyed the study.

4 Jake is standing at the workstation, and he's running reports.
   a The man standing at the workstation is running reports.
   b The man standing at the workstation and running reports is Jake.

5 They're looking for a safe location so they can try out their experiment.
   a They're searching for a safe location to try out their experiment.
   b They're looking to try out their experiment at a safe location.

6 Many people applied for the trial, but few were qualified to join.
   a Many of the few people applying for the trial were qualified to join.
   b Few of the many people applying for the trial were qualified to join.

**B** Rewrite these sentences using noun phrases. Use the words in bold to help you.

1 I speak **three** languages and **two** of **them** are Latin-based.
   _____ languages I speak are Latin-based.

2 I have **little** money, but I save **it all** … well, **almost**.
   I save _____ money I have.

3 I've read **very few** pieces of research, but this is **one of them**.
   This is _____ pieces of research I've read.

4 **The writer** draws **two** conclusions and they **both** seem dubious to me.
   _____ conclusions seem dubious to me.

5 **The researchers** interviewed **many** people. **Quite a few** had no savings at all.
   _____ interviewees had no savings at all.

6 They **can't conduct the experiment** in peace. That is annoying.
   _____ is annoying.

7 That **man** is in charge of the experiment. He's wearing a **white lab coat**.
   The _____ is in charge of the experiment.

8 Many linguists **believe language is alive**, and this is factored into their theories.
   _____ factored into linguists' theories.

► Go back to page 101.

## 9.2 Participle clauses and verbless clauses

**A** Choose the correct options to complete the sentences.

1 *Sensing / Sensed* danger, Henry shut down the machine immediately.
2 *Having already left / Leaving the building*, Danielle didn't feel like returning to get her phone.
3 Before *notifying / notified* her supervisor, Anna wanted to make sure the experiment was a success.
4 When *asking / asked* about the research, Kyle refused to reply.
5 *Too / Too being* cautious to take risks, Martin decided to stay on at his job.
6 Despite *handed / handing* in her notice, Sarah put in great effort during her last days at work.
7 *Having been told / Being told* to speed up the study, David cut corners to make his deadlines.
8 If *successful / being successful*, we can publish the results in a science journal.

**B** Rewrite these sentences using participle clauses or verbless clauses and the word in bold.

1 I understand animal behaviour better now that I've read the article. **having**
   _____.

2 The octopus hid in the coconut shell because it felt threatened. **feeling**
   _____.

3 These experiments can teach us a lot if you do them properly. **done**
   _____.

4 I guessed the answer because I didn't know. **knowing**
   _____.

5 The crow had never seen the tool before but used it perfectly. **despite**
   _____.

6 She wasn't fast enough to win the race, but she came in a close second. **too**
   _____.

► Go back to page 103.

# Grammar Hub

## 10.1 Discourse markers

- We use discourse markers to connect ideas, or to give further information regarding our attitude to what we're saying or writing.
- We use some discourse markers to join two clauses within a sentence. They can be positioned either at the beginning of a sentence (followed by a comma) or in between the two clauses. They may be used to express cause and consequence, or to describe a contrast.

| | |
|---|---|
| despite | **Despite** having a degree in Business Studies, Karla didn't get the job. / Karla didn't get the job **despite** having a degree in Business Studies. |
| owing to | **Owing to** his lack of qualifications, Omar was unable to find a job in the field. / Omar was unable to find a job in the field **owing to** his lack of qualifications. |
| whereas | **Whereas** Kim is determined to succeed, her sister lacks ambition. / Her sister lacks ambition, **whereas** Kim is determined to succeed. |

- We use some discourse markers to connect ideas in two separate sentences. These discourse markers can be positioned at the beginning of the second sentence, in which case they should be followed by a comma. Some can also be placed after the subject of the second sentence, and should in this case be followed by a comma, or at the end of the second sentence.

| | |
|---|---|
| as a matter of fact | He's doing research into Arctic animals. **As a matter of fact**, he's leaving for Greenland next week. / He's leaving for Greenland next week, **as a matter of fact**. |
| conversely | The novel was a huge bestseller. **Conversely**, the film version was never as successful. / The film version, **conversely**, was never as successful. |
| for instance | Mediterranean resorts are making a comeback. **For instance**, Mykonos is now seen as a holiday hotspot for Europe's young celebrities. / Mykonos, **for instance**, is now seen as a holiday hotspot for Europe's young celebrities. / Mykonos is now seen as a holiday hotspot for Europe's young celebrities, **for instance**. |
| in any case | It seems that no crime had taken place. **In any case**, it wasn't a matter for the police. / It wasn't a matter for the police, **in any case**. |
| moreover | Tax income increased because of tourism. **Moreover**, it has created hundreds of new jobs. / It has, **moreover**, created hundreds of new jobs. |

## 10.2 Ellipsis and substitution

- Ellipsis involves leaving out words and phrases to avoid repeating them.
- In written English, there are a number of grammatical items that are often left out.

| | |
|---|---|
| repeated subject | **He**'s into politics and (**he**) is passionate about activism. |
| repeated subject + modal | **They should** organise a campaign and (**they should**) create some positive publicity. |
| repeated subject + auxiliary verb | **We're going to** start a petition and (**we're going to**) organise a protest meeting. |
| repeated verb phrase | 'I thought you were **going on the march**.' 'Yes, I am (**going on the march**).' |
| repeated adjective | So many students are **apathetic**, but Kiera isn't (**apathetic**). |

- In spoken English, we can also leave out some grammatical items for the sake of brevity, when it's clear who/what we're talking about.

subject: *Can't believe we managed to save the forest from developers!* (= I can't believe …)
auxiliary verb: *You planning to join the group?* (= Are you planning …)
auxiliary verb + subject + verb: *Any preference as to which route we take?* (= Do you have any preference …)

- We often substitute the following words and phrases to avoid repeating words.

*do: Are you going into town? Will you post my letter if you **do**?*
*(to avoid repeating 'go into town')*

*not: I may have to organise the campaign, but I hope **not**.*
*(to avoid repeating 'that I don't have to organise the campaign')*

*do so: Deactivate the burglar alarm. In order to **do so**, you'll need to key in this code number.*
*(to avoid repeating 'deactivate the burglar alarm')*

*do it: I often read English-language newspapers. I **do it** to improve my vocabulary.*
*(to avoid repeating 'read English-language newspapers')*

*do that: I specifically asked you not to read my emails. Why did you **do that**?*
*(to avoid repeating 'read my emails')*

## 10.1 Discourse markers

**A** What is the function of the discourse markers in bold? Read the sentences and choose the correct options.

1 Large hotel complexes consume huge amounts of water, **whereas** smaller family-run hotels tend to use less.
   a  contrasting two different ideas
   b  comparing two related ideas
2 Walking holidays, **for instance**, are an environmentally-friendly choice.
   a  suggesting a possibility
   b  giving an example
3 Huge building projects tend to attract investors. **Conversely**, small businesses sometimes struggle to raise money.
   a  repeating and reinforcing an idea
   b  contrasting two different ideas
4 The room wasn't at all expensive. **As a matter of fact**, it was one of the cheapest places we stayed.
   a  adding more information
   b  giving an example
5 Farmers are warning that crops may fail **owing to** the lack of rain.
   a  offering an explanation
   b  trying to persuade someone
6 **Despite** placing adverts on various websites, Aisha didn't manage to sell her products.
   a  describing a situation
   b  contrasting two different ideas

**B** Choose the correct options to complete the sentences.

1 We haven't visited all the monuments yet. *Owing to / In any case*, Farid isn't that keen on sightseeing.
2 We managed to visit all the most important museums in the city *whereas / despite* our limited budget.
3 Because the cost of living in Venice is so high, many people are leaving. *Moreover / For instance*, many inhabitants are worried about the danger of flooding.
4 Many of the streets in Venice are very narrow. The 'Calleta Varisco', *conversely / for instance*, is just 53 centimetres wide!
5 *Owing to / Despite* rising water levels, Venice city authorities are building flood barriers to protect the city.
6 Riding on a gondola is a bucket list experience for many visiting Venice. Some say it is one of the most iconic tourist experiences, *as a matter of fact / moreover*!

▶ Go back to page 111.

## 10.2 Ellipsis and substitution

**A** Cross out the words that can be omitted in the conversation.

Dom: Do you know who I saw the other day?
Ali: No, who did you see?
Dom: Klaus.
Ali: Do you mean your old roommate from college?
Dom: Yeah! I can't believe it – I saw him again after all these years.
Ali: What happened when you saw him?
Dom: Yes. He gave me his phone number and he gave me his email address.
Ali: Are you planning to meet up soon?
Dom: He's going to be visiting the area again next month, so he'll give me a ring when he does visit the area again.

**B** Replace the phrases in bold with the words and phrases in the box.

do   do it   do so   doing that   don't

1 'Do you have time to help out at the animal shelter?'
  'No, I'm afraid **I don't have time to help out at the animal shelter**.'
2 'I'd like to volunteer with you at the weekend.'
  'That's great. You'll have to fill out this form in order to **volunteer with us at the weekend**.'
3 'I volunteer at an animal shelter every weekend.'
  'I really admire you for **volunteering at the animal shelter**.'
4 'Are you enjoying your voluntary work?'
  'Yes. I didn't know how fulfilling it would be, but now **I know how fulfilling it is**.'
5 'I've always wanted to volunteer at the cats' home.'
  'So why don't you **volunteer at the cats' home**?'

▶ Go back to page 117.

# Vocabulary Hub

## 1.1 Clothes and fashion

**A** Choose the correct word to complete the sentences.
1 There is a **dress code / uniform** at my work – for example, we aren't allowed to wear torn jeans or shorts.
2 Many people try to copy Audrey Hepburn's style – she was a real trend **setter / follower**.
3 The theme of the party is *Superheroes* – everybody has to wear a(n) **outfit / costume**.
4 You need a new pair of trousers – those are so old and **scruffy / casual**.
5 People who work in fashion usually dress boldly to **fit in with / stand out from** the crowd.
6 I like **baggy / oversized** clothes in the summer as they keep you cool.

**B** Work in pairs. Look again at both options in Exercise A. What is the difference between each option? What do they have common?

➤ Go back to page 2.

## 1.2 Experimenting with prefixes and suffixes

Add the correct prefix or suffix from the box to the words in bold to complete the sentences.

`friendly   ish   prone   proof   re   resistant   savvy   super`

1 It doesn't matter if he dropped the camera in the pool – it's **water**_____ and **shock**_____.
2 She's really up-to-date with new recording and video equipment. She's very **tech**_____.
3 The sound quality is awful and it looks like it was made at home. It's just too **amateur**_____ to be taken seriously.
4 She has a lot of experience making vlogs. She has every reason to feel _____ **confident** about her abilities.
5 He's always breaking the stuff on the set. I guess he's just **accident**_____.
6 The themes on the show are too adult. I couldn't show my children that – it's not **family**_____.
7 You've made a mess of that video. You'll have to _____ **start** it.

➤ Go back to page 8.

## 2.1 Describing art

Choose the correct words to complete the sentences. Then discuss the sentences with your partner. Do you agree?
1 Some people enjoy looking around galleries, but I find it quite **tedious / unconventional**.
2 Some modern theatre is incredibly **pretentious / groundbreaking** – it's more about making the writer feel clever than actually saying anything important.
3 Art needs to be **hilarious / thought-provoking**. Without a deeper meaning, it's just a pretty picture.
4 Some of the most **iconic / sensational** photographs can be disappointing when you see them up close.
5 When a writer uses the same idea in their work too many times, it feels really **repetitive / overrated**.

➤ Go back to page 14.

## 2.2 Compound adjectives

Make compound adjectives with the words in the box to complete the sentences. Use each word only once.

`highly   late   open   part   self   thick   well   world`

1 I work for a company now, but, in the future, I'd like to be _____-employed.
2 Travelling can introduce you to new ways of seeing the world and make you more _____-minded.
3 Sandra's looking for a _____-time job so she can study and work at the same time.
4 Sometimes as a writer you need to be _____-skinned – you can't take criticism personally.
5 Rob is a _____-motivated person who loves his job and wants to excel at it.
6 It's important that my job is _____-paid, so I have some disposable income after I pay all my bills.
7 He is definitely a celebrity in his own country, but he isn't _____-famous yet.
8 There is a _____-night convenience store below our flat that will be open.

➤ Go back to page 20.

# Vocabulary Hub

## 3.1 Sustainability

Complete the text with the words in the box.

> biodegradable   consume   emission   exploitation   neutral   offsetting   renewable

### How to be green

$^1$_____ energy from sun, wind, rain and waves is one possible solution to the environmental problems we face today. It helps us to address the over-$^2$_____ of natural resources that are finite like minerals, oil, natural gas and coal. Some businesses and organisations aim to be carbon-$^3$_____ by $^4$_____ the amount of carbon they release. There are even some zero-$^5$_____ buildings which actually create as much energy as they $^6$_____. Also using $^7$_____ materials, for example, in food packaging, is another important step because these materials break down naturally and cause less waste.

➤ Go back to page 26.

## 3.2 Verb–noun collocations

Cross out the incorrect word or phrase in each group.

1 We managed to *achieve / attain / deliver / perform / meet* our goals.
2 We have made *a concerted effort / limited progress / reasonable headway / advances in the right direction / room for improvement*.
3 They performed *impressively / particularly / reasonably / relatively / surprisingly* poorly.
4 The statistics *demonstrated / hindered / displayed / showed* a marked imbalance.
5 We should set *significant progress / realistic goals / clear objectives / measurable targets*.
6 We have seen *little movement / a deadline / a new record / regression / incremental progress*.

➤ Go back to page 33.

## 4.2 Science and research

Choose the correct word to complete the sentences.

1 What are some examples of social *findings / norms* in your social group?
2 Can you *conduct / speculate* how most people would react if they were publicly told they had a low score on a test?
3 Do you think the study above proved the theory that the researchers *demonstrated / hypothesised*?
4 What did this study *conduct / demonstrate*?
5 Can you think of another idea for *an experiment / some findings* to prove the hypothesis?
6 Is it important to read the *findings / participants* of a study to understand the conclusions?
7 Have you ever *conducted / speculated* an experiment at school or university?
8 What have you *concluded / conducted* about embarrassment by reading the texts?

➤ Go back to page 43.

# Vocabulary Hub

## 4.2 Thinking

**Choose the correct options to complete the sentences.**

1. While she is very clever, she just isn't very practical. She hasn't got much **common sense / wishful thinking**.
2. I was lying on the beach when I had an amazing idea for my business – it was an **eccentric / eureka** moment.
3. He is very **eccentric / absent-minded** – he really stands out from the crowd and doesn't mind doing things in his own unique way.
4. I'd say I'm a bit **curious / absent-minded** – for example, I left my work pass at home this morning and couldn't get into my office.
5. If you make a resolution but put no effort into planning how to achieve it, then your idea is just **wishful thinking / common sense**.
6. We need someone who can analyse and solve serious problems – in other words, **troubleshooting / overthinking** skills are essential for this job.
7. Lara always **troubleshoots / overthinks** things; sometimes she should just follow her instincts.
8. Tim describes himself as **curious / eccentric**, but I would describe him as nosy.

➤ Go back to page 44.

## 5.1 Competition and cooperation

**A** Read the definition of *outmanoeuvre*. What does the prefix *out-* mean?

> **outmanoeuvre** – definition and synonyms
> VERB (Pronunciation) /ˌaʊtməˈnuːvə(r)/
> to defeat or gain an advantage over someone by being more clever or skilful than they are

**B** Complete the sentences with the correct form of the verbs in the box.

| outdo   outnumber   outplay   outrun   outsmart   outweigh |

1. You'll need to be fast to _____ your rivals and win the race.
2. When we played tennis, she completely _____ me, and I lost every game.
3. It's not perfect, but on balance, the advantages _____ the disadvantages.
4. When I bought a new car, my neighbour didn't want to be _____, so he bought one too!
5. I managed to _____ my opponent by solving the clues faster.
6. In my class, women _____ men by three to one.

➤ Go back to page 53.

## 5.2 Reporting verbs

**Complete the second sentences with a reporting verb from the box and reported speech.**

| alleged   boasted   clarified   doubted   speculated |

1. 'The new bridge is supposed to reduce traffic congestion, but I don't think it will.'
   Daniel _____ whether the new bridge _____ traffic congestion.
2. 'Sorry – I think you misunderstood me. I didn't offer to do all the work for you.'
   Tania _____ that _____ for me.
3. 'Who knows? If you'd studied harder, you might have got a better mark.'
   Max _____ that I _____ harder.
4. 'I was brilliant at the Take or Share game! I made over £200!'
   Victoria _____ that _____ Take or Share game.
5. 'I can't prove it, but I know that Andy lied on his CV to get the job.'
   Michael _____ that _____ to get the job.

➤ Go back to page 55.

# Vocabulary Hub

## 5.2 Motivation and manipulation

Complete the text with the correct form of the phrases in the box.

act   coax   go nuts   inclined   spur   steer   tap into

### A day in the life of... a salesman

I wouldn't say my job involved ¹_____ people into buying things that they don't actually want. I would never convince someone to buy a faulty product or ²_____ against their best interests. But I totally believe in the quality of our products – they have been well designed and ³_____ what the market really wants. My job is just to ⁴_____ people towards the most appropriate products in our range to meet their needs. To be honest it's not difficult. The products sell themselves. Customers are ⁵_____ for them. It is the quality of the product that ⁶_____ me on to do my job as well as I can. If the product is no good, you're not ⁷_____ to make the same effort to sell it.

➤ Go back to page 56.

## 6.1 Journeys and adventures

**A** Complete the sentences with a word or phrase. Use the definitions in brackets to help you.

1. Can you think of a time that you went _____ (*away from frequently visited places*)?
2. How do/would you pass the time on a _____ (*long distance*) flight?
3. Do you prepare in advance before you _____ (*leave*) on a trip? What do you do?
4. Is there any _____ (*places not covered by maps*) left in the world? Where?
5. Imagine you had to camp in the _____ (*middle*) of a rainforest. What _____ (*supplies of food, drink, equipment*) would you take with you?
6. Would you like a job that required you to be a _____ (*frequent traveller*)? Why/Why not?

**B** Work in pairs. Discuss the questions in Exercise A.

➤ Go back to page 63.

## 6.2 Binomial expressions

Work in pairs. Complete the sentences with a binomial expression from the box.

by and large   far and wide   heart and soul   life or death
safe and sound   side by side   slowly but surely   time after time

1. Marco Polo travelled _____ in Asia.
2. Brothers Louis and Auguste Lumière worked _____ to create film and cinema.
3. Edmund Hillary and Tenzing Norgay were the first to climb Mount Everest and return _____.
4. The American conservationist Dian Fossey won the trust of the gorillas _____.
5. The German physicist Albert Einstein is, _____, thought to be the smartest person that ever lived.
6. Passengers on the sinking *Titanic* faced a _____ situation.
7. _____, numerous climbers have tried to reach the summit of the mountain. But all have failed.
8. Van Gogh put his _____ into his art and inventions, working tirelessly on both.

➤ Go back to page 69.

# Vocabulary Hub

## 7.1 Feelings

Choose the correct options to complete the text.

### The psychology of everyday life

Extreme and stressful situations can always be difficult to cope with. But it's actually how we deal with mundane, everyday tasks, that has the biggest impact on our well-being. Here are some tips on how to cope.

- Learn to control your emotions – be the calm and collected person rather than the [1]*hysterical / courageous / devastated* one when the pressure is on.
- Try not to fire back emails when you're [2]*humble / grumpy / resilient* – an angry message may make you feel better immediately. But, you'll be [3]*indifferent / disgusted / devastated* when your boss fires you and you're suddenly jobless.
- If you just aren't getting anywhere with something and are [4]*frustrated / devastated / disgusted*, recognise that you may need a break or even to ask for help.
- Sometimes it's important to be [5]*courageous / humble / superior* and take risks rather than play it safe. Bravery is something you can practise and get better at.
- Just because you are busy, don't be [6]*indifferent / hysterical / resilient* to other people's problems – it's important to help out the people around you.
- No matter how well you think you're doing at the moment, try to stay [7]*humble / courageous / resilient* about your achievements. Nothing annoys people more than a [8]*superior / disgusted / hysterical* attitude.

➤ Go back to page 76.

## 7.2 Polysemy

Complete the sentences with the correct form of a word. You can use some words more than once.

1. It can be quite difficult to _____ a job with the right balance between intellectual challenge and not too much _____ to succeed.
2. One of the most important _____ of barometers (which measure atmospheric _____) is to calculate the height at which a plane is flying.
3. There's too much _____ between hundreds of people who have sent in their _____ for the job; there should be a _____ to find the successful candidate instead!
4. The pilot says he will _____ the plane shortly as _____ have improved.

➤ Go back to page 79.

## 7.2 Intensifiers

Choose the correct intensifiers to complete the advice about job interviews. What other intensifiers are used?

1. It's perfectly normal to exaggerate your achievements *remarkably / somewhat*, but you should never tell *noticeably / outright* lies.
2. If you're not *altogether / immensely* sure what the interviewer is asking, it's completely fine to ask for clarification.
3. *Practically / Radically* all interviews are highly stressful, but as long as you're extremely well-prepared, it should be *relatively / utterly* painless.
4. Remember that for the interviewers, it's *practically / exceptionally* boring to hear the same answers from every single interviewee. If you give *immensely / radically* different answers, you'll stand out from the crowd.

➤ Go back to page 81.

# Vocabulary Hub

## 8.1 Health problems

Cross out one word in each sentence which does not make a collocation.
1 Tony fractured a(n) *muscle / arm / bone* when he went skiing last year.
2 Do you sell anything for a *twisted / sore* throat?
3 Some studies have claimed that *low / slow* blood pressure may be more common amongst athletes.
4 When I was running I may have *pulled / dislocated / sprained* a muscle.
5 After intense exercise your *skin rash / blood pressure / heart rate* is usually higher.
6 You can buy a number of products over the counter to help relieve skin *fractures / inflammation / rashes*.
➤ Go back to page 86.

## 8.2 Describing taste

Complete the sentences with words from Exercise A. More than one answer is possible for some sentences.
1 I love _____ drinks, but I'm trying to be healthy so I usually order sparkling water at restaurants.
2 I know I should eat more citrus fruits to get my daily dose of Vitamin C, but they are just too _____ for me.
3 Presentation is so important for me – if food doesn't look _____, I can't eat it.
4 I ate a delicious curry at the weekend, which wasn't too spicy at all – in fact, it was quite _____.
5 My dad loves blue cheese, so I get some really _____ aromas when I open the fridge sometimes.
6 I try to eat salad for lunch occasionally, but it doesn't taste of much. It's really _____ unless I put some unhealthy dressing on the top.
7 I'm trying to eat healthy snacks, like carrot sticks – they're nice and _____.
➤ Go back to page 93.

## 9.2 Verb + object + infinitive

Complete the sentences with the correct form of the verbs in brackets.
1 The scientists observed the dolphin _____ itself in the mirror for hours. (admire)
2 Snakes' heat sensors help them _____ prey _____. (detect, approach)
3 Scientists must be seen _____ procedures very carefully. (follow)
4 Oh! You're here! I didn't notice you _____! (arrive)
5 I woke up because I could feel a spider _____ on my arm. (crawl)
6 I was made _____ for over an hour before they let me _____ in. (wait, come)
7 The experimenters had the participants _____ a form before they could start. (sign)
➤ Go back to page 103.

## 9.2 Gestures and body language

Complete the sentences with the correct form of the words in the box.

beckon   fidget   glare   grin   lean   wink   nod   gaze

1 Sally was _____ across the bay, looking at nothing in particular, when the ship suddenly came into view.
2 Phillip just can't sit still in meetings – he's always _____.
3 James _____ at Emma, so she knew he was joking.
4 'Shhh … we have to be quiet … just _____ if you agree with me.'
5 The bookshelf fell over when I _____ against it.
6 Steven was so happy when he got the job that he couldn't stop _____.
7 The teacher _____ his student over to the board.
8 Elizabeth was so angry that she just _____ at them without saying a word.
➤ Go back to page 105.

VOCABULARY HUB   147

# Vocabulary Hub

## 10.1 Culture and heritage

Complete the text with the words in the box.

architectural   endangered   funding   habitat   heritage   preserve   refurbishment   settlement

### HOMETOWN GLORY

My hometown has a very rich history – it is where a famous treaty was signed and is close to the site of an ancient ¹_____. In fact some of ruins of the site are still standing today and are of special ²_____ interest as they show the precise engineering methods of the Romans.

For these reasons alone, the town is a very important part of my country's national ³_____. The nearby forests are the ⁴_____ of a lot of different wildlife, including some rare species which are unfortunately now ⁵_____. As such they have been designated as an area of outstanding natural beauty and are protected.

Unfortunately we don't receive a lot of ⁶_____ from the government to ⁷_____ areas of the old town. Some of the unlisted buildings are in real need of ⁸_____ – so please come and visit us. Tourism is a valuable source of income and helps us to keep our heritage and culture alive!

➤ Go back to page 111.

## 10.2 Word building

**A** Write the correct form of the word in brackets to complete the sentences.

1. A good politician is someone who grew up in the _____ (commune) that they represent.
2. Most politicians are more interested in _____ (person) success than helping the public.
3. Becoming _____ (act) in politics is the best way to make a difference in the world.
4. I feel _____ (passion) about politics and follow the news closely.
5. Most people's political beliefs are formed in _____ (child) by listening to their parents.
6. Many people are _____ (apathy) about politics, because they don't trust politicians.
7. The best politicians are those who had other careers before entering _____ (politics) life.
8. Local politics is often more _____ (effect) at improving people's lives than national politics.

**B** Work in pairs. Do you agree with the sentences in Exercise A? Why/Why not?

➤ Go back to page 115.

# Communication Hub

## 2.2 Students A and B

Read what your answers to the quiz say about you.

### ARE YOU CUT OUT FOR FAME?

**MOSTLY 1S**
You have a very clear vision for your future and nothing will stop you from achieving it. You welcome negative feedback as a way to improve and grow as a person. You want to be well-known, even if this won't necessarily make you rich.

**MOSTLY 3S**
You feel comfortable amongst large groups of people and don't need a lot of alone time. That being said, you would not particularly enjoy your private life being discussed online. You are fairly ambitious and would like to be respected in your field. But you also have other interests in your life which are important to you. Fame might not be for you.

**MOSTLY 5S**
You don't enjoy being the centre of attention and value privacy. For you, work is a small part of your life, secondary to spending time with friends and family. The purpose of working is to earn money to do the things you enjoy. Fame isn't for you.

➤ Go back to page 20.

## 4.1 Students A and B

### BRAIN TEASERS

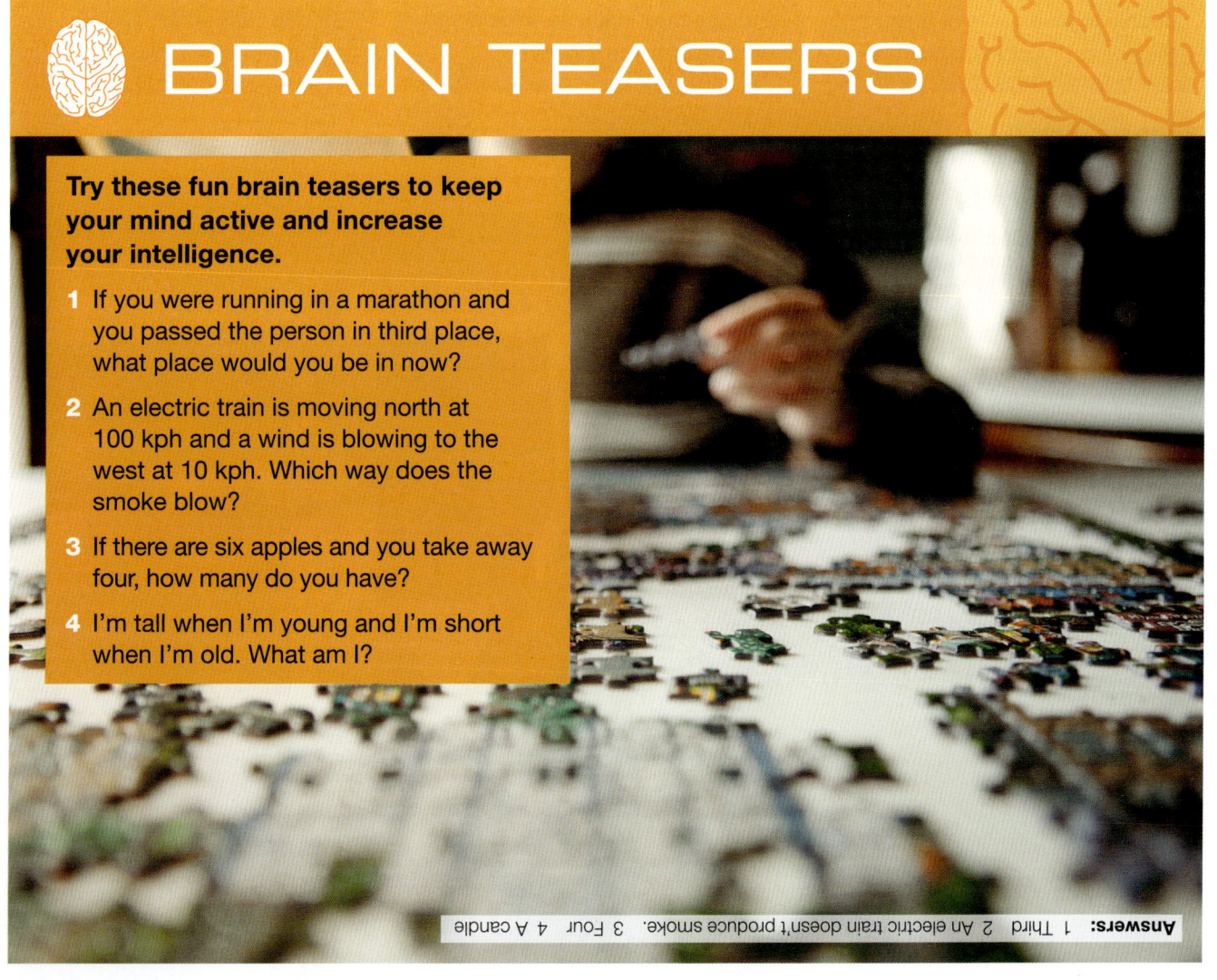

**Try these fun brain teasers to keep your mind active and increase your intelligence.**

1 If you were running in a marathon and you passed the person in third place, what place would you be in now?

2 An electric train is moving north at 100 kph and a wind is blowing to the west at 10 kph. Which way does the smoke blow?

3 If there are six apples and you take away four, how many do you have?

4 I'm tall when I'm young and I'm short when I'm old. What am I?

**Answers:** 1 Third  2 An electric train doesn't produce smoke.  3 Four  4 A candle

➤ Go back to page 38.

# Communication Hub

## 9.2 Players

You have three minutes to get ten points, but you have to work out the rules to the game by yourselves. For example, perhaps you get a point for nodding your head, for blinking your eyes or for saying a particular word (or perhaps all three at the same time). Work as a team to see if you can win ten points in three minutes. Good luck!

▶ Go back to page 105.

## 4.1 Student A

Using your own words, explain each situation to your partner. Then decide what you would do in pairs.

### Situation 1
Imagine that a company begins selling brain implants. They allow you to learn and remember information quickly. For example, some people use them to learn languages or other skills instantly. However, the implants have also caused people to lose some of their memories. Would you buy one?

### Situation 2
Imagine that a company begins selling highly advanced robots. These robots will take on any tasks that you need them to do, provide companionship for people who live alone, and protect you and your house. They are also smart enough to learn and use their initiative. Would you get one of these robots?

### Situation 3
Imagine that artificial intelligence is used for both medical check-ups and treatment in the future. The AI has a higher rate of accurate diagnoses than human doctors. You have the choice between a human doctor or an artificial intelligence system. Which would you pick?

▶ Go back to page 41.

## 4.2 Students A and B

Think of a time when you did something you regret. Use the prompts below or your own ideas. Discuss it with your partner.

- You failed a test.
- You forgot something.
- You lost something.
- You missed an appointment.
- You sent an email or message to the wrong person.
- You wore the wrong type of clothes.

▶ Go back to page 43.

Communication Hub

## 5.2 Students

Work in small groups to solve the puzzles.

### PUZZLE A: THE TAKE OR SHARE IT GAME

**You and a stranger are both offered a choice:** **TAKE or SHARE.**

If only one player chooses **TAKE**, they keep £1000.

If both players choose **SHARE**, they get £500 each.

But if both players choose **TAKE**, they get nothing.

You can't communicate with each other.

What's the best strategy if you play once?   What if you play many times?

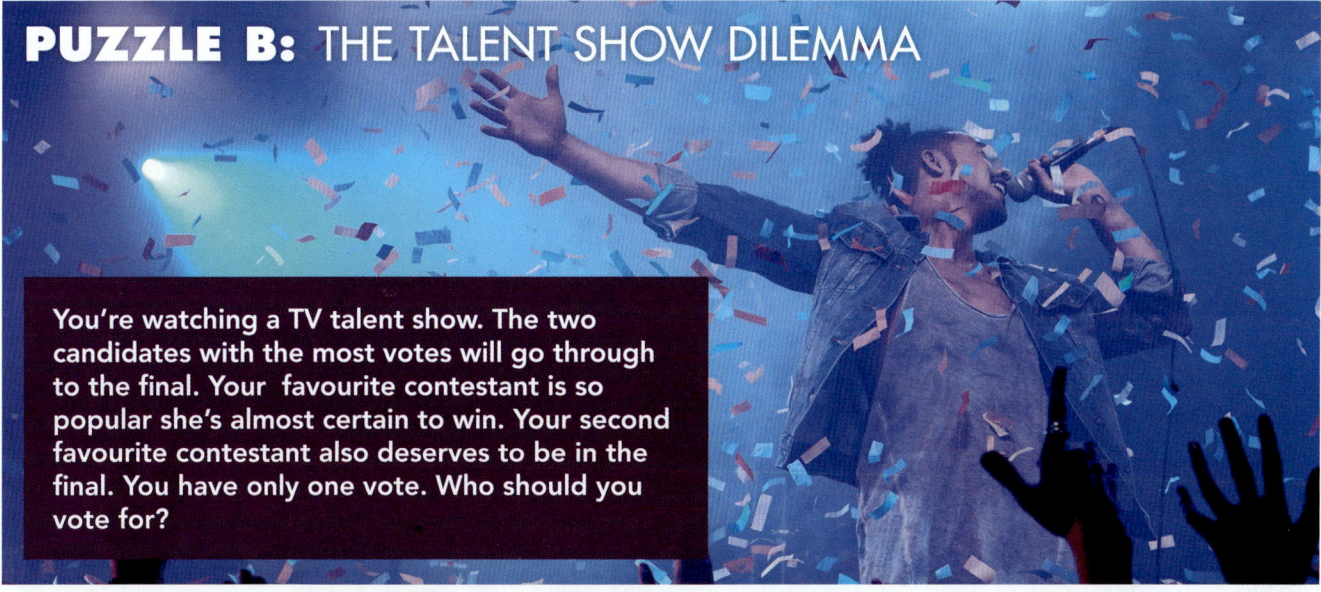

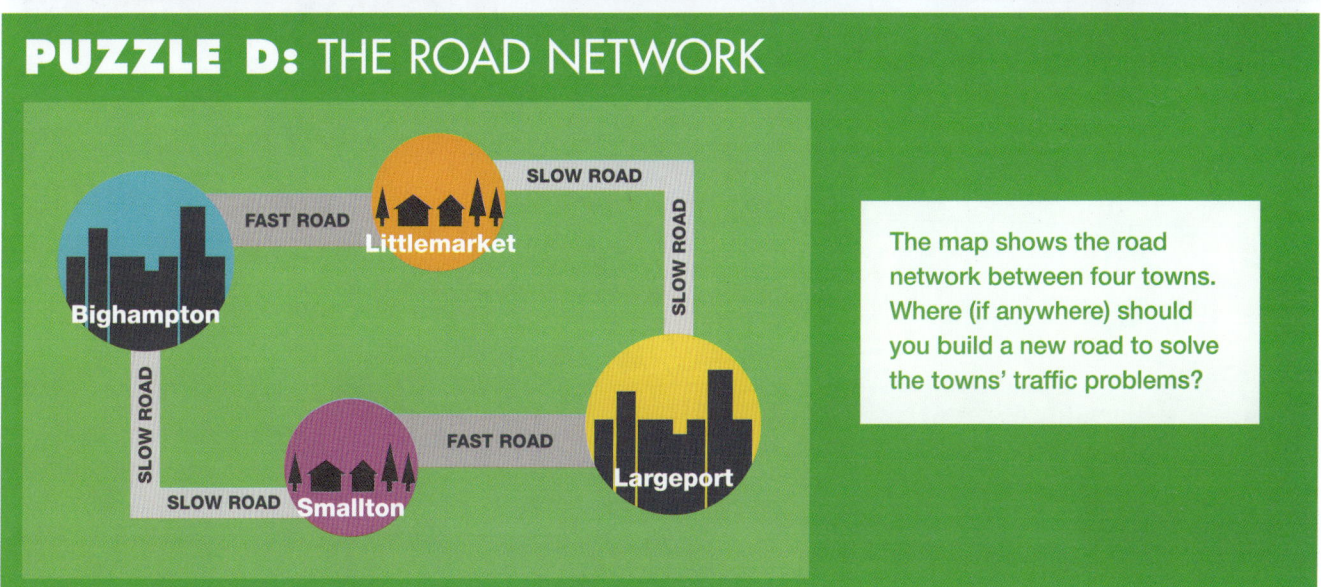

### PUZZLE B: THE TALENT SHOW DILEMMA

You're watching a TV talent show. The two candidates with the most votes will go through to the final. Your favourite contestant is so popular she's almost certain to win. Your second favourite contestant also deserves to be in the final. You have only one vote. Who should you vote for?

### PUZZLE D: THE ROAD NETWORK

The map shows the road network between four towns. Where (if anywhere) should you build a new road to solve the towns' traffic problems?

▶ Go back to page 54.

# Communication Hub

## 9.1 Students

In your groups, discuss the questions.

- Experiments have shown that speaking English encourages people to be more competitive, thanks to the connotations of English-speaking countries. What effect might your own language have on its speakers?
- Unlike English, many languages have formal and informal words for *you*, so you always have to think about your relationship with the other person before speaking to them. How might that affect your behaviour?
- The present perfect in English treats past events as part of the present. How might that affect English speakers' views of the past … and their behaviour?

➤ Go back to page 101.

## 4.1 Student B

Using your own words, explain each situation to your partner. Then decide what you would do in pairs.

### Situation 1
Imagine that a company begins selling body upgrades. You can use their technology to make you stronger, faster and more skilful. People can use the upgrades to fix their sight and hearing, or repair injuries. However, the new parts don't look natural, so it will be clear you have had upgrades. Would you use this service?

### Situation 2
Imagine that a company begins offering a memory back-up service. You can download the memories from your brain onto their servers and then view the memories whenever you want. You can also share selected memories with others. However, you don't get to choose which memories are downloaded. Everything has to be downloaded together. Would you use their service?

### Situation 3
Imagine that a highly advanced robot in the future demanded the same rights as a human. The robot argues that it is as conscious as a human being. Would you support the demands of the robot?

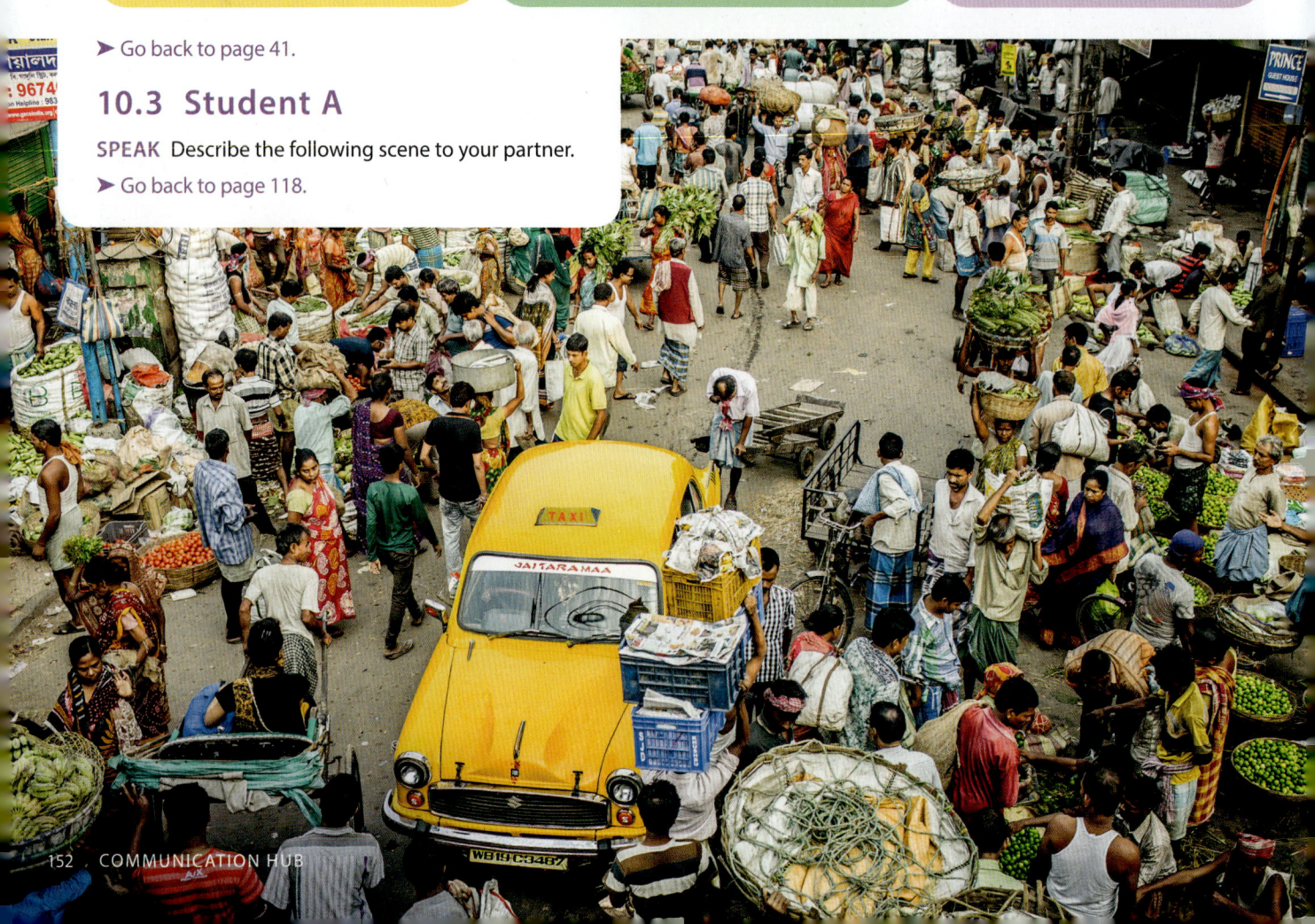

➤ Go back to page 41.

## 10.3 Student A

**SPEAK** Describe the following scene to your partner.

➤ Go back to page 118.

## 4.3 Students

Low frequency sounds, like number 1, are connected to earthy tones like browns and reds.
High frequency sounds like, number 2, are connected to violet tones like blue and purple.

➤ Go back to page 46.

## 9.2 Facilitator

The 'game' is in fact an experiment to see if you can trick the players into behaving strangely. They think they have to 'win' points, but in fact they simply get a point at regular intervals. When the game starts, count to ten slowly and silently in your head, again and again, saying 'one point' aloud every time you reach ten. Don't let the players work out the real rules – but you can share the secret with them at the end!

➤ Go back to page 105.

## 6.1 Group A

Work in small groups. Read about an historical mystery. Speculate about what happened.

### THE LOST COLONY OF ROANOKE

In 1585, an English settlement was established on a small island off the Eastern coast of the US. In the first year there, they began to run out of food, so the Mayor returned to England to get supplies – but it was three years before he could come back. He left behind his daughter, son-in-law and grandchild among the colonists.

When he returned, the colony and all 117 members of the colony were gone. The only thing left was a fence around the area and a newly built fort on the other side of the island. He never saw or heard from the colonists again.

The Mayor had told the settlers to carve a symbol into a tree if they had been forced to leave the area, but he only found the word CROATOAN. Croatoan was the name of a nearby island, inhabited by a tribe of indigenous people with the same name.

In recent years, some objects of European origin from that period were found at two different locations. Part of a sword was found on Croatoan Island and some pottery was found about 50 miles inland.

Despite modern efforts to solve the mystery, nothing of the actual colonists is known for sure. Several theories exist, but the quest to find out what happened continues.

➤ Go back to page 63.

# Communication Hub

## 4.3 Students

Both pictures are brightness illusions known as Munker's illusion. Although the shapes appear to vary in brightness, they are actually the same. It is the colours next to them that make them appear different.

➤ Go back to page 46.

## 3.2 Student B

Read the situation and prepare what you will say.

> You're being interviewed for a radio programme about progress. You feel that while there have been a lot of advances, overall life in the modern world is getting worse. You can think about the following points or use your own ideas to prepare:
> - the impact of technology
> - community
> - quality of life
> - cost of living
> - employment
> - the environment
>
> Complain to the interviewer about how life is getting worse in the modern world.

➤ Go back to page 31.

## 6.3 Students

Underline examples of summarising, repetition and dynamic words in the transcript.

> **Hydrogen atoms, carbon atoms, oxygen and sulphur atoms – these basic building blocks react and combine to make everything.**
>
> A woodland is a complex place – there are oak trees and grass and mosses and ferns, and countless animals and plants all living together in a tangled ecosystem. But there's a simpler level of description – everything is made of atoms. So an oak tree is really just carbon, nitrogen, oxygen and hydrogen and a few other bits mixed together. So, when you look at it like that, it's really not that complicated at all.
>
> The atoms that make up this woodland have been on an extraordinary journey to get here. Think of a carbon atom in this acorn. It was assembled in the heart of a star billions of years ago out of protons that were built just after the Big Bang. It got thrown out into the universe in a supernova explosion, collapsed as part of a dust cloud to form the sun and then the earth four and a half billion years ago.
>
> It will have spent a lot of time in rocks. It was probably part of some of the first living things on Earth. It would have got breathed out as carbon dioxide by someone that walked through this wood 400 years ago. It will have got into some ancient oak tree through the action of photosynthesis constructed into this acorn and fallen down to the ground. And there it is. It's got a history that goes back billions of years. In fact, a history in terms of the building blocks of carbon, the protons that goes back right to the origin of the universe. And in billions of years time when the sun dies and the Earth is vaporised they'll be thrown back out into space and probably condensed into a new world billions of years in the future.
>
> So life is just a temporary home for the immortal elements that build up the universe.

➤ Go back to page 70.

Communication Hub

## 10.3 Student B

**SPEAK** Describe the following scene to your partner.

▶ Go back to page 118.

## 6.1 Group B

Work in small groups. Read about an historical mystery. Speculate about what happened.

### THE NAZCA LINES

Approximately 2000 years ago, people living in southern Peru drew pictures of shapes and animals into the dry desert landscape by removing red rocks to reveal the white sand below.

Some of the pictures are as large as the Empire State Building, but when seen from above are very accurate. How did the people draw the pictures without being able to see them from above? And since the pictures are not visible from the ground, who was supposed to see them?

One scientist found that one of the lines pointed directly to the sun during the winter solstice.

Another scientist believes the drawings were used to mark the location of underground rivers and wells.

One image is of a spider, but this species of spider is not found in this area. It comes from the Amazon, over 900 miles away.

▶ Go back to page 63.

# 1 Writing — Write a blog post

**making your blog post successful**

**A** Look at the buttons. What do you think *skeuomorphism* means?

**B** Read *4 things you need to know about skeuomorphism*. Complete the article with the headings (a–d).

a Is skeuomorphism cool?
b Is skeuomorphism useful?
c What are some examples of skeuomorphism in real life?
d What is skeuomorphism?

## 4 things you need to know about SKEUOMORPHISM

Have you ever wondered why the best websites look fresher and smarter than yours? Do you want to learn the powerful secret of great web design? Then you need to know about skeuomorphism.

**1 ___**

Here's a simple definition: skeuomorphism involves making digital objects look like things in the real world. The earliest websites just had lots of text. Instead of a 'click here' button, you simply had the words 'click here'. But web designers soon realised that users prefer life-like buttons and switches.

**2 ___**

Examples of skeuomorphism are everywhere. Is there a trashcan on your phone for 'delete'? A cogwheel for 'settings'? An envelope for 'messages'? The list of examples is endless. Skeuomorphism even brings outdated technologies – like floppy disks and sand-filled hourglasses – back to life.

**3 ___**

It depends. Early web designers got carried away with skeuomorphism. Every button had a 3D appearance, with shadows and reflections. This led to a backlash in the early 2010s called 'flat design', which gave a cleaner, less fussy appearance. Flat design managed to appear both retro and modern … but also a little boring.

**4 ___**

Yes and no. Skeuomorphism does make things more user-friendly and intuitive. We all know that a green phone means 'start a call' and a red one means 'end a call', but what if you've never seen an old-fashioned phone? What if you're colour-blind? By all means use skeuomorphism in your web design, but don't assume your users can work out what everything means!

*Want to learn more about web design trends? Click here to sign up for our online course.*

**C SPEAK** Work in pairs. Discuss the questions in the headings.

**D** Match the objectives (1–3) with the strategies (a–g).

### Making your blog post successful

A successful blog post achieves three objectives:

1 People will find it using search engines. ___, ___, ___, ___
2 They will read it from start to finish. ___, ___
3 They will take some action that helps the writer. ___

a Include a number in your title (i.e. 7, not seven). Search engines prefer them!
b End with a clear call to action (CTA), e.g. 'sign up for our newsletter'.
c Ask questions in your first paragraph, but only answer them later in your blog post.
d Choose one key word or phrase and use it as many times as possible in your blog post.
e Use questions as section headings. Many people use questions to search.
f Speak to readers as 'you' and offer to solve their problems.
g Include lots of common search terms like 'definition' and 'examples'.

**E** Find examples of the strategies (a–g) in the blog post.

## WRITING

**A PREPARE** Work in groups. You are going to write a blog post about a trend or trends in general. Think of ideas for topics.

**B PLAN** Choose your key word or phrase (to be repeated many times in your blog post), your title and a series of questions to use as section headings.

**C WRITE** Write your blog post. Make sure the first paragraph encourages the reader to keep going to the CTA!

**D REVIEW** Read some other people's blog posts. Use the box above to evaluate the posts.

# 2 Writing
## Write a review

**W— writing concisely**

**A** Read this announcement and answer the questions.

> **Reviews wanted**
>
> Have you recently read a classic book or watched a classic film? We're starting a series of reviews of classic books and films and we want your opinions. Is the book or film as good as everyone says it is? Is it still relevant today? Please send us a review for the college paper. Write 220–260 words.

1. What should be reviewed?
2. What questions should be addressed by the review?
3. Who is the target audience?
4. How long should the review be?

**B** Read the review. Does the writer agree that the book deserves its reputation as a classic? Which parts of the review tell you this?

### Alice's Adventures in Wonderland

1. Fantasy children's novel *Alice's Adventures in Wonderland* was published in 1865. The book, adapted for film and television and translated into over 100 languages, fully deserves its reputation as a classic and is just as fun today as it always was.

2. At the start of the story, Alice sees a white rabbit wearing clothes and talking to himself. Following the rabbit, she falls down a hole into a bizarre world of strange and wonderful creatures, including a snooty caterpillar and the mysterious, grinning Cheshire Cat.

3. One of the reasons that *Alice's Adventures in Wonderland* is so popular is that it is a nonsense story. It's not a typical linear story or a story with logic and a moral. It's about the strange situations and unusual characters created by the author, and they surprise and delight readers.

4. Another reason for the book's enduring popularity is Lewis Carroll's playful use of language. The story is full of riddles, puzzles, puns and made-up words. One of the most famous examples is the 'unbirthday party' at the Mad Hatter's tea party.

5. *Alice's Adventures in Wonderland* is without doubt a classic book that has captured the imaginations of generations of children and adults. Its creative story, characters and playful use of language make it a unique story – and one that everybody should read at least once.

**C** Look at the review and identify which paragraph contains the following information.

a. an overall opinion of the work and a recommendation ____
b. key information about the work and a general opinion of it ____
c. analysis of a second positive or negative aspect of the work ____
d. a plot summary or description of the work ____
e. analysis of one positive or negative aspect of the work ____

**D** Read the review again and answer the questions.

1. Which characters from the book are mentioned?
   _____
2. How is the story of this book different to most other books?
   _____
3. What example of playful use of language does the writer give?
   _____

**E** Find features of concise description in the text. Use the information in the box to help you.

> **Writing concisely**
>
> If you need to write concisely, you can use some of the following features:
> - noun phrases: *English writer and mathematician Charles Dodgson*
> - reduced relative clauses: *Charles Dodgson, writer and mathematician, published his first book.*
> - participle clauses: *Educated at home, Dodgson wrote poems and short stories.*

## WRITING

**A PREPARE** Look again at the announcement in Exercise A.

**B PLAN** Plan your review. Use your answers to question 2 in Exercise A to help you.

**C WRITE** Write your review. Use your plan to help you.

**D REVIEW** Exchange your review with a partner. Do you have similar information? Underline any information that you don't think is correct.

**E EDIT** Read your partner's comments. Rewrite any parts you think should change.

# 3 Writing

**Write a persuasive email**

persuasive techniques

**A SPEAK** Read the email. Who is the writer? Who is he writing to? Why?

> **To:** Lakeside residential estate (group)
> **From:** Daniel Hernandez
> **Subject:** Road resurfacing
>
> Dear all
>
> a As you know, the internal roads in our estate are in a dreadful condition. Not only does this look ugly, but it also damages our cars. Furthermore, one of our loved ones may be injured by tripping on the uneven surface.
>
> b With that in mind, the housing association has set aside funds to resurface the roads. As I'm sure you remember, the roads were last resurfaced five years ago. One option is simply to use the same cheap materials again (and in five years, the surface will have deteriorated again).
>
> c I would like to propose an alternative: self-repairing concrete. Thanks to cutting-edge technology, self-repairing concrete is infused with billions of tiny limestone-producing bacteria, *Bacillus pseudofirmus*. While sealed in concrete, these bacteria remain inert, but when exposed to air they multiply rapidly. No sooner does a crack appear in the concrete than millions of these bacteria will wake up and plug the crack.
>
> d As you can imagine, although self-repairing concrete is rather expensive, it will save us money in the long run (see attached calculations). More importantly, if one serious accident can be prevented over the next five years, I'm sure you'll agree it will have been worth the extra cost.
>
> e I know you are all smart people, so let's make the smart decision. Please support my proposal at our next housing association meeting.
>
> Best regards
> Daniel

**B** Read the email again. Match the questions (1–5) with the paragraphs (a–e). Then discuss the questions in pairs.

1. What is a potential objection and how can it be overcome? ____
2. What is the most likely solution and what's wrong with it? ____
3. What action does the reader need to take? ____
4. What is the problem and why should the reader care? ____
5. What's an alternative solution and why is it better? ____

**C** Underline examples of each technique in Daniel's email. Use the information in the box to help you.

### Persuasive techniques

1. Use words like *we*, *our* and *let's* to build a connection with the readers.
2. Flatter your readers by claiming they're intelligent and knowledgeable.
3. Provide facts and figures to support your claims, in an attachment if appropriate.
4. Use emotive language and imagery to appeal to your readers' fear of loss, damage or injury.
5. Explain technical issues in simple language, but include some impressive technical terms.
6. Use *although* or *while* to link weaknesses with strengths.

**D** Work in pairs. Use the techniques in Exercise C to make these email extracts more persuasive.

1. Your biggest problem is that you spend too much money on electricity.
2. Please support me so I can solve this problem for you.
3. The road surface is so bad that delivery drivers may refuse to drive into our estate.
4. I admit this solution will be extremely disruptive during the building work.

## WRITING

**A PREPARE** Work in groups. You are going to write a persuasive email about sustainability, smart materials or voluntourism. Generate a list of ideas. Use the following questions to help you:

1. What problem are you trying to solve?
2. Who do you need to persuade?
3. What do you want your reader to do?

**B PLAN** Plan a five-paragraph email. You can use the five questions from Exercise B to help you.

**C WRITE** Write your email, using techniques from this lesson.

**D REVIEW** Exchange your email with a partner. Do you use similar techniques? Comment on how the email could be made more persuasive and underline any mistakes.

**E EDIT** Read your partner's comments. Rewrite any parts you think should change.

# 4 Writing — Write a report

**W** — hedging

**A** Study the list of twenty words for one minute. Then try to write them all down.

experiment  brilliant  eccentric
participant  professor  memory
common sense  fashion
argument  trend  brainpower  website
metaphor  conclusion  project  world-famous
iconic  obstacle  self-portrait
inspiration

**B** Work in groups. Compare the words that you remembered. Which words did most people remember?

**C** Read the report. Which words did the study find were more likely to be recalled? Why were these words more likely to be recalled?

### INVESTIGATING SHORT-TERM AND LONG-TERM MEMORY

**Introduction**
This report describes an experiment to replicate the results of an earlier study. Murdock (1962) investigated the concepts of short-term and long-term memory by getting students to memorise a list of words. He found that students were more likely to recall the words at the beginning and end of the list. ᵃHe concluded that this **may** be because the words from the beginning of the list were stored in the long-term memory, whereas the words at the end of the list were stored in the short-term memory.

**Methods**
Thirty participants (16 men and 14 women) were asked to look at a list of 20 words for a minute. They were then asked to try to recall the words.
The words that participants wrote down were analysed to see which words were recalled the most and if the position of the word in the list affected the students' ability to recall the word.

**Results**
The results confirmed Murdock's findings and showed that students were more likely to recall words from the beginning and end of the list.

**Discussion**
Murdock suggested that students studied the words at the start of the list more carefully, perhaps by saying the words out loud. ᵇ**He believed that** this meant that the words had been processed enough to enter the long-term memory. ᶜThe words at the end of the list were the words students had just looked at, so these were **likely** to be stored in the short-term memory. ᵈThis study replicated Murdock's findings and **suggests** that his theory may be correct.

**Conclusion**
It can be concluded that when given information as a list, we are more likely to recall items from the beginning and end of the list.

**D** Look at the report again and match the report headings with the descriptions (1–5).

1 Analysis of the meaning of the findings _____
2 Description of participants and what was done _____
3 The findings _____
4 A summary of the outcome _____
5 An overview and background information _____

**E** Match the rules with the four sentences (a–d) in the report.

#### Hedging
In a scientific report unless something is a well-established fact, we should use hedging to make our claims less strong and less open to criticism. Use:
1 auxiliary verbs such as *may*, *might* and *could*: ___
2 adverbs such as *probably*, *possibly* and *likely*: ___
3 verbs that that allow for some doubt, such as *seem*, *appear*, *suggest*, *indicate*: ___
4 introductory phrases to qualify, such as *We believe*, *We understand*, *In our view*: ___

## WRITING

**A PREPARE** Read about a similar experiment. Imagine you have recently replicated this experiment.

**B WRITE** Write a full report about it.

Glanzer and Cunitz (1966) did a similar experiment to Murdock, but they had two different groups. One group received the test immediately after looking at the words. The other group had a 30-second delay before they did the test and had to count backwards in threes from 99 during the delay. The results showed that although participants could recall the words from the start of the list, they could not recall the words from the end of the list. Glanzer and Cunitz concluded that this was because these words were no longer in participants' short-term memories because of the delay and the distraction.

**References**
Glanzer, M, & Cunitz, A R (1966) 'Two storage mechanisms in free recall' *Journal of Verbal Learning and Verbal Behavior*, 5(4), 351–360.

# 5 Writing

**Write a formal report**

W — using depersonalisation

**A** Read the report and answer the questions.
1 Who commissioned the report? Why?
2 What worked well in the two case studies? What went wrong?
3 Which elements does the writer recommend copying? What would the writer change?

## Using games to attract tourists to Littlemarket

### Background
At a recent meeting of the Littlemarket Tourism Board, [1]it was proposed that an investigation should be conducted into the use of urban gaming and gamification to attract tourists. This report summarises the research and provides a series of recommendations.

### Case study 1: Bighampton
Two years ago, the tourism board in Bighampton launched a series of treasure-hunt worksheets for tourists, which [2]were reported to be enjoyable by 55% of participants. However, they were found to be too easy by 25%. The games were moderately successful in attracting tourists to some lesser known attractions, but the overall impact on tourist numbers was minimal (a 1.5% rise).

### Case study 2: Smallton
Last year, the Smallton Tourism Board developed an app to gamify tourists' experience of the town. Badges could be won for visiting particular cafés, museums and other attractions. [3]In spite of widespread frustration with technical problems, the results were impressive, with some cafés and restaurants reporting an 80% increase in sales. [4]It remains to be seen how successful the app has been at boosting overall tourist numbers, but initial indications are positive.

### Recommendations
[5]It would be relatively cheap and simple to develop a series of printable treasure hunt maps. Ideally, a range of levels (beginner to expert) would be offered. However, [6]it would be necessary to invest significantly in marketing [7]to raise awareness of the games. [8]It would also make sense to use the gamification techniques from Smallton's experiment to encourage tourists to spend more money. Unlike Smallton, we should involve local businesses in the costs of developing and promoting our games.

The costs of developing an app are currently beyond our budget, so I recommend gaining experience first with a cheaper, low-tech solution and then, if appropriate, upgrading to a sophisticated technical solution in two to three years.

**B** Complete the examples with the extracts (1–7) from the report.

### Using depersonalisation
Depersonalisation involves removing people from your writing to make it more formal. Depersonalisation techniques include:

a  *it + be + adjective + to*-infinitive: *we could cheaply and easily* → ___; *we'd need to* → ___
b  preposition + noun: *Although many people got frustrated* → ___
c  changing verbs into nouns or adjectives: *55% of participants said they had enjoyed* → ___; *to inform people about* → ___
d  the passive voice: *somebody proposed that* → ___
e  other impersonal phrases: *We still don't know* → ___; *we should also* → ___

## WRITING

**A** PREPARE  Work in groups. You have been asked to write a report for a language school about using games to attract new students and improve language skills. Discuss how escape rooms, urban games, game theory or gamification could help your language school.

**B** PLAN  Imagine two or three case studies involving other language schools. Make notes about each case study in your plan.

**C** WRITE  Write your report. Use depersonalisation techniques to make it suitably formal.

**D** REVIEW  Exchange your report with a partner. Do you use similar techniques? Comment on how your partner has used depersonalisation.

**E** EDIT  Read your partner's comments. Rewrite any parts you think should change.

# 6 Writing

● Write an expository essay

W— structuring an expository essay

**A SPEAK** Work in pairs. Read the essay prompt and brainstorm possible answers.

> What are the benefits of deep-sea exploration?

**B** Read the essay. What benefits does the writer mention? What evidence or examples does the writer give for each benefit?

## The benefits of DEEP-SEA EXPLORATION

Did you know that humans have only explored 5% of the world's oceans? This means there is clearly a lot left to be discovered. There are benefits of deep-sea exploration, such as learning more about climate change, addressing the problems of food shortage, and finding cures for diseases.

First, deep-sea exploration is providing vital information about climate change. For example, researchers have been observing how rising temperatures affect the movements of sea creatures. In addition, some studies have found that the sea is able to absorb carbon from the atmosphere.

Second, exploration of the seas will help governments ensure there is enough food for everyone in the future. According to the UN Food and Agriculture Organisation, fish stocks are already getting low. However, improvements to fish farming methods will allow countries to support sustainable fishing.

Finally, exploring the seas is leading to advances in medicine to help fight disease. For example, medicines have already been discovered to help with chronic pain, asthma and even cancer. Many scientists believe we are much more likely to discover new medicines in the sea than on land.

In summary, there are many benefits to deep-sea exploration. It can help scientists to understand climate change better as they try to prevent it. It can also help people to ensure the ocean remains a valuable source of food. In addition, discovering new species of plant and animal could lead to the development of new medicines. People have already discovered a lot from just 5% of the ocean. Imagine what they could find in the other 95%.

**C** Read the essay again and answer the questions. Use the information in the box to help you.

> **Structuring an expository essay**
>
> The typical structure of an expository essay is:
> - **Introduction:** Includes a 'hook' to get readers' attention, background information and the thesis statement, which states what the essay will describe or explain
> - **Body paragraph one:** Describes or explains the first point
> - **Body paragraph two:** Describes or explains the second point
> - **Body paragraph three:** Describes or explains the third point
> - **Conclusion:** Summarises the points that were made and leaves the reader with a 'final thought'.

1 Which sentence is the hook? How does the writer get the reader's attention?
2 Which sentence is the thesis statement? What do you notice about the order of the points in the thesis statement?
3 The first sentence of each paragraph is called a topic sentence. What information is included in this sentence?
4 What kind of information is included in each paragraph to support the idea introduced in the topic sentence?
5 The conclusion contains a summary of the points made in the essay. What do you notice about the order of the points in the summary?

## WRITING

**A PREPARE** Work in groups. Read the essay prompt in Exercise A again. Come up with ideas and make a list of possible benefits.

**B PLAN** Choose the best ideas and organise them into paragraphs.

**C WRITE** Use your plan to write an expository essay. Write approximately 250 words.

**D REVIEW** Work in pairs. Edit your partner's essay. Check:
- spelling and punctuation
- use of language
- clarity of the structure

# 7 Writing — Write a cover letter

**W** — using power verbs

**A** Read the job advert.

Which skills and abilities:

1 will candidates need to prove from their qualifications and experience?
2 will candidates try to show from their life experience and character?
3 are useful but not essential?

### Research Technician – Antarctica

The **International Antarctic Research Station (IARS)** is recruiting a research technician. The job involves setting up and maintaining equipment for scientific experiments, collecting data and providing support as part of the IARS team.

No research skills are required but experience of work in glaciology, geology, meteorology or oceanology would be valuable. The main requirements are technical skills (including electrical and mechanical engineering). You will need to cope with extreme conditions (including severe weather, dangerous environments and hazardous materials), work as a reliable member of an international team and follow instructions accurately and intelligently.

Applications to: Dr Adelia Ross, IARS

**B** Read the cover letter. Which skills and abilities from Exercise A does Francesca mention? What doesn't she mention?

Dear Dr Ross,

I am writing to apply for the position of Research Technician at the IARS.

You will see on my CV (attached) that I have six years' experience as a laboratory technician at an international energy company, where I investigated energy efficiency. During this time, I gained invaluable insights into real-life research, where quick thinking and creativity are just as valuable as patience and precision.

I have explored the Polar regions many times. Last summer, I successfully led an international expedition to a remote part of Greenland, where I demonstrated exceptional organisational skills, resilience in the face of extreme challenges and, above all, the ability to work in a team.

I look forward to the opportunity of an interview.

Best regards,

*Francesca Matienzo*

**C** Read the information about using power verbs to apply for a job. Add five power verbs from Francesca's letter to the list of examples.

> **Using power verbs**
>
> In CVs and cover letters, it's more powerful to use verbs to describe your achievements (*I managed the project*) rather than nouns (*I was the manager of …*) or adjectives (*I was responsible for …*).
>
> Examples: *achieved, coordinated, designed, implemented, improved, negotiated, organised, persuaded, strengthened, updated,* _____, _____, _____, _____, _____

**D** Make these extracts more powerful.

1 I was involved in negotiations to buy raw materials.
2 My manager agreed to my idea to switch suppliers.
3 I was in charge of a team of six.
4 Our old records were out of date, so I fixed them.
5 I did general office tasks, like answering the phone and checking emails.

## WRITING

**A PREPARE** You are going to apply for your dream job or one of the jobs below. First, list the skills, abilities, experience and qualifications required for the job.

- stunt performer
- zoo keeper
- safari or mountain guide
- astronaut

**B PLAN** Draft your cover letter, using Francesca's letter as a model.

**C WRITE** Make your letter more powerful by adding at least five power verbs.

**D REVIEW** Read some of your classmates' letters. Which letters would persuade you to invite the candidate for an interview? How could you improve the other letters?

# 8 Writing — Write a summary

**W** — paraphrasing

**A SPEAK** Work in pairs. How does stress affect the body?

**B** Read *The effects of stress on the body* and circle the specific health problems the article mentions.

### The effects of stress on the body

Chronic stress can affect several different parts of the body, including the musculoskeletal system, the cardiovascular system and the gastrointestinal system.

Stress causes muscles to tense and when this happens for an extended period of time, it can cause tension and pain in the back, shoulders and head. For many people, this results in tension headaches and migraines.

It is well known that acute stress causes a temporary increase in heart rate and blood pressure. However, long-term stress means that heart rate and blood pressure remain high, potentially leading to inflammation of the arteries and an increased chance of hypertension, heart attack or stroke.

Stress can have a direct or indirect effect on the gastrointestinal system. Stress often causes people to eat more unhealthy food than they usually would. This can lead to heartburn and acid reflux, which can affect the throat. Stress can upset the stomach too, leading to digestive problems, nausea and even stomach ulcers.

In summary, long-term stress puts extra pressure on the body that can lead to health problems for various parts of the body, such as the muscles, the heart and stomach.

**C** Look at three draft summaries of the article. What are the problems with each of these summaries?

1. Long-term stress can lead to heart attacks and strokes because of the extra pressure it puts on the cardiovascular system. During periods of stress, our heart rate and blood pressure are raised. This is a natural response to stress, but it becomes harmful if it continues for an extended period of time.

2. It is important to use strategies to help you relax, so that stress does not lead to health problems with your muscles, heart and digestive system. For example, having an increased heart rate and increased blood pressure for an extended period of time can result in heart disease or stroke. Stress can also cause headaches, digestive problems and even panic attacks.

3. Chronic stress can affect different parts of the body, including the musculoskeletal system, the cardiovascular system and the gastrointestinal system. Stress causes muscles to tense, and people to eat more unhealthy food, which can upset the stomach.

**D** Read the information in the box about writing a summary. Then identify the main points in *The effects of stress on the body*.

### Paraphrasing

It's important to focus on the main points of the source text, but not just to copy the text. You need to explain the information in your own words.

1. Identify the main points in the piece of text that you want to summarise. In an academic paper, look at the introduction, the topic sentences at the start of each paragraph and at the conclusion. In a newspaper article, look at the opening paragraph and the conclusion.

2. Note down any words you need to re-use from the text (i.e. proper nouns, technical words).

3. Explain the information in your own words. Use different structures and different words to make sure you aren't copying from the text. You can also put the information in a different order.

4. Check your summary. Make sure you have not copied parts of the original, introduced new information or changed the meaning.

## WRITING

**A WRITE** Write a short summary of *The effects of stress on the body*. Do not write more than 60 words.

**B REVIEW** Exchange your summaries. Give your partner any suggestions for improvements.

**C EDIT** Use your partner's feedback to improve your summaries.

# 9 Writing — Write a conclusion to an academic report

**W** – linking in academic writing

**A SPEAK** Work in pairs. Say the following sentences aloud five times. Do they make you feel happier/sadder? Why?

1. Two new blue shoes flew to the moon.
2. These green leaves seem free and easy.
3. Our alarm can't harm the calm farmer.

**B** Read the conclusion to an academic report. Does it agree with your responses to Exercise A?

**CONCLUSION**

1. Our research set out to test the facial feedback hypothesis that our facial expressions can affect our moods. Strack *et al* (1988) famously asked respondents to evaluate cartoons while holding a pen in their mouths. Some held it between their teeth, forcing them to smile; others held it between their lips, forcing a frown. The 'smilers' found the cartoons significantly funnier than the 'frowners'. Similarly, Zajonc *et al* (1989), demonstrated a causal relationship between vowel sounds and mood: the repetition of 'smile vowels' (/e/, /iː/) and the 'aha vowel' (/ɑː/) put the respondents in a significantly better mood than 'frown vowels' (e.g. /uː/). However, recent research by Wagenmakers *et al* (2016) has cast serious doubt on this hypothesis.

2. Our own research provides limited support for the hypothesis. We found that repeating sentences with 'smile vowels' did indeed provoke a mood improvement compared to 'frown' vowels. However, in neither case were the results conclusive: the majority of respondents reported no change in mood. The one exception was that the 'aha vowel' had a significant positive effect on almost every respondent's mood.

3. Our evidence suggests that facial expressions do indeed affect mood, but it is principally the open-mouthed 'aha smile' rather than the wide-mouthed grin that has the greatest impact. This may explain the failure of Wagenmakers *et al* to repeat the effects of the pen experiment: they were focusing on the wrong type of smile.

4. If refined and confirmed by further research, the facial feedback hypothesis could be used by psychotherapists and carers to improve patients' moods. Additionally, marketers may use vowel sounds in product names to influence customers' connotations. If products such as 'New You' are renamed as 'Calming Spa', it may well be because of the effect of vowel sounds on our mood.

**C** Match the topics (a–d) with the paragraphs (1–4).

a. Analysis: What did you learn? ____
b. Implications: What do your findings mean? ____
c. Background: What question were you trying to answer? ____
d. Key findings: What information did you collect? ____

**D** Answer the questions. Use the information in the box to help you.

> **Linking in academic writing**
>
> Use linking words (e.g. *however*) to show the relationships between ideas.
> Use colons (:) to show that one idea 'explains' another.
> Use semi-colons (;) to show that two related ideas are 'equal' in importance.

1. Find a semi-colon in paragraph 1. In what way are the two ideas equal?
2. Which two linking words in paragraph 1 link all the research together?
3. Find three colons in paragraphs 1–3. How does the second idea explain the first in each case?
4. What linking word in paragraphs 2 and 3 relates expectations to reality? What grammar structure is often used with this word?
5. How does the writer link the main ideas in paragraph 4?

## WRITING

**A PREPARE** Choose one of your own ideas or a piece of academic research from this unit.

**B PLAN** Make notes about the points you will cover in your conclusion.

**C WRITE** Write a four-paragraph conclusion. Use linking words, colons and semi-colons in your writing.

**D REVIEW** Exchange your conclusion with a partner. Do you agree with their analysis? Comment on how they use linking words.

**E EDIT** Read your partner's comments. Rewrite any parts of your conclusion that you think could be improved.

# 10 Writing — Write a persuasive essay

**W** — using counter-arguments and rebuttals

**A SPEAK** Work in pairs. Look at the essay title and discuss the questions.
1 What is gentrification?
2 What do you think of gentrification? Is it a good or bad thing?

**B** Read the example essay and answer the questions.
1 What is the writer's opinion of gentrification?
2 What reasons does the writer give for her opinion?
3 What reason to support the opposite opinion on gentrification does the writer mention?

## DOES GENTRIFICATION HAVE A POSITIVE OR NEGATIVE IMPACT ON CITIES?

In cities all over the world, 'gentrification' is changing entire neighbourhoods. Some people argue that this improves the areas by making them cleaner and safer. However, on the whole, gentrification actually has a negative impact. It prices people out of the areas where they have lived for years, destroys the unique character of neighbourhoods, and it only benefits the rich.

The most obvious negative impact of gentrification is that it forces long-term residents to move away from their homes. As an area becomes trendy, landlords are able to increase the rent and attract wealthier tenants to the area. Meanwhile, lower income families are forced to move away from their friends, schools and jobs to find cheaper places to live.

Gentrification also results in the area losing its individual character. People may have first been attracted to an area by its unique shops and restaurants. However, as this area becomes gentrified, these establishments are unlikely to be able to pay increased rent. Gradually, these shops and restaurants are replaced by high street chains so the area becomes just like many other neighbourhoods in the city.

Some people argue that gentrification has a positive impact because the area becomes cleaner and safer. While it is true that gentrification leads to less crime and better facilities, the local people who deserve to benefit from these changes are unable to stay in the area. Rather than improving the city for all, gentrification only benefits the wealthiest.

In conclusion, gentrification predominantly has a negative impact on cities. It forces long-term residents from their homes, results in areas losing their individual character, and only provides real benefits for those with the most money. The government needs to find a way to ensure that redevelopment of the city can have a positive effect for everyone.

**C** Find the phrases the writer used to introduce the counter argument and rebuttal in the example essay. Use the information in the box to help you.

### Using counter-arguments and rebuttals

In order to strengthen your argument in a persuasive essay, you can anticipate the points that could be used to support the opposite side of the argument (the counter-arguments) and respond with your answer to those arguments (a rebuttal). The rebuttal must respond directly to the counter argument.

Introduce a counter argument with phrases like:
- Opponents/Supporters of …. claim/argue/believe that …
- Some studies have shown that …
- There is an argument that …

Introduce a rebuttal with phrases like:
- However, this is only partially true.
- Studies have shown this is not true.
- Nevertheless, …

## WRITING

**A PREPARE** Work in pairs. Look at the essay prompt and brainstorm reasons to support each side.

> Which is better: living in the city or living in the countryside?

| Reasons why living in the city is better | Reasons why living in the countryside is better |
|---|---|
|  |  |

**B PLAN** Decide on your best points from Exercise A and make a plan of your essay.

**C WRITE** Write a persuasive essay to answer the essay prompt. Use a counter-argument and rebuttal in the third body paragraph. Use the example essay to help you.

**D REVIEW** Exchange your essay with a partner. How could your partner's essay be improved? How effective are their counter-arguments and rebuttals?

**E EDIT** Read your partner's comments. Rewrite any parts of your essay you think can be improved.

# Audioscripts

## 1 TRENDS

### Lesson 1.1, Listening, Exercise B
**1.1  C = Carly   D = Dan**

C: So? How did the job interview go, Dan?

D: It was a breeze! I got the job. But the thing is, I start in two weeks and I've got nothing to wear. The job involves meeting important clients. But they won't take me seriously in my scruffy jeans and hoodie!

C: Sounds like you need some new clothes.

D: I know. But I'm on a tight budget until I receive my first few months' salary.

C: Well, it's easy to look good without spending a fortune. Do you have a suit?

D: No, but I saw a suit yesterday for 40% off in a sale, so I'll save almost £100 if I buy that.

C: Well, you're only saving money if you buy something you really need. If you're just buying it because it's cheap, you're throwing money down the drain. It's much better in the long run to invest in timeless classics. For example, instead of buying a cheap off-the-shelf suit that you'll need to replace in a few months, save up for a tailor-made suit that will make you look fantastic for many years.

D: OK, I admit that suit was a bit cheap-looking. But it was the only one in my size. They had some lovely suits in the sale, but they were all too tight or too loose for me.

C: Well, you can always buy oversized clothes – as long as they're good quality, and then take them in.

D: What do you mean, take them in?

C: It's when you unpick the seams, move the pieces of fabric closer together, and sew them back together. In fact, more generally, I'd say the best way to look good without spending loads of money is to learn to sew. But hang on a second. Didn't you have to wear a suit for the job interview?

D: Well, it was an online interview, so I just wore a jacket from an old suit and a nice shirt and tie to create a good impression. They had no idea I was wearing baggy tracksuit trousers under my desk!

C: Haha, no, you're winding me up! It's usually a good idea to mix and match parts of different outfits, which can save you a lot of money, but I'd say mixing a suit with a tracksuit is taking things a bit far! Do you still have the trousers to go with that jacket?

D: Yeah, I've actually got two old suits with perfectly good jackets but trousers that I can't wear! One pair is coming apart at the seams. The other is completely worn out at the knee.

C: Hmm, it sounds like you can start your sewing lessons on those trousers! Then you'll have two suits in your wardrobe for peanuts! That's actually a good example of how to go shopping in your wardrobe.

D: Sorry. Where?

C: In your wardrobe. Most people have loads of clothes that they never wear. The trick is to sort them into four categories: love, mend, sell and bin.

D: Go on.

C: 'Love' is for the clothes that make you look and feel great. 'Mend' is for the clothes that you need to adjust or repair. 'Sell' is for the clothes that you can auction online. And then 'bin' is for everything else. Basically you need to get rid of them!

D: OK, I've got loads of clothes that I could sell, but I've never used an auction website before. Do you think anyone will buy my old clothes?

C: You'd be surprised. I mean, most customers on those sites stick to the professional sellers with beautiful tailor-made sales pages created by web designers. But I actually buy most of my clothes from ugly sales pages, created by inexperienced sellers.

D: What? Are you saying I should create an ugly sales page for my second-hand clothes?

C: No, not at all. The more professional your sales page, the more you can charge for your clothes. And it needs to be a seamless process for your customers from beginning to end. So as a general rule, when you're selling clothes, it's well worth taking the time to make your sales page look good. For example, you can just use one of the off-the-shelf templates from the auction site. Choose a template that catches your eye – it's much better than creating your own site from scratch.

D: OK, sounds like good advice. And when I'm buying clothes online, to replace the ones I'm selling?

C: Then you should look out for newbie sellers with bad photos – they're usually good for picking up a bargain.

D: Aha, yes, that makes sense. So are auction sites the best place to pick up cheap second-hand clothes?

C: Sometimes, but the best place to buy them is often charity shops, even though they're pretty exhausting! You need to know where to go if you want to avoid wearing yourself out for nothing! For instance, the best charity shops are in posh, exclusive neighbourhoods. You'd be amazed what you can pick up there. The trick is to avoid shops in a trendy area or one with lots of students – all the best stuff will be snapped up immediately.

D: OK, good. What about regular shops?

C: They're fine as long as you're not too choosy – the big-name stores are often no better than others, but they charge a lot more for the same stuff! But wherever you go, don't forget to haggle to get the price down.

D: What do you mean?

C: Ask the shop assistant for a discount. I always ask, 'Is this the best you can do?' Many shop assistants are authorised to offer discounts, so it's always worth haggling. You've got nothing to lose but your pride!

D: OK. I'll give it a go. Thanks.

### Lesson 1.2, Listening, Exercise B
**1.3  D = Dora   A = Adam**

A: Hello and welcome to the latest 'Website design podcast'. Today, I've invited Dora Cho to talk about becoming a trendsetter. As I'm sure you know, Dora's video channel is the most hyper-influential source of advice on lifestyle trends on the web. Dora, are you there?

A: Sorry. I forgot to unmute Dora's microphone. Dora?

D: Hello? Can you hear me now?

A: Yes. Sorry, Dora. Shall we restart?

D: You know what? Keep going. One of the most common mistakes that new vloggers and podcasters make is to expect everything to be perfect. So they edit and re-edit everything again and again. But when things go wrong, we hear the real, authentic 'you', and that's what makes your podcast engaging. You actually need to unlearn all those rules about perfection!

A: OK. But your videos are always amazing. You seem so self-confident and relaxed. How do you do that?

D: It all comes down to experience. My first videos were pretty cheesy and amateurish. I used to be quite disaster-prone with technology: everything that could go wrong did go wrong. But after a while, it got a lot easier! I learnt everything by taking risks and making mistakes. It was frustrating at the time but you need to go through that experience. I'm a lot more tech-savvy now, but I'm still learning.

A: Great. So how did you start your vlog?

D: First of all, I set myself a target of one video every week for a year. I figured that if nobody cared after a year, I'd give up. And it did take a while to get noticed, which was frustrating. But over the months, I started to see biggish audience numbers. By the end of the year I had 7000 subscribers.

A: Wow! And now?

D: Six million.

A: Amazing! So what am I doing wrong with my podcasts?

D: Well, there's no need to be negative. The most important thing is that you've found your niche and you've created some excellent content.

A: Really? Oh, thank you.

D: Yeah, it's true. But if you want to move to the next level, you need to be really systematic. I mean, when do your podcasts come out?

# Audioscripts

A: It depends. Whenever I have a goodish idea for a podcast, then I try to make it within a few days.

D: OK, but you can't expect your listeners to check your website every day on the off-chance that you've released another episode – that's not user-friendly at all. But my followers can be absolutely sure that every Wednesday at ten o'clock, there will be a new video on my channel.

A: OK. But what if you run out of ideas?

D: I won't. I plan everything at least six months in advance, and I set alerts on my phone to tell me what to do and when. I've tried to make my system idiot-proof so that I can't mess up!

A: OK …

D: You also need to be far more social media-savvy: once you've released each episode, tell the world about it. And don't just post a link – you need to engage with your audience, too, by replying to the comments on your site. People love to feel listened to.

A: Every single comment?

D: Well, there are plenty of people who post offensive or spammy comments. The trick is to ignore them and focus on the people who want to join your community. You can also ask them what they'd like you to talk about in future podcasts. Once you've got an active community behind you, you'll never run out of ideas.

A: Right. OK, so I'll do all that. But it sounds like hard work!

D: It is hard work! Not long ago, a journalist mentioned my blog in an article about overnight successes. I suppose in many people's eyes, I am an overnight success. They probably think I'm super-lucky to have made the big time. But they don't see the years of hard work behind that success.

A: Right. So I just need to keep working hard on my podcasts, right?

D: Well, your podcasts are great, as I say, but actually I think your content would work much better as smartphone-friendly videos. I mean, you talk about website design, so we really need to be able to see what you're talking about.

A: Maybe, but I'm not as charismatic as you. I hate being in front of the camera.

D: Well, I felt awkward at first, too, but you do get used to it. I really think you should have a rethink and become a vlogger instead.

A: OK. I'll give it a go. Dora Cho, thanks so much for joining me today. You've given me a long list of jobs to do! I feel super-exhausted just thinking about it.

## 2 CREATIVITY

### Lesson 2.1, Listening, Exercise C
2.1 P = Presenter   C = Caroline

P: This week's guest on *More than meets the eye* is art historian Caroline Bishop. Caroline, thanks for joining us.

C: It's my pleasure. Thank you for having me.

P: So the painting you've picked also happens to be one of the great masterpieces. Could you start by telling us its name and a bit about the painter?

C: Sure. It's a painting by Velázquez, called *Las Meninas*. Velázquez is one of Spain's most important artists. He painted in a Baroque style, which means his paintings are very ornate, detailed and realistic. He mainly painted historical scenes and portraits. He painted *Las Meninas* after he'd been given a prominent position in the royal court.

P: And can you describe the painting to us?

C: Well, it depicts a scene in the artist's studio. In the centre foreground we have the young Infanta Margaret Theresa, the daughter of the King and Queen – the word *Infanta* is similar in meaning to princess. The Infanta is framed on either side by her two ladies-in-waiting. Then to the right we have two other women from the royal court and a dog. Behind them are the Infanta's attendants – a chaperone and bodyguard – and further in the background, there's a royal official in a doorway.

P: OK. So, we are probably looking at the Infanta's entourage?

C: Hmm … yes we can see her entourage on the right, but to the left, we can see the artist himself, standing next to a gigantic canvas. The inclusion of the artist in the painting is one of the things that makes this such an interesting piece. It seems more like a snapshot, taken behind the scenes of the royal court, rather than the typical posed portraits of the time. It was a very original composition – groundbreaking at the time.

P: So, do you know why he chose such an unconventional composition?

C: Actually, there are several theories about this – which is one of the things I like best about the painting. There's been a lot of debate about who the subject of the painting really is. On first inspection, it seems that the Infanta is the subject – after all she's in the centre of the painting. But then, if you look in the background, there appears to be a mirror that shows the King and Queen. This suggests that the artist is actually painting *their* portrait. So we, the viewer, are actually seeing the world through the eyes of the King and Queen. The Infanta and her companions are merely watching.

P: So, it's a portrait of the King and Queen, not the Infanta. Is that right?

C: Well … some people think so, yes. Even though the image of them is really small.

P: That's a very imaginative idea – and really unusual for a royal portrait I'm guessing.

C: Yes, absolutely. However … there's one other interpretation that I like. Some people believe that the scene we see is actually just the reflection in a large mirror. What we're seeing is the artist at work in his studio.

P: So this may even be a self-portrait?

C: Exactly. The point of the picture may be to show us the artist's life – this is his studio, this is what it was like when he was painting a portrait. It's actually a very complex composition. It's like a puzzle for the viewer to decide what is really happening.

P: It's fascinating – and I'm not sure which interpretation I like best. Anyway, why did you choose it as your favourite painting? Do you have a personal connection to the work?

C: Well, I first saw this painting in the Prado Gallery in Madrid over 20 years ago when I was a student. And the first time I saw it, I was astounded. It's sensational. I'd never seen anything like it. In fact, I switched to art history a couple of months later.

P: So this painting helped you to choose your career?

C: Yes, yes it did.

### Lesson 2.2, Listening, Exercise A
2.5 M = Mark   L = Lauren

L: Hi Mark, how's the dissertation going?

M: Terribly. Terribly, Lauren. I'm stuck. I've got no ideas today. Zero.

L: Oh, no. Nightmare! But did you see that article Simon shared about how people find inspiration? It's really interesting.

M: Yeah? He's always sharing self-help stuff, but…

L: No, but this one's different. It's real artists, writers, directors, musicians and dancers talking about how they come up with their ideas.

M: Hmm … So, what did they say then?

L: Oh … let me find it. Here we go. OK. This person's a fashion designer and he says, 'Inspiration can strike at any time. I sometimes get ideas when I'm out shopping or walking in the park. I always carry a pen and paper with me, so I can sketch it or write it down. Sometimes the smallest thing can trigger an idea. A flower, a smile, a colour.'

M: OK. Isn't that a bit pretentious? Can't he just use his phone to make notes? And anyway a blank notebook is still a blank notebook.

L: OK, here's an artist – he says the best time for him to get ideas is very early in the morning – when you're not quite awake and not quite asleep. He often sets his alarm for 4 am, so he can get into the right state of mind to have ideas.

M: What! Is he crazy? He must never get enough sleep.

L: Yeah, but come on, I know what he means. A few times, I've had a good idea just before waking up – usually when I've got a problem that I'm trying to solve.

M: Well, I don't think it's going to work for my dissertation.

L: OK. But here's an actual writer. Apparently, she thinks you have to be really disciplined and get into a regular routine. You just sit down and write, because if you wait for ideas to come, you'll never do anything. She says choose a time and stick to it – even if you don't feel like it or even if your writing is terrible, you just need to shut the door, remove all distractions and write.

M: Why does she keep writing if it's terrible? I don't want my dissertation to be terrible!

L: How about this then? You should immerse yourself in other things. Do something completely different – like watch a film. Then when you get back to your desk, you'll be refreshed and ready to be creative again.

M: That's the first thing that I agree with! I need to take a break. I think I need a change of scenery … right now.

L: Yeah, it doesn't hurt, does it? I also think it helps to talk to people – you know, bounce ideas around with someone and see if they can improve your idea. It can really help to get a fresh perspective on something.

M: Isn't that a bit … scary? I don't think I want to share this dissertation until it's finished.

L: Well, it has to be someone you trust. Celia and I often read each other's work, so we're used to helping each other. She also reckons that if you're working from a completely blank canvas, the possibilities can seem limitless, so she likes to impose some restrictions – such as using a particular genre or restricting herself to a particular format. I think she likes to set herself a challenge. That's pretty fun, don't you think?

M: OK, it's quite interesting – and I guess it makes sense. It must be easier to decide what to do if you have fewer choices.

L: Yeah, and I really like the idea of giving yourself a challenge like that. There's one other thing you could do. An artist here says it's important to take risks. You might not fully understand what you're doing, but you just have to trust your instincts and run with it.

M: Is she serious? How can you make something when you don't know what you're doing?

L: Haven't you ever started doodling a picture without knowing what it was going to be?

M: Hmm … I guess so …

L: Well, I think that's what she means. So … anyway, good luck with the dissertation, Mark.

M: Cheers, Lauren!

# 3 PROGRESS

**Lesson 3.1, Listening, Exercise B**
3.1 S = Saleswoman   M = Man   W = Woman

S: Excuse me, sir. Do you ride a bike, by any chance?

M: Well, I have a bike yes. Why do you ask?

S: You just look like a very fit and sporty person.

M: Really? Thank you. Well, I haven't ridden my bike for months. It's too wet at the moment.

S: Yeah, tell me about it! I bet you can't wait for the weather to warm up so you can get out on your bike, can you?

M: Er, no. I guess not. It's not much fun cycling in the rain!

S: Hmm, I know exactly what you mean. It sounds like you need some smart cycling clothes.

M: Er, sorry? I don't …

S: Smart cycling clothes are made from smart materials, which change their form depending on their environment. Let me show you an example. This cycling hat is made from an advanced material that responds to your body temperature. It's quite complicated technology, but I'll try to simplify it for you. Just imagine you're out on your bike early one morning. When you leave home, the fibres in your hat respond to the cold temperature by tightening up. That ensures there's no heat loss from your head and keeps you nice and warm. But as you warm up, the gaps between the fibres in your hat automatically enlarge to allow air to flow freely around your head, to cool you down. But then let's imagine it starts to rain. As the hat gets wet, the water strengthens the fibres and the gaps close to keep your head dry. Amazing, isn't it?

M: Yes. It sounds very clever.

S: It is clever! This technology is straight out of the laboratory. You won't find these in any shops for years!

M: Really?

S: No. We're still at the testing stage. Hey, would you be willing to test it for us? We'd absolutely love to hear how you get on with it. It would be incredibly useful for us.

M: Er, possibly. What would it involve?

S: You wear your hat for a few weeks while you're cycling, and then you fill in a five-minute questionnaire about your experiences. And of course you get to keep your hat at the end! Would that be OK?

M: Really? Yeah, why not?

S: Great! Thanks. Here's your hat. Congratulations! I just need you to sign this form to formalise our agreement.

M: OK, no problem.

S: Thanks. We're planning to sell the hats for £50 in the future, so I think you've got yourself an excellent deal there, sir. I can see you're a very smart negotiator!

M: Am I? Yes, I suppose so. Thanks a lot.

S: No problem. Actually, maybe there is a problem. Did you say you never go cycling in the rain?

M: Yes. Why?

S: Ah … well we really need people to describe their experiences of wearing the hat in different weather conditions over the next couple of weeks, including rain. I'm so sorry – this is really embarrassing. Shall I take the hat back?

M: Er, no. I don't mind cycling in the rain once or twice. I'll just have to get a bit wet, I suppose!

S: Really? Oh that would be amazing if you could. And you know what? Maybe I can help you out there. You see, we also have some smart cycling jackets. They're made of tiny fibres that flatten when they're wet, making the coat completely waterproof, and they open up again when dry, enabling your skin to breathe. Again, they're not available for sale for a while, but maybe I can make an exception for you. Do you mind waiting a second while I phone my boss?

M: No, not at all. Go ahead.

S: Great! Oh hi, Debbie. Listen, I've got a gentleman here who's interested in buying the cycling coat. I know we're not allowed to sell them yet, but … No way, huh? Are you sure? He's going to help us test our hat. Really? Oh, that's great. Thanks, Debbie! I owe you one. Good news! She says she's willing to make an exception, just for you.

M: Oh, great. Thanks. Er, how much is it?

S: Well, we're planning to sell them for £500. But … hmm … maybe … I can offer you … a special price … to thank you for your help. I'll give you 10% off … would that be better?

M: Yes, I guess so.

S: Excellent. So that's £450, please. Will you be paying by cash or credit card?

M: Er, credit card, I suppose.

S: Yes. Of course. Just put in your PIN here.

S: OK, perfect. Thanks. And here's your coat. Thanks so much for helping us out with the testing. I really appreciate it.

M: You're welcome. And thank you. You've been very kind. Goodbye.

S: Goodbye.

# Audioscripts

## Lesson 3.2, Listening, Exercise B
**P = Presenter   B = Bob   M = Mary   J = James   C = Callum   S = Sonia**

**P:** Hello, and welcome to *The Progress Show*. According to a recent survey, despite amazing progress in technology and sharp increases in living standards, many of us believe our quality of life has actually decreased! So this week, I interviewed some people in the street about their lives. I asked them, would you say the world is generally getting better or worse? Let's hear a few extracts from those interviews.
So Bob, would you say the world is getting better or worse?

**B:** Worse, definitely. When I was a teenager, we always showed respect for older people. For example, no sooner had an older person got on the bus than we all stood up to offer the person a seat. I was on a bus the other day, and it was full of teenagers, but not one person offered me a seat. Only after they'd all got off the bus could I finally sit down.

**P:** So Mary, what's your view?

**M:** I'd say it's getting worse for people of my age. People of my parents' age had it much easier. There was plenty of work for everybody, and flats and houses were much cheaper. But everyone of my age seems to be struggling for money. No way could I ever afford a flat. It's not fair!

**P:** James, what do you think?

**J:** I feel like I'm going backwards sometimes. I mean, when I was younger, life was simple. None of our neighbours had much money, and neither did we. But we didn't need much, so we were content just to get on with life. But these days, if you don't post endless selfies of your perfect lifestyle on social media, you feel like a reject from society. It's very frustrating and stressful.

**P:** Callum, what's your take on this?

**C:** On balance, it's probably getting worse. You see such terrible things on TV all the time – crime, wars, diseases! I don't remember anything like that from my childhood. Mind you, I didn't watch much TV when I was a kid and I certainly didn't read any newspapers.

**P:** Sonia, how about you?

**S:** Worse, much worse. I remember when I was in my early twenties, life was brilliant. Not only did I have great friends, but we also did cool things all the time … and the sun always seemed to be shining. Nowadays, life's just work work work … and the weather's always terrible too!

## Lesson 3.2, Listening, Exercise D
**Pre = Presenter   Pro = Professor**

**Pre:** Let's turn now to my guest, Professor Nila Martinelli, an expert in psychology. Professor, is the world really getting worse?

**Pro:** No, not at all. However you choose to measure people's well-being, life for the average person is getting better. But the key word there is 'average'. By no means am I suggesting that life is wonderful for everyone everywhere. But the vast majority of the world's population really is better off, year after year.

**Pre:** OK, so why do so many people say the opposite?

**Pro:** Well, it's all due to a psychological process called declinism, which is a feeling that things are declining, or getting worse. Declinism has a number of separate causes, including something called the inequality paradox. Let me give you an example. Say you live in a community where everybody has terrible healthcare and education, and so on, but overall people just accept that life is hard. But now imagine that 20% of the people suddenly become a lot better off, with comfortable lifestyles and so on. Those 20% push the average up, so according to statistics, the population seems better off. But in fact the remaining 80% feel much worse than before, because they're now aware of what they're missing.

**Pre:** Aha. That makes sense.

**Pro:** Another reason is the so-called reminiscence bump. Scientists have conducted plenty of research on this subject which shows that we build up our strongest memories in our late teens and early twenties. Our memories of early adulthood stay with us for ever. This is why so many people are nostalgic for that time in their life.

**Pre:** Ah … so it's almost as if we rewrite the events in our memories in order to perfect the picture of our younger days!

**Pro:** Exactly! One of my favourite phenomena is something I call the them-and-us delusion. If you were a well-behaved child, you're likely to remember that most other kids of your age were similarly well-behaved. But that's probably because you didn't notice their bad behaviour at the time. Or you've simply erased their negative attributes and bad conduct from your memory. But when you look at a group of people from the outside, what do you notice most? The noisiest, worst-behaved ones. That explains why so many people think that kids today are worse than their own generations.

**Pre:** Yeah, I suppose you're right. I don't remember much about my childhood!

**Pro:** No – and that's normal. Children simply fail to notice things obvious to adults. When I was a child, never in a million years did it occur to me that my parents were worried about money or job insecurity or whatever. But that doesn't mean they never talked about those things. This is something that we might call the invisible struggle phenomenon: we don't see the problems that other people face, so we think we're the only ones with such problems. We tend to attribute other people's success to luck and we overlook all the problems they've struggled with. And of course that's a major source of inter-generational conflict: young adults always suspect that earlier generations had it much easier!

**Pre:** Aha. I see what you mean.

**Pro:** There's one last aspect of declinism, and it's called the window-on-the-world effect. It arises when people become aware of the terrible things that happen around the world. Centuries ago, people were blissfully unaware of wars and diseases in distant countries. But nowadays, we see such things on a daily basis on the news, on social media and so on. So it's not that terrible events are necessarily becoming more frequent, but rather that we're aware of those events. And for me, the fact that more and more people care about global tragedies makes it more likely that we'll do something about them. And that's my main reason for optimism that the world really is getting better, and will continue to do so.

**Pre:** Hmm … Professor Nila Martinelli, thanks very much for joining us.

# 4 INTELLIGENCE

## Lesson 4.1, Listening, Exercise B
**H = Host   Dr = Dr Carter   A = Amanda**

**H:** On this week's episode of *Ask an Expert*, we're talking about boosting your brain power. These days many products claim to make you smarter. But is it really possible? To answer the question, I'm joined today by two experts: Dr Ramona Carter, a leading neuroscientist, and Amanda Saraha, a life coach and the author of *How to be smarter*. Thank you for joining me.

**A:** Thanks, John.

**Dr:** Thank you, John.

**H:** So first up, Amanda, the big question. Can people really make themselves smarter?

**A:** The short answer is yes, John. But the first step may actually be believing it's possible. Researchers have shown that when a group of students are told it's possible to become more intelligent, they can retain more of what they learn.

**H:** Dr Carter, do you agree? Can we make ourselves brighter? One way that's very popular is brain training games.

**Dr:** I've got to admit, I love them. But I'm sceptical about whether they have any long-term effects. The problem is that the effects are probably not transferable. So for example, if you do a lot of Sudoku, the maths puzzle where you write the numbers in boxes, it's most likely that you will just become better at playing that game.

A team from Cambridge actually tried to shed some light on the impact of brain-training games. They had thousands of participants, so this was a big study doing brain training activities for at least 10 minutes a day, three times a week for six weeks. They tested them before and after. And the results showed no improvements in their test scores. In other words, their study showed that brain training didn't actually work.

**A:** Actually, if you don't mind me saying, that was just one study. Another study looked at older people playing a game that involved multi-tasking – they had to drive a car and look out for specific symbols as they drove. In this study, the participants showed that not only did they get better at the game, but that they also improved their attention and working memory.

**Dr:** Yes, you're right. But it's worth noting that this study specifically involved a video game rather than a typical brain-training game. Playing video games may affect our cognitive abilities according to research. But these kinds of games may prove to be more beneficial than dedicated brain-training games.

**H:** So overall the findings about playing games are a little inconclusive at the moment. So, what else can we do to boost our brain power?

**A:** There are actually lots of things you can do. For example, have you ever wondered why so many high achievers boast about starting the day with a workout? I strongly believe that the exercise they are doing makes them smarter and more competitive.

**Dr:** Well … I'd be cautious about making a direct link between high achievement and exercise, but there is a pretty clear consensus that exercise is good for the brain. Some scientists believe that exercise can help to promote the growth and formation of neurons in the hippocampus – so, as I mentioned before, if we retain the new cells that our body produces, it could affect our ability to think and remember.

**H:** Hmm … Is food another factor? Recently, we've seen a lot of media stories about super foods, food that you should eat to boost your brain power – fatty fish, blueberries, even chocolate. Is this true, Dr Carter?

**Dr:** Erm, the research is actually fairly inconclusive. Some studies have shown that eating a healthy diet has an impact on thinking ability, but claims that particular foods can impact your intelligence are mostly exaggerated or misleading.

**H:** Do you agree, Amanda?

**A:** As Dr Carter says, we may still be in the dark about the science behind it, but I personally believe that the food we eat has a huge effect on every aspect of our lives. I know a lot of people who strongly believe that changing their diet has made them smarter.

**H:** OK. So maybe I do need to rethink my lunch choices. And is there anything else we can do to boost our intelligence. Amanda?

**A:** Well, we haven't talked about this yet, but it's actually really important to take some time out and switch your mind off for a while. You need to disconnect from your phone and your computer and let your mind wander.

**Dr:** I completely agree with this. Getting enough sleep, taking some time to rest, sitting quietly or meditating has a big impact on reducing stress and anxiety, and it also helps you think. There are studies that back this up – they have shown that students who daydream do better on standardised tests than those who remain completely focused on task.

**H:** So, resting can boost your brain power? That's good to know!

### Lesson 4.2, Listening, Exercise B
**4.2  C = Chair   E = Ella**

**C:** So the motion is: 'Intelligence gives people the greatest advantage in life.' Now I look to Ella to open the case against the motion.

**E:** Thank you very much. It's an honour to speak against the motion tonight. Right, it's easy to see why so many people believe being intelligent makes your life better. After all, we see intelligent people thriving at school. We see them getting onto the university courses they want. We see them graduating with good academic qualifications. And on top of that, we see the importance the world gives to qualifications.

So, it may seem strange for me to stand here and argue that intelligent people aren't necessarily at an advantage in life. However, that is exactly what I'll do. In fact, there are several clear disadvantages in having a superior intellect.

Let's start with a lack of common sense. And let's talk about a chess champion. Not just any chess champion, but a chess champion that was also a child chess prodigy. She must be smart, right? Well, talk to her mother. According to her, she often locks her car keys inside her car. The 'nutty professor' – smart but absent-minded and eccentric – is a common stereotype of highly intelligent people. Some scientists believe that geniuses' brains are wired differently. While highly intelligent people are curious about complex puzzles and are able to troubleshoot, they can't deal with more mundane tasks. So Ms Chess Champion could beat 15 chess players in a row … but she can't drive herself home.

Another problem faced by intelligent people is an inability to socialise. We've all known that friend at school or university. They're ready to answer in the physics class, they ask the lecturer countless questions and their voice drowns out everybody else's in the seminar. Then you take them to a party. Suddenly it seems like wishful thinking that anyone will talk to them again. Ever. Probably because they're still talking about physics. There are a few reasons why highly intelligent people are thought of as socially awkward. Firstly, they find small talk tedious. You find them correcting other people's mistakes or trying to engage in a passionate debate at a casual social event. Secondly, they are incredibly self-conscious. This means they tend to overthink things and appear awkward.

And finally, there's the burden of expectation. You've got a reputation to protect. If everyone thinks you're a genius, they expect you to be successful and make an impact in the world. Sometimes the pressure is just too much. Highly intelligent people can end up dropping out of education altogether and trying to hide their intellect to fit in. Or they're afraid to look stupid. So they avoid asking questions when they need to, or they try to skip the basics when they learn something new, which, of course, only creates problems down the line.

In summary, if you think that being smart means lounging in a bath tub waiting for a eureka moment, then think again. There are a lot of downsides to intelligence. Geniuses can lack common sense, find it difficult to socialise, and feel pressure to live up to expectations. I've always said myself that intelligence and happiness don't necessarily go together. This is no surprise to people who lock their keys in their car, haven't got any friends to drive them and are too scared to ask. In fact, being highly intelligent makes life more not less difficult.

# 5 GAMES

### Lesson 5.1, Listening, Exercise B
**5.1  J = Joe   O = Olga   L = Lin**

**Part 1**

**J:** OK, so we've been locked in. So where's the key?

**L:** Found it! It's at the bottom of this measuring cylinder.

**J:** Really?! That was easy!

**L:** Yeah, but there's a metal bar across the top with a combination lock attached to it. No way will we get that big key through this narrow gap.

**O:** So we need to figure out the combination to remove the bar, right?

**L:** Exactly. But even if we could do that, my arm's nowhere near long enough to reach the key at the bottom.

**O:** Can you tip it upside down?

**L:** Nah, it's attached to the wall. It can't be moved.

**J:** Try pulling it really hard.

**O:** Seriously?! That's cheating! Anyway, we'll get thrown out if anything gets broken! According to the instructions, we're not allowed to use force to move things!

**J:** I don't remember being given any instructions.

**O:** We were made to sign a form at the reception desk. Those were the instructions, Joe!

# Audioscripts

J: Ah, I wondered what that form was.
L: Didn't you read it?!
J: Er, sorry. I just signed it.
L: Unbelievable! Anyway, there are microphones all over the place, so we're probably being listened to right now!
J: OK, so we need to get the key out of the cylinder without touching it. But that's impossible.
O: Not necessarily. Look. There's a cork attached to the key.

**Part 2**

O: I reckon the cylinder needs to be filled with water. Then the cork will float to the top, lifting the key with it.
L: Well, there's some water in this big vase, but nowhere near enough to fill that measuring cylinder.
J: What about this cooking oil? Do you think the cork will float on oil?
O: Absolutely. Bring it over here.
J: Hmm, I can't. The jug's fixed to the shelf.
L: Typical! Could we use the vase to transfer the oil?
O: No. It needs to be something small enough to fit inside the jug and scoop out the oil. There must be a cup hidden somewhere. What's in that chest of drawers, Lin?
L: Let's have a look. Some electric scales, a bath towel and, hmm, there's no handle on the bottom drawer. I can't open it. Any ideas?
J: Er, maybe it'll open if we press that switch on the wall.
L: It's just a light switch, Joe! It won't … Oh amazing! You just turned all the lights off! Excellent!
J: Wait! I did it! Look up! There's a secret message on the ceiling! It must have been written in luminous paint – it's only visible in the dark. But it's just one word: sugar.
O: Really? There are some sugar cubes on the shelf, but how does that help us?

**Part 3**

L: This is ridiculous. We've been stuck in here for nearly an hour. We should've been given more clues. Shall we give up?
J: Give up?! No way! I told all my friends I'm brilliant at puzzles. If we give up now, I'll be made fun of for weeks. There must be a clue somewhere – something we're missing.
O: I've got it! Something must have been hidden inside those sugar cubes! We need to dissolve them in water!
J: Yesss! There's some water in that vase.
O: Brilliant! OK, great. They're dissolving. And I was right. There's something there. What is it? Something metal? Aha! Two screws!
L: Screws? What are we supposed to do with them?
O: We can screw them into the holes in the drawer and use them to pull it open. Just a second.
J: You did it! You've found the cup! We're free!
L: Are you joking?! We still need to remove the metal bar from the cylinder, which means working out the combination to that lock.
J: Ah yeah, I forgot.
L: Joe! We've got two minutes left! Think of something!
J: Stop shouting at me! I can't think when I'm being shouted at!
O: I suppose at least we can transfer the oil to the cylinder while we're thinking. Pass me the cup. Thanks. Ooh! There's something in the jug!
L: Yeah right! There's nothing there apart from the oil. You need to get your eyes tested! Oh!
O: I was right! A glass ball. Maybe we're supposed to weigh it.
J: Brilliant! But it's covered in oil, and so are you! Be careful not to drop it!
O: Aha, that's what the towel's for! We need to clean the oil off it first!
L: OK, but hurry up! We've only got 60 seconds!
O: Calm down! OK, it weighs one kilogram 327 grams. Try that combination, Joe! One three two seven.
J: One, three, two, seven. Yes! It worked. Quick, bring the oil over! How much time have we got?
L: Forty-five seconds! Come on! Hurry up!

### Lesson 5.2, Listening, Exercise C
**5.4 P = Presenter**

P: So? What did you make of puzzle A – the Take or Share game? The fairest outcome would be for both of you to choose SHARE, and to win £500 each. Sadly, it's more complicated than that. By choosing that option you're risking losing everything. It turns out that the best strategy in a one-round game is to be selfish, because you have a 50/50 chance of winning £1000, which is better than a 50/50 chance of winning £500. The problem is, your opponent can be assumed to be having the same thoughts, so you'll both probably end up with nothing anyway!

This example comes from Game Theory, which involves using mathematical models to solve problems where your choices affect – and are affected by – other people's choices. It allows for more accurate predictions and estimates.

Coming back to puzzle A, things get really fascinating over several rounds, because now you can reward your partner's kindness, or punish their selfishness. For example, if you share the money in the first round, you're implying that you're willing to cooperate. It turns out that one of the best approaches over several rounds is to share in round 1 and then spend the rest of the game copying your opponent's previous move. However, it's important to acknowledge that this strategy doesn't always work.

Let's turn to puzzle B – the Talent Show Dilemma. If there's a clear favourite, you might conclude that voting for her would be a waste of your precious vote, because she's expected to win by a landslide anyway. Supposedly then the most appropriate solution is to vote for your second favourite contestant, to make the final more interesting. But if everyone follows the same strategy, no one will vote for the favourite, and she'll be eliminated! This type of thing is reported to have happened many times in real life – not just in talent shows, but also in important elections. So in such situations, I'd urge you to resist the temptation to vote tactically, and to vote for your own favourite.

What about puzzle C – the Food Truck problem? The answer seems obvious, right? You should put your truck at point B and instruct the other truck to move to point D – or vice versa. That way, you serve half the town each, and all the town's residents have one food truck fairly close. Wonderful, except that the other owner has no incentive to move her truck from point C. If you park at point B, she can simply assert that she's staying in her prime spot in the town centre, and end up with three-quarters of the town's customers. The only way for you to get 50% is to park right next to her at point C! Even if a hundred new food trucks arrived, they'd each be better off by clustering together in a single point.

Finally, what about puzzle D – the road network? To reduce congestion, we need to build a new fast road between Smallton and Littlemarket, right? It's common sense, isn't it? But let's check. In the original network, there are two routes between the two big towns, so half the traffic is likely to choose each route. But in the new 'improved' network, there's now one obvious route that everyone's going to choose. So it'll have almost twice as much traffic as either of the old routes, and the whole network will have much worse congestion than before!

# 6 DISCOVERIES

### Lesson 6.1, Listening, Exercise B
**6.1 P = Presenter   K = Kyle**

P: Today we're talking about unusual travel challenges. Forget remote beaches and idyllic islands or precarious mountain treks and volcano hiking. None of that is enough to impress anybody these days. If you really want to stand out from the crowd, you need a travel challenge. At least that's what travel journalist Kyle Chen, who's been following this trend closely, is here to tell us today. Welcome to the show, Kyle.

K: Thanks for having me, Jo.

P: So … first of all, what exactly is a travel challenge?
K: Well, basically, it's travelling with a goal or some sort of self-imposed restriction – or both in some cases.
P: OK. Can you give us some examples?
K: Sure. So you can limit yourself to a particular method of transport, you can visit locations with a theme, or you can choose a particular route.
P: Actually, that sounds kind of fun. But why do you think these kinds of challenges are so popular all of a sudden?
K: Different reasons I guess. Well, in general, I think people want to be different. Perhaps they want to have a goal to make their trip more interesting. And, I think for some of them, they want to share their adventure. Or maybe they're doing something for charity, or hoping to write a book.
P: So, can you tell us about some interesting challenges that people have done?
K: OK. Well, this was a pretty ambitious one. A guy called Adam Leyton challenged himself to visit as many countries as possible in 24 hours using public transport.
P: Woah! I'm guessing you can't visit that many countries in 24 hours, though?
K: Well, amazingly, he visited 12.
P: Twelve countries in a day!
K: Right. It wasn't an easy 24 hours by the sounds of it either. He came up against a few challenges. He had no time to sleep, on the whole, except for a couple of hours on a night train. But he had to wake up, and get off and on the train, to set foot in the Czech Republic. He had to jog to the border with Hungary and only had 22 minutes to get from there to the Austrian border.
P: That's sounds quite … intense. What gave him the idea to take on the challenge?
K: Supposedly, he wanted to break a record but he also wanted to raise £900 for charity.
P: Hmm … it does sounds like an incredible trip. But … the fact is, you need some spare time to plan a challenge like that. What are some other challenges you've come across?
K: Well, one of my favourite challenges is a guy called Dixe Wills. He decided he was going to visit places in Great Britain, except he was only going to visit places that started with the letter Z. And he was going to visit all of them.
P: How many places is that?
K: There are 41 apparently! He wrote a book about it called *The Z-to-Z of Great Britain*. It's a great book, actually. It's about all these obscure places you might never have heard of – small farms in the middle of nowhere, a rock on the Isles of Scilly.
P: Hmm. That sounds like an interesting read. What else have people done?
K: Well, another really quirky one is Daniel Tunnard, a British man who lives in Buenos Aires. He decided to ride all of the 140 bus lines in the city.
P: One hundred and forty bus lines? Why?
K: It's a travel challenge. It took him about six months. Remarkably, he was sometimes travelling for 14 hours at a time.
P: OK. That actually doesn't sound like much fun at all to me.
K: Hmm … me neither. But you have to admire his dedication. He set himself a goal and then he went through with it, taking three bus routes a day. He also blogged about his experiences – in English and Spanish – and he published a book about them. Actually that's a really fascinating read.
P: Good for him. So how do these people fund their trips, on the whole?
K: Well, I think most of the examples I gave were self-funded. Mind you, travelling on the buses was actually very cheap. I think it cost about £55 altogether.
P: Right, got you.
K: However, some people ask for donations through crowdfunding sites like GoFundMe.
P: Isn't that a bit … cheeky? Surely, you should pay for your own adventures.
K: I think it's OK. The idea is that if people enjoy reading your blog or looking at your photos, they can make a small donation. People don't have to give anything unless they want to.
P: And what would your advice be for someone thinking about trying a travel challenge?
K: OK, first it's super important to be realistic about what you can do. Think about your budget. Think about how much time you can spare. Think about what you would be comfortable doing. The most important thing is to enjoy yourself. You don't have to travel far to have an adventure.

### Lesson 6.2, Listening, Exercise C
6.4 **P = Presenter**

P: Today, I'd like to talk about someone who I particularly admire. In my opinion, he's far and away one of America's greatest inventors. His innovations have fixed everyday problems but also probably saved thousands of lives. In addition, he was one of the first African-American inventors to gain public recognition for his work. His name was Garrett Morgan and he was a prolific inventor and entrepreneur who lived between 1877 and 1963. And while you may not all know his name, you're likely to have experienced his innovations.

One of Morgan's early successes was actually an accident. He was repairing a sewing machine in his shop when he noticed that some oil he was using had straightened the hairs on a cloth. Realising that he might be on to something, he decided to test the oils on something bigger. So he borrowed his neighbour's dog and used the oils to straighten its hair. It worked. So well, in fact, that his neighbour didn't recognise his own dog and tried to chase it away. Morgan bottled his new invention, labelled it 'G.A. Morgan's Hair Refiner' and he was soon selling it far and wide.

His second big success, a safety hood, turned him from an innovator into a hero. Morgan had noticed how smoke inhalation made the work of firefighters both difficult and dangerous. His solution was a hood worn over the head with two tubes that extended to the ground, where the air was breathable. He soon had an opportunity to test out his invention. An explosion in a tunnel near his home trapped 32 workers underground with smoke, dust and poisonous gases. With emergency services unable to enter the tunnel, it was truly a life-or-death situation. Morgan and his brother Frank raced to the scene and went in side-by-side, each wearing one of Morgan's safety hoods. It was a tense moment, but they soon re-emerged safe and sound with survivors. Morgan's fame began to spread slowly but surely, with his device being used by fire and police departments across the country.

Another of Morgan's life-saving inventions was an improved version of the traffic light. By and large, in the early 1920s, American roads were dangerous places. They were filled with horses, carriages and wagons – and increasingly, the newly invented automobile. On top of this, there were only two traffic signals – stop or go. Time after time there were stories of injuries and fatalities in traffic accidents. One day, Morgan and his family saw such an accident – a collision between a car and a horse-drawn carriage at a busy intersection. The driver of the car was knocked unconscious, a little girl was thrown from the carriage, and the horse had to be put down. Determined that accidents like that shouldn't happen, Morgan's innovation was to add a third light – a 'caution' light. This gave vehicles that had entered the intersection enough time to get out before the signal changed to 'go'. Morgan sold the patent to the General Electric Motor Company, which installed the new traffic lights in cities all over the country. As a result, roads became safer and many lives were saved.

So why is Morgan so widely admired? Not only did his inventions save the lives of millions, but he also put his heart and soul into the community, even running for the city council. So while his life was a classic rags-to-riches story, it was also the story of a man who took a leadership role and truly cared about others.

# 7 EXTREMES

### Lesson 7.1, Listening, Exercise B
**7.1** **A = Arjun  C = Catina  T = Tony**

**T:** Welcome back to *The Breakfast Show* with me, Tony Scott. Now I'd like you to meet a real-life superhero, Arjun Prasad. Good morning, Arjun. What's your story?

**A:** Good morning. Well, I was driving home from work about three months ago, not really paying attention to the other vehicles, when suddenly I heard a loud bang from the road behind me. I looked in my mirror and saw a car had run over a bicycle. The cyclist was still trapped under the car, which was leaking fuel onto the road.

**T:** Sounds terrifying! So the car could have exploded at any second, couldn't it?

**A:** Exactly. So I ran over and lifted up the car while the other driver pulled the cyclist free. As soon as she'd freed the cyclist, I put the car down again. Then together we carried the cyclist to safety and called an ambulance. And we were just in time – the car exploded a few seconds later. A spark must have caused the fuel to catch fire.

**T:** My goodness! Now, you said you lifted up the car. But that's incredible. I mean, you're a big guy, aren't you? But a car!

**A:** Yeah. It's weird, isn't it?

**T:** It certainly is. This seems like a good point to introduce my second guest, Catina Ivǎnescu, a professor of kinesiology. Catina, how is it possible for a person to lift a car? I mean, a car weighs, what, a tonne and a half, doesn't it?

**C:** Good morning. Yes, a typical family car weighs between 1500 and 2000 kilograms. The world record for weight-lifting is just over 500 kilograms.

**T:** Are you saying that Arjun lifted over three times the world record?

**C:** No, not at all. If he'd lifted the car above his head, that would have been a superhuman feat. But in fact Arjun just lifted part of the car a few centimetres off the ground. Three or even all four of the car's wheels were still on the ground, supporting most of the car's weight.

**T:** Right. So Arjun's achievement is nothing special, then?

**C:** Far from it! First of all, as Arjun said, it was an incredibly dangerous situation, with a high risk of explosion at any second. So Arjun's actions were unquestionably courageous. There's no doubt that the cyclist escaped serious injury thanks to Arjun's heroic actions. But in addition, it still takes exceptional strength to lift a car, even by a few centimetres.

**T:** OK. Let's conduct a little experiment now. We have here in the studio a car of the same model as the one you lifted, Arjun. Could you lift it for us now?

**A:** Er, not really. I've had a bad back for several months, and the doctor advised me against doing any more heavy lifting.

**T:** Oh. That's a shame!

**C:** Why don't you lift it, Tony?

**T:** Me? Er, OK. Wow! That's heavy! There's no way I could lift that!

**C:** Well, not here and now. But who knows? Maybe if you were in the situation Arjun found himself in, you might be able to. It's all about something called 'hysterical strength': the strength that you get in extreme situations.

**T:** So that's what helped Arjun, then, was it? Hysterical strength?

**C:** Exactly. Basically, we're all a lot stronger than we think we are. But when we push our muscles to the limit, it's really painful.

**T:** Yeah, I know. I was in too much pain to lift the car – it was agony!

**C:** But that pain is just our body's way of telling us to stop exerting ourselves before we break anything. We feel it when our muscles are operating at around 60% of their potential. But, you could, theoretically, push yourself a lot further without damaging your muscles.

**T:** OK. But surely it would hurt so much that you'd want to stop.

**C:** Exactly. But in a high-stress situation, your body is flooded with adrenaline, which blocks your body's pain sensors – but only temporarily. That's how Arjun was able to go way beyond 60% of his strength. He didn't notice the pain until the adrenaline had worn off.

**A:** Exactly. I literally didn't feel any pain at all until about an hour after the accident. And then every muscle in my body was in agony!

**T:** I'm sure. Er, I'm just wondering, Catina. We can't harness this strength in everyday life, can we?

**C:** Well, world-class athletes are able to harness it to some extent. During training, they can often push themselves up to 80% of their potential. But in high-stress situations, such as when they're chasing an Olympic medal, it's often possible to go much higher. That's why so many world records are broken at such events, rather than in regular training sessions. The adrenaline blocks the pain, allowing you to go way beyond your normal limit.

**T:** Aha. OK, one last question, Arjun. What happened to the cyclist?

**A:** She made a full recovery. When I met her last week, after a few weeks in hospital, she said if it hadn't been for my actions, she might not be alive today. But I don't feel like a hero – I'm just a normal guy, aren't I?

**T:** Well, I'm not so sure about that, Arjun! Anyway, let's have a break now, shall we? We'll be back very soon.

### Lesson 7.2, Listening, Exercise C
**7.3** **RS = Recruitment specialist**

**RS:** OK, so let's look at those questions now. Interviewers often use the 'desert island' question to determine what sort of person you are. A practical survivor type might take a knife or even a satellite phone. A more creative dreamer would take something original and fun. There's no correct answer – it depends what type of employee they're looking for. Just don't pretend to be something you're not. Focus instead on the image you want to convey about yourself.

Next, the 'dinosaur' question tests your ability to avoid obvious answers. Ninety per cent of people say T. Rex, the first dinosaur they think of. But unless the employer is looking to recruit cold-blooded predators, T. Rex would be pretty unsuitable as a potential employee. Almost any other answer is much better – as long as you justify it.

The 'weakness' question is an old classic. Whatever you do, don't claim to have no weaknesses, as you'll come across as arrogant and lacking in self-awareness. A good trick is always to describe a weakness that you've overcome.

With the 'stapler' question, the key is to think beyond the obvious applications, and to explore the properties of the object in question. I wouldn't recommend saying 'a paperweight' – it's what everyone always says.

OK, so the 'pizza' question tests your ability to make estimates and work out a plan. So don't just say any old number that pops into your head. You don't need to produce an accurate answer – which would be about 150 million in this case. But of course it's better if you're in the right ballpark, which in this case would be between around 75 and 300 million.

Next, the 'not on your CV' question is a great opportunity to remind the interviewers that you're a real person, not some invented character whose life revolves around landing this particular job. It's fine to get personal, but don't forget to bring your story back to how you're suitable for the job.

Finally, for the 'worst enemy' question, it's always worth mentioning that you don't have any enemies. But resist the temptation to leave it there; talk about perceived weaknesses that are actually strengths. Demonstrate your ability to see yourself through others' eyes – a crucial skill for any employee.

### Lesson 7.2, Listening, Exercise D
**7.4** **I1 = Interviewer 1   O = Oscar   I2 = Interviewer 2**

**I1:** What would you take with you to a desert island and why?

**O:** Er, a notebook and a pen. I find writing poetry immensely calming, so an extended stay on a desert island, without any other people to distract me, would really get my creative juices flowing. I'd be utterly devastated if I couldn't record my ideas on paper.

**I2:** Thank you. If you could be any dinosaur, which dinosaur would you be?

O: Oh, a pterodactyl, a flying dinosaur, soaring high above the plains. The views would be spectacular, and the sense of freedom would be quite exhilarating. But much more importantly, compared to the ground, the sky would be a relatively good place for staying out of harm's way!

I1: Right. What's your biggest weakness?

O: Hmm, well I tend to be somewhat disorganised. When I was a student, I often missed deadlines. But then I learnt some remarkably simple techniques, and I've improved noticeably since then. For example, I make a to-do list every day, and I can't have any rewards until I've cleared my list. It takes quite a lot of self-discipline, but it's so satisfying to know that, at long last, there's nothing hanging over you.

I2: Thank you. Name four uses for a stapler, without the staples.

O: You could use it to pick up tissues without getting your hands dirty! You could also use it as a hammer for bashing things. I suppose you could also give it to a child as a toy – the child might have fun pressing it and listening to the noises. And I suppose you could also use it as a paperweight, to hold down papers when it's windy.

I1: Hmm. How many square metres of pizza are eaten in the US each year?

O: A standard pizza is, what, thirty centimetres across? So you could easily fit nine inside a square metre. In fact, if you cut them up, there'd be room for perhaps three more in the spaces, so, twelve. That's a year's supply for me. I'm not altogether sure how typical I am – I guess some people would eat that many in a single month! But if we assume I'm not radically different from the average American, then we're looking at around one square metre per person per year. The USA has around 300 million people, so that's my estimate: 300 million.

I1: Not bad. What's the most interesting thing about you that we wouldn't learn from your CV?

O: Well, I have six younger brothers and sisters, who are all quite adorable. I'm the oldest, so I've spent most of my life looking after them while my parents were working. It's been quite challenging, because I never had any time to myself and it was often practically impossible to study, but it's also incredibly rewarding when I see how far they've come.

I2: Great. How would your worst enemy describe you?

O: Hah! I'm not the sort of person who has outright enemies. It used to irritate me when people treated me badly, but I've learnt that the best trick is to ignore them and move on! I know some people are jealous of what I've achieved and they think I'm lucky. But they haven't seen all the struggles I've been through. The people who matter know that I deserve any luck that has come my way.

I1: OK, great. Thanks. That's the end of the interview.

# 8 WELL-BEING

### Lesson 8.1, Listening, Exercise B
8.1  C = Cheryl   J = Jake   L = Luke

L: Hey, Cheryl.

J: Hello, Cheryl. What you doing?

C: Oh, hey guys. Check out my brand new … smart watch! What do you reckon?

L: Cool. I've been meaning to get one of those. Is that switched on, Cheryl?

C: Erm … maybe.

J: Smart watch eh? Hmm … not a hundred per cent convinced about those. I mean if I want to check my email I can just look at my phone.

L: Yeah, yeah … but you can use it whenever you exercise to monitor the amount of activity you do.

J: Didn't know you were so big on fitness Cheryl.

C: Yeah, sure. I mean … I do like to keep fit … and … well, OK so … You'll never guess what … I've just been commissioned to write an article about wellness technology.

L: Amazing!

J: Cool. Congratulations. But what's wellness technology?

C: Good question. So wellness technology is … technology with which we can improve our health and well-being.

J: Did you just read that somewhere?

C: Might have done. But you get the idea. There are lots of other devices you can get to track things. Actually, you can monitor whatever you need to keep an eye on: your breathing, temperature, glucose levels in your blood, amount of sleep, pretty much everything!

J: Yeah. And it sounds a bit like information overload to me.

C: Well, yes and no. Sure more information doesn't necessarily mean better health. But I've just read several news stories about people whose lives may have been saved because their smart watch alerted them to a problem. For example, on this smart watch take this handy … heart rate tracker.

L: Eighty-five beats per minute. Isn't that quite high …

C: Not for me, Luke. No. And anyway I'm a bit stressed. I'm meeting the person writing the article with me for lunch today. I'm supposed to share my ideas. But I think I'm out of new ideas!

L: Well, what about the smart swimsuit? Have you heard of that?

C: Hmm … tell me more.

L: Hang on – here it is. It's a swimsuit with a tracking tag embedded, so you can log your time and how far you swim. It will start tracking all that whenever you put the swimsuit on.

J: I don't know. What happened to just going for a swim? People are obsessively tracking everything these days. Writing down everything they eat or do. It takes over your life – when really all you need to do is take some exercise and eat healthily.

L: But I don't think wellness technology is just about fitness fads. For example, monitoring devices can help show your doctor the big picture so he or she will be more likely to pick up on any problems. And it goes beyond just tracking. Like the smart pill bottle.

C: The smart pill what? Let me write this down.

L: It's a pill bottle for medication, like the Adhere Tech bottle. It glows blue when it's time to take your medication. And … if you forget … it starts flashing red. It can also text you or email you to remind you to take medication.

J: OK, maybe that could be quite useful for my grandpa.

L: There are a few health devices like that now. I was also reading about this thermometer. It's basically a thermometer which a smartphone can be attached to. Here it is. It says … this device has an automated diagnosis feature whereby it checks the symptoms of the person to whom it's attached against a database. I'll send you a link to the review. And look at this – this could be a great quote for your article. 'As tech gets smarter and people get smarter about tech, this could be the decade in which we revolutionise healthcare.'

C: Yeah. Yeah. I think that would work as a strapline. Great! Thanks, guys. One last question though. Is this thing really switched on?

### Lesson 8.2, Listening, Exercise B
8.3  L = Laura   B = Bill   R = Rohan   J = Julie

L: Hello, everyone. This is *First Past the Post*, the sports performance podcast. My name is Laura Ford …

B: And I'm Bill Williams.

L: This week, we're talking about sports psychology. A lot of the big teams have sports psychologists these days. But what do they actually do? This week we set out to find out more.

B: First up, we spoke to Professor Rohan Kumar, a lecturer in sports psychology. Here's what we discussed …

L: So Rohan, could you explain what a sports psychologist does?

R: Certainly. Essentially, our job is to help athletes perform at the peak of their abilities. We do that by offering training and therapy. Training usually means things like encouraging positive thinking, whereas therapy could be supporting them with off-field issues – this is particularly important in the case of long-term injuries.

L: You mentioned working on positive thinking. How exactly does that work?

R: Well, athletes, even elite athletes, suffer from the same fear of failure that we all do. They have times when they doubt their abilities or get cold feet because they're anxious about competing. Our job is

to help athletes cope with these feelings, so they can perform to the best of their abilities.
- L: So what kind of training do you do with them?
- R: Well, I said before that positive thinking is important – but that doesn't just mean encouraging people to imagine winning a game or winning a trophy. It's actually more about visualising your performance, thinking about the individual steps that you need to take, and imagining doing each one of those steps in exactly the right way. It's all about staying calm and focused, so they can give it their best shot.
- L: So you encourage them to break things down into smaller goals?
- R: That's right. It helps people focus by thinking about these smaller goals rather than getting distracted by the big picture. We also work on self-talk, which means trying to get control of that little voice inside your head that says you're not good enough or that you're having a bad day. We train athletes to use positive self-talk to build self-confidence and self-belief – and if it's a team game, to talk out loud and encourage those same feelings in the rest of the team.
- L: That's been really helpful. Thank you for your time, Rohan.
- R: You're very welcome.

### Lesson 8.2, Listening, Exercise D
**B = Bill    J = Julie    L = Laura**

- B: After Laura spoke to Professor Kumar, I spoke to Julie Matic, a sports psychologist working with a local football team. I should mention that Julie was speaking to me from a training session, so there's a bit of background noise during this interview.
- B: Julie, thank you for taking the time to talk with me today.
- J: No problem.
- B: So, can you tell me a little about your role with the team there?
- J: Well, before I started here, the team had been going through a bad period, so one of the first things I needed to do was to help the team get over their fear of failure. I've been helping them to think about failure in a more positive way, so they don't dwell on the fact that they failed, but they try to learn from that experience, so that failure becomes a positive thing. Nobody can win every game, so it's not a disaster to lose – as long as you just think about what you can do differently next time.
- B: What about working with individual players? What kinds of things do you focus on?
- J: Well, the most important thing is to get to know the individuals, and encourage the manager to do the same, so that we can work out the best way to get the most out of each person. When people think about coaching, most people have a stereotypical image of a coach shouting at the players, but that's very outdated because many players won't respond positively to that kind of coaching. Different players need different approaches – some people need a lot of guidance, some need a lot of praise, others need to feel trusted and important. It's important to talk to the players – to listen to them and find the right way to work with them.
- L: Apologies again for the sound quality on that interview, but she said a lot of really interesting things. I completely agree that it's important to think about the right kind of coaching to suit individual players. I need someone to nag me and tell me to up my game, but I know that's not everyone's cup of tea.
- B: Yeah, actually I find that kind of coaching ends up distracting me because I get so angry with the coach. It means I don't concentrate on the game and I end up playing even worse! I prefer a more supportive approach.
- L: Yeah, I can imagine that! So we also interviewed …

## 9 BEHAVIOUR

### Lesson 9.1, Vocabulary, Exercise B
**M = Man    W = Woman    A = American**

- M: I could do with some new wheels but they'd set me back at least ten grand … and I'm completely skint.
- A: Hey, can you lend me ten bucks? Ah, sweet. That's awesome, dude.
- W: I don't mean to whinge, but the office do last night was a total shambles. I was so gutted!
- M: This bloke offered me a brand new telly for fifty quid, so I'm like 'Sounds dodgy to me – it's probably nicked or something.'
- A: I wanted to hang out with my buddies tonight but I'm totally beat, so I guess I'll just chill out and crash instead.
- W: I'm well chuffed cos I got myself a new flat. So I'm sorted now.

### Lesson 9.1, Listening, Exercise B
**L = Lisa    G = Greg    J = Jake    H = Helen**

- L: Er, hello.
- H: Hey. Come on in. I'm Helen.
- J: What's up? I'm Jake.
- G: Good morning. How are you doing? I'm Greg.
- L: Good, thanks. I'm Lisa. Are you all here for the psychology experiment too?
- G: Yeah. The organisers offered us ten quid, so we signed up.
- L: Yeah, same here.
- J: I don't know what they're testing, though. Do you?
- L: Something about perception skills and stuff like that. Are we supposed to wait for the experimenters?
- H: Nah, there were two blokes here earlier, psychology professors or whatever, and they were like 'sorry but we've got to go and teach.' They left some questions in an envelope.
- G: Total shambles! Shall we get cracking?
- J: OK. Task 1: Which line is the same length as the one on the left? Easy. It's line B, innit?
- H: Yeah, definitely B. It's obvious.
- G: Yeah, it's line B. Lisa?
- L: Er, yeah. Line B.
- H: Hey, those doughnuts look kind of yummy. Do you think they're for us?
- L: I suppose so. Look, there's a note. It says this plate's for the 12 o'clock group and this is for the 11.30 group – that's us.
- G: Sorted! Mmm, yummy!
- H: What's the next task? Let's see: AFC or PTU?
- G: PTU, no question. What about you, Jake?
- J: Definitely PTU.
- H: Yeah, me too. Lisa?
- L: Er, yeah, PTU, I suppose.
- J: Great. Those doughnuts were well yummy. Shall we have some more?
- L: Well, the others are supposed to be for the next group.
- H: Yeah, but we could just eat them and hide the note!
- J: Yeah, whatever.
- G: Fine with me. Lisa?
- L: Oh, go on then. I mean, they are yummy!
- G: Sorted! Well done Lisa! You passed the test!
- L: What are you on about?
- H: Sorry, Lisa, but it wasn't about perception at all. It was about social pressure and conformity: how groups influence our behaviour, and so on.
- L: How do you know? Aren't you participants like me?
- J: Nah, we're the experimenters. We were only pretending. Sorry.
- L: So what do you mean, I passed the test?
- G: OK, so the first part was the lines. Did you really think it was line B?
- L: Not really. It seemed obvious it was line A, but then you all seemed sort of convinced it was line B. I thought my eyes were playing tricks on me in some way!
- H: Yeah, that happens to more or less everyone. Sometimes it's easier to follow the crowd, in a sense, than to trust your own eyes!

L: So it was line A after all?

H: Yeah, of course it was! OK, so the second test was AFC versus PTU. Why did you go for PTU, Lisa?

L: Cos you all chose it! I don't even know what PTU stands for. What is it?

J: PTU? Pretending to understand! Most people hate admitting they don't understand something, especially when everyone else is nodding their heads, or something like that, so you pretend. But maybe everyone else is pretending too! They're all kind of too embarrassed to admit they don't know what's going on!

L: So what's AFC?

J: Ask for clarification! Always ask, even if it makes you feel stupid!

G: Enjoy the doughnuts, Lisa?

L: Yeah, they were yummy.

G: Yummy? That's a strange word! Why do you say that?

L: Ach, you got me again! You all called them yummy, didn't you? I never say 'yummy'! Gutted!

G: Yeah, sorry. We wanted to influence your choice of words. We used loads of slang too, and stuff like that, to get you to conform to our style of speaking.

L: Ah, yeah. I always thought 'yummy' was uncool, but when you all started using it, I thought maybe it was cool again!

H: Nah, yummy is always a lame thing to say!

J: How did you feel about eating the other group's doughnuts, Lisa?

L: Not good. But you all convinced me it was fine. It was some kind of trick again, was it?

J: Yeah, sorry. That was an example of 'groupthink', where people make bad decisions as a group that they wouldn't make as individuals. That's why we agree to things we don't want to do. And it's why many business teams make such terrible decisions.

L: OK. And what was with that humming at the end?

H: Hah! That was the last task. We wanted to make you copy us. And it worked!

L: Yeah, I know. I felt kind of stupid cos I didn't know what was going on, so I just joined in. You must think I'm some sort of sheep, copying everything you did!

G: Chill out, Lisa. Most people are just as bad as you! Anyway, cheers for taking part. You were wicked! Want another doughnut?

### Lesson 9.2, Listening, Exercise B
**9.6 P = Presenter   M1 = Man 1   M2 = Man 2   W = Woman**

P: Hello and welcome to *Human Behaviour*. Today we're looking at one of the most famous experiments of all time.

In the 1940s, the leading behavioural psychologist, B F Skinner, conducted a remarkable experiment. Some hungry pigeons were placed in a cage with a mechanism that delivered food.

The twist in this particular experiment was that the pigeons' actions had no effect whatsoever on the mechanism, which simply delivered food at completely regular intervals, regardless of what the pigeons did. The pigeons, of course, didn't know this, so they kept pecking and pushing and so on in a desperate attempt to make the mechanism deliver food. Inevitably, there were occasions when food appeared immediately after the pigeon had performed a particular action. That was enough to convince the pigeon that it was that action that had caused the food to be delivered, so the pigeon kept repeating it again and again. And of course, every time the mechanism delivered another serving of food, the pigeon became more and more convinced that it could influence the mechanism with its actions.

According to Skinner's report, the pigeons swung and moved around a lot, making it look like a kind of bizarre pigeon dance. Surely humans wouldn't believe such actions could influence something beyond our control … or would we?

In fact, when the experiment was repeated on humans, who received points instead of food, the results were almost identical. By the end of one experiment, the participants were convinced that they'd got a point for a particular combination of shrugging, fidgeting and rocking back and forth. What never seemed to occur to them was that the points were simply awarded after completely random lengths of time. If they'd just sat there and waited, they'd still have won the points just the same, without making themselves look ridiculous in the process. But of course, it wouldn't have been so entertaining to watch.

Does anything like this happen in real life? Let's hear from a few people we interviewed on the street this morning to find out.

M1: I'm a big football fan. I try to watch all my team's matches on TV. In fact, pretty much whenever I miss a match, my team loses! So I make sure I'm sitting by the TV in good time for each match, wearing my lucky football shirt and scarf, to bring my team luck! And it definitely works – well, most of the time, at least.

W: It started when I was a youngster, and my aunt gave me a lucky hamster mascot before a big test. I forgot to take it with me for my next test, which was a disaster! So ever since then, I've always used mascots in exams.

M2: I always buy my lottery tickets at exactly 11.41 on a Thursday morning. I know it sounds crazy, but every time I've won any money on the lottery, it's after buying my ticket at that time. Unfortunately, it doesn't always work, for some reason, but it certainly seems to improve my chances of winning.

P: I'm sure it does. Anyway, join us again next week on *Human Behaviour* …

## 10 SOCIETY

### Lesson 10.1, Listening, Exercise B
**10.1 D = Denise**

D: Walking along the streets of Beijing, you really get the sense of a city going through a rapid period of change. Huge skyscrapers dominate the skyline, while construction work continues all around. As the city evolves, its population has swelled to over 21 million, making Beijing one of the most populated cities in the world. And the more people there are, the more challenging it becomes to provide comfortable environments for people to live and work in.

Fortunately, researchers at the Well Living Lab on the northern outskirts of Beijing are conducting an extensive research project to identify ways that building design can make people healthier, happier and more productive. And if people feel better about their environment they have a higher inclination to interact positively with the people around them. Inside an unassuming office building, human guinea pigs are being carefully monitored inside a simulation of a typical office environment. I talked to environmental psychologist Wang Wei about how this kind of research can help with building design.

### Lesson 10.1, Listening, Exercise C
**10.2 W = Wang   D = Denise**

D: So, Wang Wei, what research is being done at the Well Living Lab here in Beijing?

W: They're looking at how small changes to the environment, such as changes to the lighting, air quality or noise levels affect people. They're observing people's emotional responses and using wearable technology to monitor people's physical reactions.

For example, recently they've been looking at what kind of light makes workers most productive. They experimented by using different kinds of light. They found that people strongly preferred daylight to electric light – and, as a matter of fact, other research has shown that people have a tendency to be less productive if their desk is more than 7.5 metres away from a window. They also found that certain kinds of blue lighting can have a positive effect on workers' moods.

D: What other things have psychologists learnt about office environments?

W: Some fascinating research has focused on shapes and lines. Apparently, people feel more comfortable in places with round shapes and curved lines. On the other hand, straight lines and sharp edges have been shown to create feelings of fear. Other research has

# Audioscripts

looked at colours. Red walls have been shown to be better suited for tasks that require accuracy and attention to detail – perhaps because people associate the colour red with danger, so they're more alert. Conversely, blue walls suit creative tasks – in fact, people trying to be creative in rooms with blue walls had twice as many ideas as those working in rooms with red walls.

**D:** And what have we learnt about the design of the city?

**W:** People living in cities tend to have higher levels of stress, so unsurprisingly a lot of the research has looked at what can be done about this. One interesting study showed that people are more relaxed when they see lively and interesting shop facades, whereas plain, monotonous facades make people anxious and give them the urge to hurry past. Other studies have looked at how spaces can facilitate more communication – because cities can be very isolating places. Some ideas include arranging spaces that encourage interaction between strangers, such as providing more seating in communal spaces. It sounds simple, but many places have had this kind of seating removed in recent years and people didn't realise the impact this would have.

**D:** If you don't believe the importance of thinking about these details, you only need to look back at the story of the Pruitt-Igoe housing complex that was built in Missouri in the US in the 1950s. When it opened, the complex was lauded as magnificent architectural design. Yet, when people actually began to live there, several problems with how people interacted in the space became evident – for example, the wide spaces between the different apartment blocks in the complex meant people in different blocks had little chance to interact. This meant there was no sense of shared community between residents of different blocks, and as a result, the complex quickly became a hostile and unpleasant place to live in. The project's failings were a reminder for architects to think not just about the look of buildings, but also about how people would interact within the spaces they create.

Today, architects and designers are much more aware of the importance of psychology when designing buildings. Various studies, like the ones being carried out in Beijing, are looking at how places make people feel and act. This research is vital for creating the buildings of the future. With so many people living close together, the environment should encourage positive feelings.

### 🔊 Lesson 10.2, Listening, Exercise B
**10.4**  R = Robin   J = Joanna   Mr E = Mr Evans

**J:** A few weeks to go and then we're done with uni for good. Can't quite believe it.

**R:** Me neither. The end of an era. So … you going to work at your dad's company then?

**J:** Hmm … hope not. Not if I can help it, anyway. But yeah … may need to. Any idea what you're going to do?

**R:** Well, funny you should ask that. I've just been trying to sort out my CV and looking for some interesting stuff to apply to. The thing is I really want to do something to help people. But I haven't seen too much of that sort of thing.

**J:** Really? Oh OK, thought you were going to apply for something in business though, like one of those management trainee schemes.

**R:** I don't know. I don't think all that is really for me. I'd like to make some kind of a difference to the world. You know my cousin works for a charity, right?

**J:** Oh yeah?

**R:** Yeah, a clean water organisation. Anyway, we've been talking a lot recently about all the stuff she's doing and it kind of made me want do something similar too.

**J:** Oh, OK got you. But you wouldn't earn that much working for a charity. At least not at first. Any other ideas?

**R:** Well, yeah I thought about politics too.

**J:** Hmm. Don't know. I mean all they seem to do is argue with each other. Just don't know how much of a change you'll be making.

**R:** OK … and there's also social work. You know, looking out for children, vulnerable people …

**J:** Hmm OK…

**R:** I take it you're not convinced then?

**J:** I just think that looks like a tough job, coping with lots of difficult situations. I couldn't do it myself personally. I was thinking … what about teaching? You'd be a great teacher. You could train to be a teacher or just volunteer in your spare time.

**R:** Yeah … I guess.

**J:** Hey, there's Dr Evans. Isn't he the new career's advisor? Why don't you talk to him?

**R:** Good idea. Hang on sec … Excuse me, Dr Evans. Would you have a moment for a quick word at all?

**Mr E:** Oh hello Robin. Sure. How can I help?

**R:** I was wondering if you could offer me some advice. I've just been considering what to do after graduation.

**Mr E:** OK right. So what are you interested in doing?

**R:** Well I think … first and foremost I want to do a job which involves helping people, you know, that are less fortunate than myself. So I was quite keen on applying for a position with a charity.

**Mr E:** Aha. OK. So my first question then would be: what kind of charity do you have in mind?

**R:** So, ideally one that campaigns for clean water … or maybe disease prevention.

**Mr E:** So second question: what do you see yourself doing for them?

**R:** Well … I'd like to be assisting with making policy, I guess.

**Mr E:** OK let me just stop you there. Of course that is one area of charity work. But it's highly competitive. And you don't have experience or a specialist qualification. You're more likely to be involved in fundraising, persuading people to donate money, at least initially. And even then, it would definitely strengthen your application if you can show some commitment to their particular work.

**R:** Like volunteering perhaps. I was thinking about some kind of voluntary work.

**Mr E:** You should definitely do it.

**R:** Brilliant, thanks Mr Evans. I can look into it.

**Mr E:** But let me get to my final point. You should bear in mind, that working for a charity isn't the only way you can help people. If you're likely to be helping the organisation get money, you may actually be able to make more of a difference pursuing a career in business. Especially with your background. Then you can commit to donating a portion of your salary to your chosen charity.

**R:** Right … I hadn't thought of that before.

**Mr E:** Yes, there's a very, very interesting book about a Wall Street trader, called *The Most Good You Can Do*. If you haven't read it, you should do. The guy was a philosophy student, quite brilliant in fact. Just like you he was thinking how to make a difference. He decided that the way he could make the biggest impact was by working hard in finance and donating money to charity. He's been able to donate over $100,000 a year to his chosen charities – and as a result touched many people's lives.

**R:** Thank you, I'll look it up. And thanks for the advice Mr Evans, it's much appreciated. I definitely have a lot to think about.

**Mr E:** You're welcome.

**J:** So, come on then. What did he say?

**R:** Not what I expected. At all. He said it might be better to get a normal job, you know, an office job and that.

**J:** Told you so.

**R:** No, but then give the money to charity.

**J:** Oh. Great.

**R:** Yep, that's what he said. Apparently, there's a guy who does that and has given over a hundred grand a year away.

**J:** No way!

**R:** Yeah I know. Crazy, right?

**J:** Well, it's kind of good advice. The bit about an office job. I'd do that. I'm just not sure about the giving away part.

Macmillan Education
4 Crinan Street
London N1 9XW

A division of Springer Nature Limited

Companies and representatives throughout the world

Language Hub Advanced Student's Book ISBN 978-1-380-01755-0
Language Hub Advanced Student's Book with Student's App
ISBN 978-1-380-01750-5

Text, design and illustration © Springer Nature Limited 2020
Written by Jeremy Day and Graham Skerritt

The authors have asserted their right to be identified as the authors of this work in accordance with the Copyright, Designs and Patents Act 1988.

The right of Kieran Donaghy to be identified as the author of the Speaking Pages in this work has been asserted by him in accordance with the Copyright, Designs and Patents Act 1988.

First published 2020

All rights reserved. No part of this publication may be reproduced, stored in a retrieval system, or transmitted in any form or by any means, electronic, mechanical, photocopying, recording, or otherwise, without the prior written permission of the publishers.

Designed by emc design ltd
Illustrated by Daniel Limón (Beehive Illustration) p50
Cover design by Restless
Cover illustration(s)/photograph(s) by Getty Images/Luís Henrique Boucault (bg), Plainpicture/Cavan Images
Picture research by Emily Taylor

Authentic video footage supplied by BBC Studios Distribution Limited
Café Hub videos produced by Sharp Focus

Authors' acknowledgements
Jeremy Day would like to thank the team at Macmillan Education for their support.
Graham Skerritt would like to thank the students who tried out activities and gave invaluable feedback. Thank you to the Macmillan Education Editorial team for your excellent comments and suggestions. And thank you to my family for your patience and support.

The authors and publishers would like to thank the following for permission to reproduce their photographs:

**Alamy**/Zoltan Gabor p65, Suat Gursozlu p156(icons), Phillip Roberts pp16–17, Science History Images p69, Visions of America p14(b), David Wall p155(t), Westend61 p2(tr); **BBC Studios Distribution Limited** p34(a, b, c, d, e); p58(a, b); **Getty Images** pp2(bl), 64, 77(3), 94–95, 106(b), 10'000 Hours p112, AFP/Adem Altan p109, AFP/Ronaldo Schemidt p118(tl), Anadolu Agency p52, Andersen Ross Photography Inc p30(james), Ascent Xmedia pp74–75, Axelle/Bauer-Griffin p20(bl), Peter Barritt p15(e), Nathan Benn p61, Ira Block p67(tr), Bloomberg p37, Nikolay Bogdev/EyeEm p153, Claudia Burlotti p30(bob), Caiaimage/Tom Merton p45(b), Jon Cartwright pp104, 105(tr), Matteo Colombo pp82–83(background), Ian Cuming pp70–71(background), Robert Daly p32, Markus Daniel p110(bl), Nick David p18(tl), Steve Debenport p66, Lea Dettli/EyeEm p58–59, Enrique Díaz/7cero pp10–11(background), 88–89, Digital Vision p77(5), Erik Dreyer p97, Richard Drury p30(callum), Michael England p70(c), ER Productions Limited p163, FatCamera pvi, Clare Fieseler p115(bl), Filadendron p160, Flashpop p151, Freemixer p29, Goldfaery p87(tr), Grandriver p76(2), GrapeImages p5(b), Jorg Greuel p7, Paul Harris p33, Hero Images pp30(sonia), 31, 91(b), 98, Hill Street Studios p18(tr), Dave Hogan p149(tr), Hoxton/Martin Barraud pp114–115(background), Hoxton/Sam Edwards p44(b), Imagemore p76(1), Image Source p55(cm), 106–107(background), iStockphoto/Ellerslie77 pp1, 94(tr), Izusek p158, Azman Jaka p4(b), Johner Images p85, Jupiterimages p45(cl), Jason Kempin p21(cm), Daniel Knighton p20(br), Peetatham Kongkapech pp62–63, Roos Koole p4(mr), Justin Lewis p44(cr), Lilly3 p18(bl), Littleting/Pradthana Jarusriboonchai p82, Maica pp54–55, Martin-dm p9, Maskot p8, MECKY p49, Ty Milford p79(b), Laurence Monneret p43, Moodboard p105(tm), Morfous p78(bl), Jessica Nelson p149(b), Aaron Oberlander p155(br), Orchidpoet p110(tr), PeopleImages p42(paul), 88(tr), Javier Pierini p150, Piola666 p15(c), Photo_Concepts p53, PhotoQuest p21(bm), Pixelfit p5(ml), Busakorn Pongparnit p118-119(background), Dave Porter pp34–35, Norman Posselt pp22–23(background), Franz Pritz p73, Purestock/Punchstock p90, Gavin Quirke p152, Ken Redding p77(4), RichVintage p100, Tim Robberts pp42(caroline), 56, 105(tl), Alexis Rosenfeld p161, Jenny E. Ross p67(br), Saenman photography p14(a), Elizabeth Salleebauer p154, Audrey Saracco/EyeEm p164, Anup Shah p103, Jordan Siemens pp86–87, Skynesher pp18(br), 80(b), 91(cl), SolStock pp10(t), pp117, 116(cl), Paul Souders p162, SpVVK p113, Stocktrek Images p79(tl), SuperStock p13, Thehague p111, Camille Tokerud p116(br), Topical Press Agency p62(tr), Adina Tovy pp46–47(background), Tuan Tran p30(mary), Universal History Archive p70(a), Vctor Vargas/EyeEm p118(tr), Vasantytf p87(cl), Westend61 pp3, 42(gianni), 51, 81, Josef P. Willems/LOOK-foto p25, Yumehana p92(cr), Tim Zurowski p102(tr); **Hero Images** p116(bl); **iStockphoto** pp39(r), 70(b); **PhotoDisc** pp40–41(background); **Powerstock** p102(b); **Rex Features/Shutterstock**/Mikael Buck p22(tl), Hufton Crow/View p16(cm), George Frey/EPA p15(d), Neil Hall/EPA-EFE p22(tr), Solent News pp26, 27(c,b); **Shutterstock**/Domino p57(illustrations), Gorodenkoff p40(bl), Margouillat photo pp92–93; **Stockbyte** p80(stapler); **Thinkstock** p80(pizza), 92(tr)

Commissioned photographs in the Café Hubs by Sharp Focus pp11, 23, 35, 47, 59, 71, 83, 95, 107, 119

The author and publishers are grateful for permission to reprint the following copyright material: Graph from 'Vinyl LP Sales and Market Share' by British Phonographic Industry, 2017. © BPI (British Recorded Music Industry) Limited 2019. All rights reserved. Reprinted with permission of British Phonographic Industry, p6; Extract from 'Tim Smit: how we made the Eden Project' by Anna Tims. Originally published in The Guardian, 29 September 2014. © 2019 Guardian News & Media Limited or its affiliated companies. All rights reserved. Reprinted with permission of Guardian News & Media Limited, p16; Extract from 'Life In An Underwater Skyscraper' by Rex Features. © Rex Features Ltd. 2018. Reprinted with permission of Rex Features Ltd. UK, p27; Extract from 'Architect Unveils Plans For Spectacular Eco-Friendly Resort' by Rex Features. © Rex Features Ltd. 2018. Reprinted with permission of Rex Features Ltd. UK, p27; Extract from 'The 'Lily Pad City' - 03 Jul 2008' by Rex Features. © Rex Features Ltd. 2018. Reprinted with permission of Rex Features Ltd. UK, p27; Extract from 'From Forest Bathing to 'Halotherapy': 5 Ridiculous Wellness Trends' by Loulla-Mae Eleftherious-Smith. Originally published in The Independent, 7 October 2016. © Independent Digital News and Media Limited 2019. Reprinted with permission of Independent Digital News and Media Limited, p92; Extract from 'Political activism is as strong as ever, but now it's digital – and passionate' by Ethan Zuckerman. Originally published in The Guardian, 15 October 2013. © 2019 Guardian News & Media Limited or its affiliated companies. All rights reserved. Reprinted with permission of Guardian News & Media Limited, p120

These materials may contain links for third party websites. We have no control over, and are not responsible for, the contents of such third party websites. Please use care when accessing them.

The inclusion of any specific companies, commercial products, trade names or otherwise does not constitute or imply its endorsement or recommendation by Springer Nature Limited.

Printed and bound in Dubai
2024 2023 2022 2021 2020
10 9 8 7 6 5 4 3 2 1